HARDPRESS.NET
HOME OF HARD-TO-FIND BOOKS

The Grand Extensive Plan of Human Redemption

by James Kershaw

Address:
HardPress
8345 NW 66TH ST #2561
MIAMI FL 33166-2626
USA
Email: info@hardpress.net

48

3/6

THE

GRAND

EXTENSIVE PLAN

OF

Human Redemption.

THE GRAND *EXTENSIVE PLAN* OF HUMAN REDEMPTION,

From the Ruins of the Fall,

Including the Times of the Restitution of all Things:

COMPRISING

The Time of the MILLENNIUM, SATAN's LITTLE SEASON, and the SÆCULA SÆCULORUM, or the AGES of AGES, till Time is no more;

IN TWELVE FAMILIAR DIALOGUES,

BETWEEN

DIDASCALOS, a Teacher, *and PHILOTHEOS,* a Friend or Lover of Truth.

BY JAMES KERSHAW.

"I also will shew mine Opinion," *Job* xxxii. 10.

"Many shall run to and fro, and Knowledge shall be increased," *Dan.* xii. 4.

Louth;

Printed and Sold by SHEARDOWN and SON, and may be had of most other Booksellers in Town and Country.

MDCCXCVII.

[*Entered at Stationer's-Hall.*]

[illegible]

ADVERTISEMENT.

THIS question, Whence came Evil? *or whence originated that perpetual war between the very elements, between animals, between men? Whence errors, miseries, and vices, the constant companions of human life? Whence good to evil men and evil to the good? and Death to all?*

This question, the solution of which has been so puzzling to the wisest men in all ages, have driven some to deny either the existence of God, or at least of a Governing Providence. Lucretius *assigns no other reason for his denying the* System of the World to be the Effect of a Deity, *than that* it is so very faulty. *B. 2d. V.* 180.

Others perceiving so great a Mixture of Good and Evil, have supposed a Malevolent *Principle or God, directly contrary to the Good one. These have deduced from the Good Being, nothing but Good; and from the evil Principle, evils of every kind. Such were the* Manicheans, Paulicians, *and other Heretics. And there are some at this day who suppose this* Herculian *difficulty unsolved by both Divines and Philosophers; that this Gordian knot is yet tied. The Author of this* Essay *proposes the following Plan to the Judicious Public, and commits it entirely to that*

Bar to pass sentence how far he has succeeded in untying it. The attempt is founded entirely upon Revelation; the Author supposing all other Keys incapable of unlocking the Cabinets in the house of David, and of exploring the Treasures of divine Wisdom in the Mysteries of Providence.

It is wrote in a kind of familiar Dialogue between Didascalos, *a Teacher, and* Philotheos, *a Friend or lover of God.*

PREFACE

To the Reader.

Philotheos. MY dear Didascalos, What is the Original of Evil, of which we see and feel so much in this "Present evil Age?" *See Gal.* i. 4.

Didascalos. We may justly suppose, That Evil, whether moral, spiritual, or physical, can never be the immediate Production of infinite power, purity, and goodness. The Fountain of purity and essential goodness can never yield such bad and bitter streams as have deluged the world in every age, and found their way into every human, brutal, vegetable, mineral, and elementary body.

"Evil cannot from God proceed,
"'Tis only suffered, not decreed."

But suffered or permitted most certainly it is. Since Adam was banished Paradise, no Golden Age ever existed, except in Poets' fancies.

——"When men, yet new,
"No Rule but uncorrupted Reason knew,
"And with a *native bent* did good pursue;
"Needless were written laws, when none opprest;
"The law for man was written in his breast.
"No suppliant crouds before the Judge appear'd;
"No Court erected yet, nor Cause was heard;
"But all was safe, for Conscience was their guard."

What

What *native bent* to good had Cain, when he cruelly slew his Brother, "Because his own works were Evil, and his Brother's Righteous?" 1 *Joh.* iii. 12.

Phil. If we say, That God *could not* have Prevented evil, where is His Omnipotence? or, That He *would not*, how is this reconcileable with his Goodness? both being essential to the Creator of all things in heaven and earth.

"Some have supposed, That all Evils owe their existence solely to the necessary relations and circumstances of created Beings. That no system can be created but Evil will unavoidably insinuate itself into, even in opposition to the will of the Creator. The reason is, because they suppose it cannot be excluded without working contradictions; not to effect which, is no diminution of Omnipotence. This argues no defect in the Power of the Creator, but a supposed *imperfection* in all created Beings.

The *Stoicks* imagined, That the Untractableness of *Matter* was the cause of evil. That God would have made all things perfect, but that there was in Matter an evil Bias repugnant to His Benevolence, which drew another way; and from hence arose all manner of Evils. From whence it is inferred, That how many evils soever force themselves into the creation, so long as the good preponderates in the scales of Providence, the whole is a work well worthy of infinite Wisdom and Benevolence." And notwithstanding these necessary imperfections in things, the whole, nevertheless, in some sense, may be said to be perfect. Hence it is supposed, that the infinite power and goodness of God are fairly reconcileable both with the wickedness and misery of his creatures, from the impossibility of preventing them. This is the kind of Faith most worthy of the human Understanding, and most meritorious in the sight of God; as it is the offspring of Reason,

as

as well as the Parent of all Virtue and due Resignation to the just but inscrutable dispensations of Providence." *See* 2 *Letters of a Free enquiry into the nature and origin of Evil*, 3d. *Ed. Let.* 1*st.*

Didas. But my dear Phil. This account does not accord with the discoveries of Revelation. Very far from it. Unto Moses as an author, and the New Testament as his Expositor, we stand indebted for a true solution of this weighty problem. Sin, or moral evil, is the root or fountain of Spiritual and Physical evils of every kind and degree every where.

Adam was that *One Man* by whom Sin entered into the world, and Death by Sin. Ever since his days the world has been full of sin. From Cain to this day, murders and miseries in all nations and ages have abounded. What are all the Histories of Mankind, but Records of these incontestable Facts? These facts have been always observed, confessed, and lamented, by a few of the wisest and most moral in every age. How many false and futile hypothesis have men invented, to explore the cause, and to prescribe a cure! Here human Reason is nonplussed. Divine Revelation alone has discovered these momentous subjects. The Author of our Being, in compassion to our otherwise invincible ignorance, has condescended to teach and instruct us in the Cause, the Case, and the only Cure, by a Revelation.

Phil. If, as some, you say, have supposed no system can be created but evil will unavoidably, and contrary to the will of the Creator, insinuate itself into it, on account of the necessary *Imperfection* of every thing created; or, according to others, a natural Bias to evil exist in the things created, Must not Omniscience have known this necessary imperfection and insuperable Bias to evil? And in such a case, can we suppose essential and infallible Truth could consistently have pronounced every created thing *very good?* *Gen.* i. *Ult.*

Didas. By no means. So that the Origin of Evil, can never be consistently accounted for from the works of Creation. To attribute it to any natural Bias or Imperfection in the Creature, what is it but plainly to Palm it upon the Creator? On the other hand, To refer it altogether to the subtility and deceitful agency of invisible evil spirits, is entirely to exculpate man. But to ascribe it to a concatenation of different causes, is both reasonable and most certainly the Truth. The short of it is,

The Serpent deceived Eve; the example and persuasions of Eve prevailed with Adam; and though the Creator was no Agent in the deadly criminal action, yet his divine Wisdom and Power did not think proper so to interfere as to prevent it; for such interference was contrary to Adam's free-agency, and state of probation in which his Maker had placed him as a candidate for a happy immortality; and in consequence, must both greatly have degraded man, and defeated His own designs in so placing him. Besides, in case of such an event, His secret Counsel had determined upon a Plan of Grace and Providence, to bring a far greater Good out of so great an Evil. This is the "Mystery of God," (*Rev.* x. 7.) and which will only begin to be publicly exhibited upon the stage of Time in the Days of the voice of the seventh Angel, when *he shall be about to sound.* In the mean time it is in the womb of futurity, and wrapt up in promises, prophecies, and types, and very little understood by most People at present, or even in past ages.

Phil. But that Adam's free-agency was never intended to be controlled, and actually was not, is evident, by his Maker giving him a positive Law, with penal sanctions; and punishing him for Voluntarily transgressing it. But does not the Doctrine of of the Abſolute Decrees of God, now that man is fallen, ſuppoſe him to be as much a mere machine as if he had originally been created one, or his Freedom afterwards controlled?

Didas. Moſt certainly it does. For if God has *abſolutely* "Ordained whatſoever comes to paſs," then that Ordination muſt be the prime and principal Mover in every Action, whatever Inſtrument be employed in its performance. And if ſo, beyond all doubt

"Whatever is, is Right."

Whether ſinning, or ſuffering for ſin, are equally of divine appointment. And according to this, all evil, Moral, Spiritual, and Phyſical, muſt have their root and fountain in that Decree. The preſent appearances of Providence; His Diſpenſations in paſt ages; together with ſome important paſſages of Scripture, all being miſconſtrued, have induced many of the moſt pious and well-meaning Perſons to embrace ſentiments, almoſt ſubverſive of that Religion they intended to promote. They have, in general, contracted the ſcale of Redemption and Salvation within ſo narrow a compaſs, as entirely to exclude the far greateſt part of Mankind, not only without the limits of the Redemption which is in Jeſus, but alſo, by a ſecret Decree of their Maker, have conſigned them to endleſs and unſpeakable Torments, whether Chriſtians, Jews, Heathens, and even dying Infants.

Phil. If the divine Decree were indeed the real though ſecret Cauſe of human ſalvation, would it not have better comported with the known Attributes of the Deity, to have compriſed the far greateſt part of mankind, rather than ſo few, within its ſaving limits?

Didas. Both reaſon and humanity naturally ſuppoſe ſo, and ſcripture gives its ſuffrage to the ſame benevolent

benevolent ſuppoſition. What Decree can Sovereign and eſſential Love paſs upon Mankind, but what is expreſſive of ſovereign Will? But is not this Will the Determination of infinite goodneſs, and regulated by unerring wiſdom?

Phil. Certainly. But has not God a *Secret* and a *Revealed* will?

Didas. We know of none exiſting any where but in human fancies. If God has a ſecret will, is it poſſible that it ſhould ever contradict Revelation in any one inſtance? If not, what have we to do with it? If it does, what is Revelation good for? What Revealed ſubject can we fix upon, the Truth of which we ſhall not doubt? By what criterion can we poſſibly determine wherein this two-fold will agrees or diſagrees? Does not this diſtinction lead directly from Chriſtianity to Scepticiſm? How many thouſands it has lead into it, who can tell?

Phil. But do not the Arminians, ſo called, who profeſs the beſt and moſt liberal Principles, ſuch as general Redemption, aſſert man's free-agency, and Chriſt's Univerſal atonement; nevertheleſs, upon the whole, firmly believe, That very few adults, in compariſon, will ever get to heaven out of any age or nation?

Didas. This is the general belief. And however Calviniſts and Arminians differ widely in other things, yet their general *concluſion* is, That *very few* will be finally ſaved. Certainly, with regard to mankind, the *iſſue* is nearly the ſame, if nine out of ten go to hell; of the Torments of which, take the following account:—" Si omnes homines nati ab Adam uſque ad hodiernum diem, &c. If all the men born, from Adam to this preſent day, or to be born from him, ſhould live to the laſt day; and all the ſpires of graſs that ever ſprung out of the ground were men; and they were to ſhare amongſt themſelves *one* Puniſhment for a *mortal ſin* in Hell,

equally

equally shared amongst them; *one particle* of that pain attached *to each man*, would surpass all the Torments of the holy Martyrs, and all that Thieves and Malefactors ever suffered, put together." So much for the Torment. Let us attend to their *duration*. "Tanta sunt æternitatis spatia, &c. Such is Eternity, says a Divine, That if a damned Person in a thousand Years were to squeeze one tear from his Eye, it would afford water enough in Time to drown the whole world." To which may be added, that when this period arrived, eternity would be as far from ending as ever! Let it be here most seriously considered, as above noticed, that it matters little upon the whole, if such multitudes actually go to hell, whether it be from their own fault solely, or from some Secret Decree of God, consigning them thither.

Originate from whatever Cause it may, the Idea shocks reason and humanity to reflect upon it; and from either the Calvinian or Arminian conclusions, where shall the sensible thinking mind find an Asylum from the horrid, but unavoidable Idea? That God, whose very essence is love, and darling attributes goodness and mercy, should merely, for his own Glory, ever pass such *a horrible Decree* as the one supposes, is naturally impossible; because such a dire Decree is a plain contradiction to His divine nature. If we acquit Him of such a design in making Mankind, how shall we vindicate omniscience, omnipotence, justice, and mercy, in the Government of Mankind? If, on the other hand, supposing Universal love and redemption true, which certainly is the case, yet nevertheless if mankind is so Providentially placed, and in such circumstances, and the obtaining the benefits of that Redemption be attended with such difficulties, and suspended upon such Terms as to be out of the reach of the bulk of the world, which is notoriously the case

where

where the Gospel of Jesus never comes; then upon the Gospel Plan, if history be true, the dreadful conclusion is as unavoidable upon this as upon the Predestinarian hypothesis; more especially with respect to the heathens.

Carefully examine both these and some other systems; consider the *Torments*, and the *Duration* of those torments, which such systems consign over the bulk of Mankind to suffer; and reconcile them, if you can, to the known Attributes of the Deity. If this is impossible, as I think it is, then these conclusions must, in this case, be as false as those Attributes are true; at least in my judgment, so far as I can see.

To avoid the consequences of these sentiments, which are obvious to every thinking mind, some have roundly denied the existence of any hell at all: Others, who admit of its future existence, yet deny its endless duration. Some suppose the Wicked will finally perish, or be annihilated at Death, or after the Resurrection. Others again suppose, That the duration of Hell will be temporary, and its sufferings Salutary and Curative; and by amending the delinquent, will prepare him in Time to become an Object of Mercy and final Salvation; while some have maintained, very strenuously, the Natural mortality of the Soul as well as the body. These, and many more hypothesis, have been maintained by men of piety and learning, and all to vindicate the Justice of the divine Œconomy with Mankind, and free their own minds from those disagreeable, painful sensations, which are necessarily excited, by seriously reflecting upon the subject, as commonly understood and believed. Here let the Reader pause a moment, and survey a spectacle most horrid in itself—Behold the greatest part of thy fellow-creatures for ever suffering in *Pur Asbeston*, in fire inextinguishable! shrieking and crying like peals of rattling Thunder! Are these shrieks and cries of the Reprobate, unison with the hallelujahs of the Elect; or do their Discords heighten the harmony in the ears of God, Angels, and Saints? Reader! wouldst thou wish to join the concert, and to endless duration maintain thy Part in it? O horror of horrors to think of! Yet true it is, that this was an essential Article in the Creed of Calvin, "That God, in Predestinating from all Eternity one Part of Mankind to everlasting Happiness, and another to endless Misery, was led to make this distinction by no other motive than his own *good pleasure and free will.*" Was not this a Manichean Deity?

The Doctrine of Absolute Predestination, however modified or softened by palliating expositions and distinctions, always appeared to the Author of this Essay, as inferring Reprobation by unavoidable consequence—A doctrine, so far as he can remember, he was never so much as once tempted to embrace. That the decided Judgments and Sentiments of many Pious and Learned men flowed in that channel, was evident; but not more evident than surprising to him. He always apprehended the current of scripture-truth to flow in an opposite channel, and run to a very different shore. This current always carried his Judgment along with it, and forced him to draw very different conclusions. Nevertheless, the History of Providence seemed to form a contrast with Revelation; and how to reconcile them appeared to him, for many years, a very difficult, if not impossible task. Both Books lay open to inspection. That in Fact they were not contradictory, he always believed; but how to render them consistent, he knew not. No Author, within the narrow compass of his reading, afforded the least satisfaction. Till at length, except History, he nearly laid all aside; being determined

entirely

entirely to think for himself, how widely soever he might differ from others.

In this dilemma, there appeared two open avenues affording satisfactory prospects: The one was, daily and devoutly to address the Father of Lights, to give Wisdom and spiritual Understanding in His word and will; the other, To "search the Scriptures of Truth," altogether unbiassed, and wholly detached from all parties, or principles of other men. Such a conduct had not been long pursued, before it afforded a satisfaction, in vain expected from any other method formerly pursued. If the Author thinks differently from others, it is because he cannot help it. As a Man, and a Protestant, he claims it as his birth-right to think for himself; and as candidly allows the same liberty to others.

The Plan here recommended is extensive; including both the Old and New Creation; the Paradise of Adam, and the Paradise of God; the Ruin of the World by the First, and its Restoration by the Second Adam, to almost infinitely superior happiness and glory above its primeval state; attempting to demonstrate, That Time is only in its most early stages, and the World itself in its infant state; that the Principal scenes of Providence being wrapt up in Prophecies and Promises, are not yet unfolded; that few, except those of an afflictive kind, will ever be seen until the next advent of the Redeemer: That His own Times, the Times of Refreshing, and the Times of the Restitution of All Things," will then commence, and begin to unfold THE MYSTERY OF GOD, according to the unanimous Voice of all the Prophets. Mysteries that will astonish men and angels, as they will be gradually unfolded in their proper Seasons as Time runs its successive Stages, agreeable to those Ages that were Constituted, in Fact, when Christ was appointed the Heir of all Things, (*Heb.* i. 2.) upon the

the Rebellion and Disobedience of Adam, who was the true heir of the primitive world, (see *Psa.* viii. *comp. with Heb.* ii. 5.) as Christ is of the future.

The following *Essay* begins with some Cursory Observations upon the Book of Genesis—the Creation, and the Fall of Man: Both these treated of something at large, in five Dialogues.

Part II. Enters upon the Principal Design: Opens up the subject of the two Adams, as Type and Antitype, in Expository Remarks upon *Rom.* v. 12 *to* 21. Proceeds to enquire into the extent of human Redemption, and the Duration of Time; suggesting Reasons to suppose, that the Salvation of Mankind, though not *absolutely Universal*, nevertheless will be much more extensive than is Generally supposed by Arminians themselves: An Account of the Resurrection. An attempt to prove, that those Heathen who never heard the Gospel in this life, will hear it when they rise again from the Dead, in the time of Gog and Magog, &c. and what will follow their Destruction, &c. &c.

The whole is submitted to the Judgments of the candid lovers of Truth among all Denominations of Christians. He, who made the heart, knows, That the Love of Christ, of Souls, and of Scripture Truth, have been the only Motives to the present undertaking. The Author has but one Request to make, which is, That the Reader would "Judge nothing before the Time." Now, he thinks, that the Time to form a judgment will be when he has attentively Read the whole, and honestly weighed it in the Balances of unbiassed Reason and divine Revelation, as contained in the two Testaments in their Original Languages, if he is able to read them: At the same time, to let Humanity, and not Popular Prejudices, hold the Scales.

The Author hopes that no expressions, militating against Christian love, has fallen from his Pen.

His design is not to litigate, but, if he can, to enlighten the Reader's Mind, so as to prevent future litigation, that has so often wounded the vitals of Religion. He proposes a plan to the public, which, if its foundations are firm, he humbly hopes will rationally account for some of those Herculian difficulties in Grace and Providence, which have driven different men into different extremes. The Author has been long convinced, That Truth is uniform—Right Reason is uniform: That this Reason, Revelation, and Providence, harmonize: That God is the Author of all the three. That a coalition of these three, all acting in concert, would form a Band, or three-fold Cord, that Free-Thinkers of every Denomination united, could never break. But where is that Received system that unites them all in perfect harmony? For instance, He who believes the Bible, must acknowledge, "That there is Salvation in no other name than that of Jesus Christ;" and that "He that believeth shall be saved, &c." But take *all ages* into the account, and the Name of Christ has never been heard of in five parts out of six. If this be denied, where are the histories that prove the contrary? If it be granted, "How shall they believe in him of whom they have not heard?" If it be said, that "God can save them for his sake, without either hearing or believing." Then what great difference is there between Christianity and Deism? Here let Reason ask, If he *can* save five parts out of six, why not the whole? These systems, you see, are at variance one with another, and both with the Truth. "But, says the Deist, He can save all the World, if he pleases, by his own Free Grace." Here Revelation is set aside. Nay, says the Predestinarian, "He has Decreed to save the Elect, a few, and to Damn all the rest." Here humanity shudders; reason recoils, and scripture contradicts. But says, the

the Arminian, "Christ died for All—there is Mercy for all." And yet confesses after all, That very few will be finally saved. Here both Reason and Humanity recoil again. The Universalist says, "That all shall be saved." But where do the Scriptures plainly say so? Now an *Orthodox* Plan, that steers wide of all these difficulties, and many others too tedious to mention, and at the same time, instead of contradicting, confirms every article of the Creed, harmonizing Providence, Revelation, Reason, and Humanity, must certainly merit attention. Such is the Essay before us; and as such is committed to the censure or approbation of the public, by a lover of Scripture-Truth, a Believer of the whole of that Truth so far as he understands it, and a well-wisher of all Mankind."

"THE

"THE later Jews make such Reckoning of
"the Book of *Genesis*, that they have numbered
"the very letters of it, which, they say, amount
"to 4395. The three first Chapters thereof are
"the Fountain of all the following Scriptures, and
"the common catechism of the Churches of both
"Testaments; in explaining and applying whereof
"are spent all the Sermons and other labours of
"the Prophets and Apostles."

TRAP'S TREASURY.

DIALOGUE I.

Being a short Introduction to the following Work, in a few cursory Observations on the Book of Genesis; wherein, among other Remarks, the Reader will find hints sufficient to inform him, that Patriarchs, both Antediluvian and Postdiluvian, had an Alphabet written by the Hand of God in the legible Characters of their own lives and deaths; by which, in succession, they might spell the Immortality of their own souls, their existence in a future state, together with a future Resurrection of the Body.

AS the promised Seed, by whom the Redemption of the world was to be effected, flowed in a current of blood from the first fountains of mankind, so it is easy to observe, that all down the holy line in succession, that Seed was typically pointed at as by an Index, almost at every step.

But before we notice these things, let us speak a word or two about the Writer of this Book, and notice a few of its more remarkable contents. And first,

1. *Moses* was the inspired Penman of the Pentateuch, God's great Secretary, or the amanuensis of the Holy Ghost: and all that Free-Thinkers, or Deists, have said to the contrary, is vain and futile in every unprejudiced eye capable of judging.

He was the seventh in descent from Abraham the friend of God. A great beauty when born; a circumstance no doubt that greatly contributed to his adoption by Pharoah's Daughter when she found him in the Bulrushes. He was a Courtier, and initiated into all the Learning of the Egyptians, at that time the most polite and learned nation of the world. Here he spent forty years, or one third part of his days, in high life.

But all the gaudy glare of a splended Court his judgment knew how to estimate, which shewed his option to be most excellent; choosing rather to suffer affliction with the people of God, than to enjoy all the pleasures of sin for a season; justly esteeming the reproaches of Christ greater Riches than all the treasures of Egypt, though at that time perhaps, the richest kingdom in the known world.

Thus dead to the world's pleasures, riches, and honours, he was duly prepared not only for the cares, fatigues, and toils of a Shepherd's life, and for forty years an exile in the land of Madian; but the much heavier toils and troubles for forty more, though exalted to be King in *Jeshurun*, the Vice-gerent and Law-giver of Jehovah, advanced on the Sacred mount to converse with his Maker as a man with his friend! Singular indulgence!

It is probable those forty years he was an exile in *Madian*, in the centre of his life, he might employ and improve his leisure time in writing the Books of Genesis, and of Job.

II. *Genesis* is a History, but at the same time contains a mystery; the former of Providence, the latter of Grace. Here we have a rational, and sufficiently satisfactory account of the Creation of Matter, out of nothing; that matter moulded into ten thousand Forms, and the whole put into Motion; some animate and Rational, others animate and

and brutal; others vegetable swarming with life; some inert, but all in motion active or passive! Stupendous thought! *Gen.* i.

If we look into the systems of the most renowned Philosophers, or the most authentic profane historians, according to some of them the World was formed by a fortuitous concourse of Atoms; or according to the wisest of them, it furnished its own Matter to the Author of it. It therefore, according to them, neither depends upon God for the essence of its Being nor original estate; yea, it even ties him up to Laws which himself cannot violate. Highly absurd! But without inspiration, nothing but hypothetical conjecture can possibly exist. Tradition can have no place without it, seeing mankind was not then in Being.

Philotheos. Moses with the utmost propriety began his history with an account of the Creation. For if the God of his People Israel had not Created Matter and the essences of things that had no preexistence, he might have recommended Him as a wise Artificer, but by no means as an Omnipotent and all-wise God or Creator, the only proper Object of worship and adoration.

Didas. It is true. But according to both Reason and Revelation, *Elohim* created heaven and earth, and all things that are therein, (*Act.* xvii. 24.) "Visible and invisible, whether Thrones or Dominions, or Principalities, or Powers." (*Col.* i. 16.) i. e. every body or every being, whether corporeal or intellectual; every enormous Globe that exists in the universe; with every inhabitant thereof; and gave Laws of Motion unto them all; bowling them around their respective Orbits! Could any power less than Omnipotent form them? or less than infinite Wisdom Contrive them? Who but an Omniscient Being can comprehend them? And let Reason say, What could induce such an

all-perfect

all-perfect God to make them at all, unless it were to make every intelligent Being happy by a communication of his own exuberant love and goodness unto them, as well as to manifest the glory of his own perfections?"

Phil. From the history which Moses has recorded, we are taught to consider the Universe, as well as Mankind, as under the fostering hand of the great Creator. Brought out of nothing by His Word; preserved by his goodness; Governed by his wisdom; when deserving, punished by his justice, yet pardoned and saved by his mercy, when penitent; and the whole subject to his Dominion and powerful Authority.

III. *Didas.* It is true, the scriptures no where say, that the Universe, in all its parts, is coeval in time as to existence; it rather intimates the contrary. Millions of millions of ages may have intervened between the Mosaical creation, and that of the first system in the Universe. But what are these ages, were they multiplied as far as arithmetical progression could carry them, compared with the existence of that immense and infinite Being, who has no Relation to either Time or Space! And yet, From the "Beginning of the creation which God Created," (*Mar.* xiii. 19.) who can number the Ages? *Eternity past* Moses seems to express by one word reaching higher than the first creation of Matter. This is the first word in the Bible, which St. John translates into Greek in the first words of his Gospel. In both places it is englished IN THE BEGINNING. But how can words express eternity? Let this Duration be what it may, it was in this Beginning that God Created all things. Time with us commenced with the first appearance of Light, which God called Day: this will continue as long as the Sun and Moon will continue to measure it, after which it will be absorpt in *Eternity to come!*

IV. The Book of Genesis contains a history of Providence for the space of about 2369 years; and as it is by far the most ancient, so it is by far the most excellent, and admits of no competitor in any nation or language. The Author held it up as a Mirror of Providence, in which all the Nations that read it may read a history of Facts that speak plainer than written laws, before any written laws had a being. As God's ways are equal and uniform, individual persons, families, countries, and kingdoms, may here see what they have to expect in equal circumstances. A world shall be drowned in water; fertile countries and populous cities consumed by fire; and the sword shall shed the blood of millions, and cut off opposing kingdoms, as of Egypt and Canaan, &c. when they forsake Jehovah, and worship other Gods. Ignorance and infidelity quarrel with holy writ, for commissioning the sword, upon certain occasions, to cut off women and children with Male offenders. Alas! can any thing but perverseness frame such objections against sacred Writ? May not the Deist turn Atheist upon the same grounds that his Reason denies Revelation in this instance? Where the scriptures supply one instance of such a promiscuous exterminating command, the book of nature supplies twenty; witness the histories of Earthquakes, Pestilences, Famines, &c.

On the other hand, we here find a Righteous Noah, at the command and under the protection of heaven, with the whole world in epitome, embarked on a little floating Timber, ride out a storm for many months together, in the utmost safety; and was thereby advanced to be a common Father of the present world of Mankind.

A Righteous Lot shall arrest the executing hand of an Angel; restrain the pointed shafts and darts of avenging thunder and lightning, until he escapes to a place of safety! Here you see a persecuted pious Joseph called out of a prison to govern a kingdom; to teach the Egyptian Senators Wisdom; and by his prophetical knowledge, and prudent management as a Minister of State, save near half of the World from perishing by famine!

Phil. How instructing and affecting these short Memoirs of the Pious Patriarchs! Their steps were marked with Divine approbation, and afford striking examples for Posterity to follow. What a contrast this history affords, between the conduct of the righteous and the wicked, and the consequences of that conduct!

Didas. True. But as this is not a time of Retribution, he who would rightly interpret both sides of the question, ought to consider the divine Conduct here in a typical light, and as a pattern which the Judge of All will follow in future at the Times of the Restitution of all Things.

From the Infancy of the old world, to its maturity in vice and wickedness, were 1536 years. This year a respite of 120 years were granted it, by its Maker, for Repentance and Reformation. Alas! in vain. At last, grown grey and hardened in sin beyond recovery, its Death-warrant was signed in heaven: This was executed by drowning it in 40 days time, at the age of 1656. By the time of the death of Joseph, about 713 years after, the descendants of Noah, in the new World, were almost universally sunk in Idolatry and Superstition, except his Family.

Phil. And pray, my dear *Didas.* what were the Principal events recorded in the former of these Periods?

Didas. *First* the Creation, and Generation of the Heavens, and of the Earth, and of all things therein. *Secondly*, The Formation of man out of the Dust; the inspiring him with Life; the Plantation

tation of Paradise for his kingdom before the Fall; his giving names to the Cattle; the Formation of Eve, and consequent Marriage of the innocent Couple, after the Law of life and death had been promulged by his Maker. *Thirdly*, Eve's Dialogue with the Devil in the body of a serpent; that Dialogue issuing in her deception and sin; her example and persuasion of Adam to sin also. Hence the Origin of evil, moral, spiritual, and natural. *Fourthly*, The apprehension, trial, conviction, and sentence of the guilty pair to labour, sorrow, and death. Here the door was opened at which Death entered into the world, and the guilty couple were expelled Paradise, and re-admittance denied them; but this was not until they had heard the Gospel of the Woman's seed preached in their hearing; which, no doubt, they believed, and were repriev-ed from Death, &c. in consequence. *Fifthly*, The birth of Cain, which Eve took to be the *Man Jehovah*, or the promised Seed. This affords a strong probability, that she had some knowledge that Jehovah was to be that Seed, as in fact he was when incarnated. This was followed by the birth of Abel. *Cain* signifying *gain* or *acquisition*. He was of that wicked One, and type of the Serpent's Seed in all ages: *Abel* signifying a *Mourner*. He was Righteous, and Type of the Woman's Seed collectively. Here the Enmity discovered itself; and the righteous fell by the hands of the wicked, as they have done in all ages ever since, and will so long as the Dragon reigns. As Abel had no issue, so Cain's Descendants perished at the Flood, type of the Destruction of the Beast and false Prophet; (*Rev.* xix. 20.) who, having walked in the way of Cain, will be cast into a lake of Fire, when the days come which the Flood typified, at the next coming of the Son of Man.

The two typical Persons thus cut off, the present

Race

Race of Mankind sprang from Seth, a Substitute, (as his Name signifies) in the room of Abel. Agreeable to the typical characters of his two Brothers, the Descendants of Seth, in both worlds, have been in a perpetual state of enmity. Cain Ruled over Abel—an example followed by every age; as all History testifies, where professors and profane have not coalesced in vice.

Phil. Bishop Cumberland supposed, that Cain was the first Idolater, worshiping the Sun, Fire, Light, &c. according to *Sanchoniatho*. And *Maimonides* thought, that Idolatry overspread the old world, as we know it did the new.

Didas. True. And it is probable that one design of Moses was to confute idolatry, by shewing, that all the heavenly bodies, and every element, being the objects of their adoration, were, in fact, only Creatures of the One True God: Consequently that the Creator, and not his Creatures, ought to be Worshiped.

As the first Transgression threw open the sluices of *Tartaros*, Satan's Residence, (2 *Pet.* ii. 4.) and thereby not only opened a communication between this visible and that invisible world, but, alas! erected this world into a Principality of the Devil, who is the Prince of it, by the confession of Christ himself, (*Joh.* xiv. 30.) so also, all the Idolatry of both the old and new world, was no other than a worship which ultimately devolved upon the Devil himself, by whatever mediums it passed through to reach him. It is therefore no wonder that we find the "God of this World" (2 *Cor.* iv. 4.) offering the world and all its Glory and Authority to the Son of God, for one single act of Worship; (*Luk.* iv. 5 to 8.) seeing that the greatest part of Mankind had hitherto, and then did worship him. His former success with Adam and his Posterity emboldened the fiend in this astonishing Temptation. No

doubt

doubt when he propofed to furrender all the kingdoms of the world to him for a fingle act of worfhip; to diveft himfelf of all property in, and authority over them, was the leaft thing in his thoughts; His defign was to devolve the Viceroyfhip upon the Son of God, while he maintained, as an Emperor, the fupreme Authority; and of courfe his hellifh Pride foared fo high as to have made the Son of God his Vaffal! But, bleffed be God, he here met with more than his match. It was for this Purpofe the Son of God came into the World to deftroy the Works of the Devil. This Truth there is reafon to believe, that the Devil was not altogether a ftranger to, which made him make fuch great tenders down unto him of his honour and property.

If thefe facts be true, and who that believes the Bible can deny them? Is it any wonder that the world was drowned with a double Deluge; firft, of all manner of impiety and wickednefs; and then of water? This was quickly followed by a general confufion of Languages; and that by Heaven exhibiting upon Earth a lafting fpecimen of Hell upon the plains of Sodom, "Suffering the vengeance of eternal Fire." *Jude*, 7. The Deftruction of Egypt, and of the nations of Canaan that quickly followed, were Types of the Deftruction of Spiritual Egypt (*Rev.* xi. 8.) and Sodom, when a greater lake will make its appearance than that in the days of Abraham. *Rev.* xix. 20.

Phil. Hence it is evident, That the Fall of the Firft Man, and the confequent introduction of the Dominion of the Devil over the World as a God and tyrannical Defpot, are fufficient to account for all the evils of every kind, that have, do, or ever will afflict the world.

Didas. True. And Philofophers may Tenter and Rack their brains, and ranfack Nature as long as they pleaſe to reſolve this grand queſtion, *Pothen ton Kakon? Whence came evil?* But where will they find a better, or one ſo full and true as the above? All the evils of this "Preſent evil Age," (*Gal.* i. 4.) ſpring from theſe two fountains.

The Tree that formed the Teſt of Adam's Trial, carried, in its very name, the ſymbol of the State that taſting it would introduce into the World. From the name of this Tree, one might reaſonably ſuppoſe, that Good and Evil might be equally poiſed in human and the world's experience. But were it poſſible to draw a Map, or write a hiſtory, in which might be ſeen all the Good and all the Evil that the World has ſeen and heard, ſuffered and enjoyed, from Adam to this day, it would be found that the evil would greatly exceed the good in every age and nation. I know that this is ſtrenuouſly denied by many both Philoſophers and Divines. All the treaſures of learning have been exhauſted, all the powers of Reaſon and Wit have been exerted, to prove the contrary. All this has been done by ſome of the beſt of Men, and that from the beſt of Motives, viz. "To vindicate the ways of God to Man." How far this end has in fact been attained, after all that has been ſaid, and that upon every Hypotheſis, however plauſible in appearance, let libertiniſm and the vaſt increaſe of Libertines bear witneſs at this day. Be this as it will, the preſent Eſſay will exhibit ſcenes tranſcendently glorious, and open an Avenue into future Ages of long continuance; in which, divine Philanthropy will act a part ſuch as will aſtoniſh the moſt expanded, generous, and elevated Minds; and confound every narrow contracted ſcheme of human invention; and that by a moſt copious diſplay of Nature Renewed; Paradiſe Reſtored with almoſt infinite improvement; Evil of every kind deſtroyed, or expiring; and the greateſt

eſt Good that human nature, in a new world, is capable of, for ages enjoyed; with a great probability of ſtill farther advancement in honour and happineſs. It is this Reſtoration, that will take place in *Ages to come*, and on this ſide Eternity, but after *this preſent evil age* is over, which will vindicate the conduct of Providence in the preſent; ſilence every objection; and make it evident, that, taking the whole compaſs of Time, and every tranſaction of Providence in it, the whole will appear worthy of God, and aſtoniſh Men and Angels with its glorious completion. This will be ſeen in the ſequel of this *Eſſay*, D. V. In the mean time, the *equilibrium* of good and evil is not to be found. Evil preponderates in the ſcale of preſent enjoyments, take the world in general. Evil elections, ariſing from free-agency, natural propenſions, bad examples and temptations to vice, &c. increaſe the multitude and ſwell the magnitude of miſeries of every kind, in the preſent ſtate of things, by increaſing human guilt, which ſeems to accumulate with growing knowledge in this age eſpecially.

However, let us change the ſcene, and brighten the black ſhades of this affecting picture of human miſery, by laying a few lines upon it taken from ſome typical characters drawn by the Pen of Moſes.

Let us begin with the morning of the old world, which, as you heard, continued 1656 years, and then was buried in water.

1. Abel, the *ſecond* man born of woman, the firſt being of that wicked one. Thus Shem was younger than Japhet; Abram than Nahar; Iſaac than Iſhmael; Jacob than Eſau; Joſeph than Reuben or Judah; and Moſes than Aaron, &c. Yet theſe had the Birth-right or the Bleſſing, although the younger.

Phil. And what then, I pray, my dear Didas.?

Didas.

Didas. What then! Can you ſuppoſe that infinite wiſdom ordered all theſe younger Brothers to have the pre-eminence and the Bleſſing without any deſign?

Phil. I ſuppoſe not. Wiſdom ſhines in all God's ways.

Didas. True. Remember then, "The firſt man is of the earth, earthly: The ſecond man is the Lord from heaven. That was not firſt which is ſpiritual, but that which is natural; (like Cain, &c.) afterward that which is ſpiritual." 1 *Cor.* xv. 46, 47. Thus, in the world's childhood and youth, did its Maker inſtruct it in theſe important Truths, by the pictures and living characters in their own Children in the moſt diſtant and intereſting of all events. Such is that of our Reſurrection. And this divine conduct, in preferring the *Younger* before the *Elder*, moſt certainly typified this Glorious event, and that by the ſame rule that Iſaac and Jacob typified the Goſpel, while Iſhmael and Eſau, the elder brothers, typified the Law as a former Diſpenſation.

Abel! his heart and life were Righteous; his offering by faith accepted, even faith in his Antitype—the proto-ſhepherd and proto-martyr of Mankind; his blood was ſpilt by his wicked Brother, becauſe he was better than himſelf; whoſe blood called for vengeance upon the murderer; and yet evidenced his Juſtification by faith as a martyr. Allowing the facts, will Reaſon admit that a Righteous Abel ſhould fall a ſacrifice to the ambition and envious reſentment of a wicked brother, being the only two ſuch in the world, unleſs a future ſtate exiſted, in which to reward the martyr and puniſh the murderer? Hark! the blood of Abel, (the firſt human blood that was ſhed) is turned Vocal! It cries aloud from the newly-curſed ground, addreſſes in the moſt convincing manner,

and

and demonſtrates by its cries, a life different from that which the Murderer took away, and preaches the life and immortality of departed ſpirits to all poſterity acquainted with the fact. *See and comp. Rev.* vi. 3 *to* 11.

In this righteous mourning martyr, we ſee, as in a glaſs, the mourning man of ſorrows—he falls under the murdering ſentence of his Brethren by Roman hands, while his blood ſpeaks better things than that of Abel, uniting its cry with his dying groans, "Father, forgive them, for they know not what they do." Abel, the proto-ſhepherd in the world, innocent as the flock he watched over, died as innocently—ſo did the great Shepherd and Biſhop of ſouls, with this difference, that the latter laid and paid down his life a ranſome for his ſheep. Herein both type and antitype, that original enmity between the two very different ſeeds eminently appeared, which in every age has filled the Church with martyrs, and inundated the world with human blood? Where is the ſoil that has not ſucked it in?

2. *Seth* ſignifies a Subſtitute, being put in the Place of Abel. He was the Second head of Mankind; and ſince the extinction of Cain's Family at the Flood, the world of Mankind have all deſcended from him. Thus was Jeſus Chriſt the Righteous, *firſt*, Subſtituted a Second Head of Mankind with reſpect to the world to come. He is therefore called *Abi Gned*, or *a Father of the World to come. Iſa.* ix. 6. "For as in Adam all die, even ſo in Chriſt ſhall all be made alive," viz. in another age, by a Reſurrection from the dead. *Second*, Abel was cut off by the envy and malice of Cain, who was of that wicked one, and Seth Put into his place—Chriſt was cut off by the envy and malice of his brethren, but roſe again in human Nature a Father of a world to come, like Seth. What will

our Resurrection-bodies be, but Substitutes in the room of those we should have Derived from Adam in case he had never sinned, only much more Glorious; and then naturally immortal?

3. *Enoch* signifies *Teaching, dedicating.* He walked with God as many years as we have days in a year: And having lived not above half as long as his contemporaries, took his flight bodily into the invisible world, as a kind of first-fruits of human nature, being the first of the kind thus highly honoured. *See Gen.* iv. 24. *comp. Heb.* xi. 5. Thus the great *Teacher* or Prophet of the church, whose both life and death were *Dedicated* solemnly to God's service, and man's salvation, having not lived above half the common term of the life of his Contemporaries; and having called at the Gates of Death, and like Sampson, in a sense carried them away, so as not to hinder the egress of all mankind in his own proper Seasons; at length took his flight upon the wings of the wind, and entered *bodily* into heaven itself, being the first-fruits from the Dead of human nature; in which he is invested with all authority in heaven and earth, at the Right Hand of the Majesty on high, Glorious Emanuel! Now, my dear Phil. Can we reasonably suppose, That the Antediluvians could be ignorant of the Translation of Enoch?

Phil. By no means; nor yet of his exemplary and uncommon piety and converse with God before his translation.

Didas. Suppose you, my dear Phil. had been a witness of his walking with God upon Earth, and of his bodily Translation into heaven, what conclusions would your reason have drawn from such an extraordinary Phenomenon?

Phil. I should certainly have concluded, That there were other beings, to us invisible, inhabitants of other worlds; by whose agency, above any

known

known law of nature, he aſcended above the clouds, probably into a happier world than that he left behind. That therefore his ſoul muſt be immortal, or capable of intercourſe with thoſe ſpiritual beings among whom he was going to reſide. And that as his body did not die upon earth, that this muſt paſs into a ſtate of immortality, by ſome change, to me unknown, after he left this world.

Didas. A very rational concluſion indeed! more eſpecially as Moſes introduces the Maker of Man breathing into his noſtrils *Niſhmath chajim*, the breath of LIVES, as principals of vitality, ſufficient to denominate him the Image and Offſpring of God. So that the natural mortality of the body admitted, as its natural component parts originate from the Duſt, and therefore its very *ſtamina* mortal; yet who can believe that the whole of what Jehovah-Elohim breathed into him is mortal alſo? The fruit of the Tree of life was intended to immortalize the body; but could it therefore immortalize the ſoul? If not, if the ſoul was not naturally immortal, by what means muſt it become ſo, in order to be a companion, and a living actuating principle to the body?

4. *Noah*, ſignifying *Reſt and Comfort*. Both him and his family *lived in two Worlds*. Is it poſſible to find any fact, either ancient or modern, that can afford a clearer figure of a world dying and riſing again? At the death of the old world, the Ark, like the Grave, preſerved the remains of human Nature: But behold! the following year, this remnant appears again upon the ſtage of time, and a new world of mankind ſprings out of the Ark out of thoſe who had been buried in it ſo long, as if lodged in their graves, yet alive all the time they ſeemed to be loſt.

Phil. Inſtructive figure indeed! They ſurvived the wreck of nature, and ſtand the Types of the dead,

dead, who ſhall riſe at the Reſurrection of the juſt, as the deſtruction of the old world was a figure of the deſtruction of the preſent.

The above curſory obſervations appear ſufficient grounds for the Patriarchs to found their faith and hope of a happy immortality upon, and that the ſoul lives when the body is dead.

This will appear plainer ſtill, by adding two or three inſtances, by which it will appear, that they did actually poſſeſs ſuch a faith and hope. The firſt inſtance ſhall be Abraham, the father of the Faithful. But as his faith in this very ſubject is conſidered in the following Eſſay, ſhall only at preſent obſerve, That it is not reaſonable to ſuppoſe, that Abraham ever imagined that the ſhedding the blood and burning the body of Iſaac would put an end to the exiſtence of his ſoul; which certainly muſt have been the caſe, if it expired with the body. But being perfectly reſigned to this ſingular requiſition of his Covenant-God, he haſtened to tranſact the bloody Tragedy; until He, who could read the heart, obſerved the voluntary ſacrifice virtually offered; which being in his eye tantamount to an actual offering, accepted the will for the deed. The victim was releaſed, and the Father received him as alive from the Dead. *Heb.* xi. 19. Did not Jacob receive his Joſeph in Egypt much the ſame way? Suppoſing him to be actually dead, the hoary afflicted Patriarch cried, "I will go down into *Sheol* unto my ſon." *Gen.* xxxvii. 35. Sheol in Hebrew is *Hades* in Greek: Both ſignify properly the place of ſeparate ſpirits, but hid from mortals.

Phil. Don't many ſuppoſe, that Jacob intended no more than to go to him into the grave?

Didas. But let Reaſon aſk, is the grave the ſepulchre of the ſoul as well as of the body? If not, was the body all that Jacob intended to viſit? Is the body the whole of man living or dead? How ſtrangely

ſtrangely diſappointed would Jacob have been, if neither his own nor the ſoul of his darling had ſurvived the body! But farther, the tranſmiſſion of the bones of Joſeph, and the burial of Jacob in the promiſed land, ſufficiently evidenced their faith and hope, not only of the Deliverance of the whole nation out of Egypt at the time appointed, but of the future Reſurrection of their bodies; and that they Looked for a city that hath foundations, whoſe builder and maker is God; for he hath (or will) prepare for them a City, (*Heb*. xi. 10, 16.) a continuing City yet tô come. This City was included in the Promiſes made to theſe Patriarchs. Their Faith gave them not only a demonſtrative rational evidence of the real exiſtence of the things promiſed, but they anticipated the enjoyment of them, though afar off, with regard to time, and left the world with unſhaken confidence of the power, goodneſs, and veracity of him in whom they believed.

But again; how was it poſſible for thoſe Patriarchs not to believe in a future ſtate of immortality, who were, upon every important occaſion, favoured with viſits and meſſengers from the Court of heaven? Frequently Jehovah himſelf condeſcended to viſit them. It has often been a query with many, whether they were not better acquainted with another world then, than we are now. And the preſumption ſeems to lie in favour of that ſide of the queſtion.

Did not the Philoſophy of Moſes in a manner illuſtrate this important Truth? Let the Deiſtical and Socinian Philoſopher deny the fact, or elſe Demonſtrate, How the firſt and Parent-Seed of every Plant contained *in embrio* every ſeed and every plant that from the creation to this day the prolific Womb of Mother Earth has ever produced? When he has reſolved this difficulty, and demonſtrated

demonſtrated *how* this operation of nature is performed: A Trinity in Unity; a God in human fleſh; Original ſin; imputation of ſin and righteouſneſs; the ſatisfaction for ſin that moral divine Juſtice demanded and obtained by the redemption that is in Jeſus; the natural immortality of the ſoul, &c. &c. Divines will demonſtrate beyond a poſſibility of contradiction.

On the other hand, let the Country Ruſtic, who neither has nor pretends to poſſeſs erudition, conſider that "All fleſh is Graſs," which Autumn cuts down, Winter withers, but its Roots being buried in the Earth, it lives under ground, and riſes with the returning ſpring in all its verdant or variegated blooming beauties. Here, in every field and every flower, the Peaſant may ſee every year his own Death, intermediate life of his ſoul, and future Reſurrection, as certain as the ſpring returns. The ſetting and riſing Sun repreſents the ſame every returning day. The Blind has ſtill a more natural illuſtration, ſanctioned by Scripture language—He ſleeps, he dreams, he awakes, and riſes with the riſing morn! Thus Univerſal nature around us, unite with experience and give their ſuffrage with ſacred Writ, and, without one diſſenting voice, proclaim Man's Immortality in Reaſon's Ear! But let us touch upon a few more topics in few words, and then cloſe theſe curſory Obſervations.

1. The Promiſed Seed flows in a current of Blood from the Mother of all living down to Judah the Son of Jacob. This divine Genealogy is full of myſtical inſtruction, as is elſewhere to be ſeen. It is not only the Chronologer's clew in the Labyrinth of ancient Time, but the Key to Prophetical numbers in both Teſtaments. *See the Author's S. Chronology*.

2. The *Geographer* may trace out the original diviſions of the earth; the ſettlement of the ſeventy nations

nations according to their respective Families, under the Leaders of Colonies, into those settlements. A pleasing employment this to occupy the leisure hours of the learned Antiquarian.

3. The *Linguist* may find an Epoch for the Grammatical Variations and Divisions, in different Languages, a few of which to learn has cost him so much time and trouble.

4. The Divine, the Philosopher, the Statesman, and Historian, in the History of Providence, may each find an Index that will point them to subjects worthy their deepest attention, and which will richly repay them for the most laborious investigation.

5. Who can read this instructive book, without seeing, as if written with sun-beams, the righteous Governing Providence of that God who made all things, and that both general and special, over all things that he made? But it should never be forgotten, that this Providence always Governs with an eye to a future state of Things. Without this Key,* the Divine Conduct is altogether Enigmatical. How otherwise can Reason account for what this book plainly proves, viz. That the most innocent and upright are, for the most part, the greatest sufferers in the world; that suffering innocently is God's High-road to honour and happiness; and that such are the greatest favourites of heaven; witness Abel, Isaac, Jacob, and Joseph. This is farther evident from observing, that "The Basest of Men," (*Dan.* iv. 17.) for the most part, possess the greatest Authority, and often weild the sceptre of Government in this evil world, witness Cain, Nimrod, Pharoah, &c.

These Remarks, being founded upon incontestible Facts, in the eye of reason, demonstrate a Governing Providence here, and the existence of a future world of Retribution, which, among other

things,

things, the Parable of Dives and Lazarus was intended to illuſtrate.

Laſtly, Moſes, no doubt, intended to inform his Brethren of their Divine Right to the Promiſed Land. Thus he introduces Jehovah, ſaying, "The Land is mine." It is therefore termed, "The Lord's Land," *Hos.* ix. 9. Emanuel's land; That is, Chriſt's Land, *Iſa.* viii. 8. And hence it is termed "The Holy Land," *Zech.* ii. 12. And frequently the Land which God Gave to them and their Fathers. The original Right is indefeaſible, but a temporary forfeiture has taken place, "Until the Times of the Gentiles be fulfilled," (*Luk.* xxi. 24.) on account of their Rejection of the Meſſiah. In future, they will moſt aſſuredly repoſſeſs it, notwithſtanding what Dr. Allix and others have ſaid to the contrary.

Here we muſt not fail to obſerve, That it is by the Righteouſneſs of Faith alone the Title ſtands Good. It was upon this Righteouſneſs that the Promiſe was made or founded, which conſtituted Abraham the Heir of *Koſmos* or the World, *Rom.* iv. 13. Therefore the Jews will never *peaceably poſſeſs it*, until they commence Believers in Jeſus. For want of this Faith, they were cut off from their own good Olive Tree, expelled from their Inheritance and are wanderers among the Nations, and will be ſome conſiderable time yet.

It is ſufficiently evident from the Prophecies, that the Jews will not generally believe in Jeſus until they ſee him at his next advent. Then he will bleſs them, by turning them from their iniquities; the Beginning of the Reſtitution of all things will then commence; at which Time He will Reſtore the Kingdom of Iſrael. The Canaan poſſeſſed by their fathers, was a Type and Earneſt of this Reſtored inheritance, as this will be of a ſtill more glorious one in the ſupernal Heavens. Happy Gradation!

DIALOGUE II.

Containing a few Obſervations upon the Creation; as given us by Moſes.

Philotheos. MY dear Didaſcalos, as you have before obſerved, that God created heaven and earth, and all things therein, viſible and inviſible, pray what are we to underſtand by *heaven and earth* in *Gen.* i. 1.?

Didaſcalos. The whole ſyſtem of the univerſe in general; but more particularly our ſolar ſyſtem; being the proper ſubject of the Moſaic creation. A genuine belief of this firſt Article of our creed, lays the foundation of all Religion both natural and revealed. *Elohim* or God, gave Being by his Word to all the enormous Globes in the univerſe, not excepting the central Suns, and launched them all in liquid ether throughout the vaſt immenſity of ſpace, each in its orbit revolving around its centre, and that with a velocity almoſt exceeding our narrow conceptions, and altogether unaccountable by Mortals.

The ſolar ſyſtem is included in the *Magnus Orbis*, or that vaſt circle which the *Georgius Sidus* deſcribes in his revolution round the ſun. This is the common Centre of all our planets, lately diſcovered to be ſeven in number. They have ſuch a near relation one to another, by the laws of gravitation, &c. we may very reaſonably ſuppoſe, That they were formed out of the ſame maſs of matter, originally Created together, and formed in their proper Order, nearly, if not exactly, at the ſame time; the Sun being the firſt in that Order. As to the ſtars beyond the limits of the ſolar ſyſtem, the Moſaical account of the creation ſeems to give no farther information, than that God Created them. Our Planets God appointed the moon's assistants in ruling the night. But the fixed stars, it is hard to conceive what influence they can have upon our earth, any farther than what their light affords, being at such an immense distance. We are told that a ray of light moves at the rate of ten millions of miles in a minute. And that a ray of light emitted from the brightest Star, maintaining the same velocity, would not reach the earth in less than six years time. If this be true, how far does it surpass human understanding to comprehend, or to account for!

When God laid the foundations of our earth, "The morning Stars sang together, and all the Sons of God shouted for joy," *Job* xxxviii. 6, 7. This seems to more than intimate their priority in time, and therefore to be no part of the mosaical creation, but beyond its limits, in regard to space.

The *Tekom* of Moses, or the great Deep, seems to include all the space of the solar system, and to have contained the materials or Elements of which the sun and all the Planets were made, to have been in apparent, if not real confusion. The whole was *void* of all settled order, beauty, inhabitants, or decorations of every kind, a shapeless mass as yet unmoulded into any regular Form. The Elements constituting the present system, mingled together, heavy and light, fluid and solid, earth, air, fire, and water, with all their different salts and sulphurs; and the whole in pitchy darkness, penetrable only by His eyes before whom darkness is as the day. God could have made a world by Word in a moment, with all its rich furniture. But to render both his own attributes and stupendous workmanship more conspicuous and intelligible, he proceeded in a regular and beautiful gradation

dation in our earth, from the less perfect, to the more perfect, which amazing performance ravished the celestial spectators into extacies of joy and praise! That truly sublime Command, so justly admired by *Longinus*, "Let there be Light," brought forth light out of darkness, and rendered visible the prolific mass to the admiring crouds of heavenly Courtiers, no doubt spectators of this astonishing scene. See! see! my dear Phil. how by the spirit's incubation, the once-stagnant mass is all in motion throughout the vast deep! Behold! the heavy terrene parts, within each planetary orbit, sink to their respective centres. And while the grosser and more dense particles subside, the the lighter and more tenuous ascend towards the surface of each forming globe within the system. Motion, in every direction, might now be seen, as if the whole mass had been inspired with life and vitality.

The second mandate of creative power produced a *Firmament*, an ærial expansion, probably around every planet within the *magnus orbis*. It includes within its limits the whole region of the Air and Ether, from the surface of the earth to the fixed stars. Here our winged tribes sport and play, (*ver.* 20.) near our dwellings; here the lamps of heaven burn with resplendent sparkling lustre, (*ver.* 14, 17.) held out by the hand of Elohim, though at such immense distances, to guide the mariner circumnavigating the globe, and lend their lights to the benighted traveller.

Now, probably, the waters were collected throughout the vast profundity, and surrounded the surface of each watery planet contained within our system, being restrained by the pressure of the air within their due limits on their respective surfaces. Thus the Omnipotent architect "Divided the waters which were *under* the firmament," upon the

the ſurface of each reſpective globe, "From the waters which were *above* the firmament" or atmoſphere of that globe; each atmoſphere confining the waters of its own particular Planet upon its own ſurface. By this diviſion, each planet would have its own waters confined to its ſurface by the ſurrounding atmoſphere belonging to it. The laws of repulſion and attraction now taking place, the planetary waters would be kept aſunder, and confined within their own limitted bounds by their reſpective atmoſpheres throughout the ſyſtem.

Phil. God having thus circumfuſed the planetary waters around their proper ſurfaces, and confined them within their due bounds by their reſpective atmoſpheres, the whole region of the air would become pellucid, and capable of tranſmitting the ſolar beams in every direction throughout the vaſt expanſe; illuminating each planet in the ſyſtem in proportion to their diſtance from that fountain of light ſituated in the centre, and encircled with every Orbit.

But, my dear Didas. Is it not uſually ſuppoſed, That the waters *above* the firmament only mean the clouds, as vehicles of rain?

Didas. True. But my dear Phil. may remark, That then there was no rain, the humid ſtate of the earth for ſome conſiderable time requiring none. And ſome have ſuppoſed, That the Miſt, mentioned by Moſes, precluded the neceſſity of rain; and that the firſt that fell, drowned the world. But however that might be, take the word firmament in which ſenſe you pleaſe, how can it poſſibly be true? Will waters float in Ether, where there is no denſity of air to ſupport them? But ſo they muſt of neceſſity do, according to that hypotheſis, if the waters *above* the firmament mean only rain water; for the firmament extends to the fixed ſtars, (*Gen.* i. 14, 18.) or we could never ſee them.

them. I therefore conclude, That the waters *above* the firmament mean the planetary waters belonging to thoſe planets which are above the atmoſpheres of the reſpective globes in the ſyſtem, as their orbits are farther and farther from the ſun, encircled one within another, at greater or leſs diſtances.

The firſt of all viſible things was light; and that light concentrated in the Sun; whoſe beams immediately ſo far penetrated through the horrid gloom, as to reach the ſurface of our globe, and that on the firſt day; a day meaſured by its own Diurnal Motion, and of the ſame duration that it was afterwards. Light is a property that makes every thing viſible that is ſo. A bleſſing this which diſcovers all the viſible beauties in the univerſe; conſult *Pſa.* lxxiv. 16. *Pro.* xv. 30. *Eccles.* xi. 7. The firmament is the only medium or vehicle to tranſmit light from the central ſun to every planet, and to ſuch as are ſecondaries to them. The air is ſo ſubtle and tenuous as to fit it for animal reſpiration; and yet, though porous, ſo denſe as to buoy up in its interſtices a very large quantity of vapours, ſo ſtrong as to carry the heavy-loaded cloud into diſtant regions; and when violently agitated, rends all before it; ſo elaſtic, if expanded by heat, &c. as to move mountains from their baſes. 'Tis a principal inſtrument in the adminiſtration of providence, by its maker termed *heaven*, but by Him never, in particular, termed Good, as the reſt of the parts of the ſix days works were.

Hitherto the earth was wrapped up in a watery veſt. But now the earthy particles ſubſided; the waters leſs turbid, and more liquid; the third command was iſſued by Omnipotence, "Let the waters under the heaven (or firmament) be gathered together into one place, and let the dry land appear," which the light would now diſcover. The waters ſtood above the mountains, but at His command

mand

mand they fled, at the voice of His thunder they hafted away. They go up by the mountains, they go down by the valleys, into the place which God had founded for them, (*Pfa*. civ. 6, 10.) both at the Creation and at the Flood.

Phil. It was an eafy thing for Him to fhut up the ftupendous ocean with doors, faying, "Hither-to fhalt thou go, but no farther; and here fhall thy proud waves be ftayed." *Job* xxxviii. 10, 11. *comp. Prov.* viii. 28, 29.

Didas. True. And it is owing to this word, more powerful than ramparts of ftone or fteel, that the boifterous ocean knows its bounds. Hitherto we have contemplated a fteril unproductive world yet forming under the foftering wings of the brooding fpirit, which, by its divine incubation, made earth pregnant with vegetable and animal life.— This day, a fecond command iffued from the *Elohim*, the facred *Three*; "Let the earth bring forth grafs;" the earth heard, and felt the influential word! Grafs, the firft of vegetables and of moft abundant and extenfive production, feemed fpontaneoufly to rife; and, like a verdant carpet, covered the new footftool (*Ifa.* lxvi. 1.) of its Majeftic maker, variegated with all the beauteous Tints that virgin flowers could exhibit! But again, "The herb yielding feed; the *herb* for meat and medicine, the *feed* to propagate its kind in every adapted climate and in every age. Once more, "The fruit-tree yielding fruit after his kind." Every kind and fpecies of delicious fruits, that adorn the orchard, or bedeck the feftive Table of the Prince in every part of the world to this day, owe their origin and continuance to this prolific word! Finally, "Whofe feed is in itfelf upon the earth." *ver.* 11. Inexplicable myftery! Every tree and every plant lives *in embrio* in its parent feed! Yet more myfterious ftill—The primitive,

or

or firſt made ſeed, contained in itſelf all the future productions of its kind ! ! ! Nor time, nor change of ſoil or climate, will ever change the eſſential qualities of any ſeed, ſo far as obſervation reaches.

Phil. What a change! Enwrapt in waters; involved in impenetrable darkneſs; one word diſperſes the darkeſt ſhades; a ſecond diſmantles earth of its watery veſt; a third dreſſes it up in all the gorgeous ſumptuous cloathing that nature, in her prime, could poſſibly produce! Behold, now the moſt variegated plants and flowers deck the face of nature; emit their virgin odours; whoſe delightful tints and inimitable filmy embroidery as far excel the royal robes of Solomon, in all his glory, as the works of God exceed all human art!

Didas. Fruit-trees now begin to teem with their reſpective fruits; plants and flowers, being male and female, whoſe *farina* to propagate their kind, promiſe their duration to all future generations, for the pleaſure and profit of animated beings. Seed was the more immediate work of God. Experience has abundantly demonſtrated, that no formative power, reſiding in any ſoil without ſeed, can poſſibly raiſe either herb or plant. But is any thing too hard for Him, who, with equal eaſe, can ſummon an atom or a thouſand worlds, with one word, into exiſtence? Surely no.

However the uſe of the creatures may be given, or rather lent to mankind, certain it is, that they will forever remain the unalienable property of the Divine Proprietor, the great *Poſſeſſor* of heaven and earth. *See Hoſea* ii. 9. *Matth.* v. 45. How then dare ſuch Tenants at will as mortals are, either venture to alienate or abuſe, to the wanton and profligate purpoſes of rebellion againſt God, the very property he has lent them, for His ſervice, for a ſeaſon?

Phil. The employment of ſecond cauſes, appears

pears to me rather to increaſe than diminiſh the wonders of vegetable productions, *Deut.* xxxiii. 14, 16. How aſtoniſhing is it to obſerve, that a little plot of ground, whoſe ſoil is the ſame, will afford a *pabulum* or different nouriſhment for a hundred plants of different genuſes and ſpecies, with all their vaſt varieties of colours, odours, and uſes, both for food and phyſic! Behold what millions of animals of various kinds, cattle upon a thouſand hills and in fruitful vales, the verdant graſs ſupplies with paſturage, as well as herbs for the uſe of man!

Didas. Yes, my friend; and the whole proceeds from that original command which mother earth received from her Maker, "Bring forth Graſs," from the moſs upon the wall, to the cedar in Libanus, in ſpight of the ſeverity of ſoils or ſeaſons, each ſeed will, by nature, produce its own kind! This uniform and exuberant production of nature has continued for a ſeries of near ſix thouſand years, yet all that time labouring and groaning under an influential Curſe for the rebellion of Man! How manifold are thy works, O Lord! in wiſdom haſt thou made them all!

From this footſtool of heavenly Majeſty, let us, my dear Phil. for a moment raiſe our eyes up towards the chambers or pavilions, in which the Throne of the high and lofty one, who inhabits eternity, is erected. To demonſtrate that earth, and all its primitive produce, and *virtually* all her produce ever ſince, owed their exiſtence and perfection, not to planetary influence, or ſecond cauſes, but their Maker only, they were all in exiſtence before the Omnipotent *Fiat* was iſſued, which ſaid, "Let there be lights in the Firmament of the Heaven." Thus ſpake the Father of lights, and it was done! This firmament extends into the higheſt regions of ether that we are acquainted with.

with. This ether, with the more denſe air, make the medium and vehicle of ſight and ſound. Hence the ſolar, lunar, and ſtarry beams, find an eaſy paſſage from planet to planet, and keep open a communication between very diſtant worlds!

In this diaphanous and heavenly mirror, let us, my dear friend, contemplate the attributes of its Maker. In its height, behold the majeſty and ſupremacy; in its brightneſs, the holineſs and glory; and in its vaſt immenſity, the ſpirituality, omnipreſence, and univerſal providence, of Him whoſe preſence fills heaven and earth!!

It is now very well known, That the Sun is the parent of day, the palace and fountain of light. From thence the morning ſtar gilds her horn; the planetary globes derive their luſtre; and the moon, her brighteſt beams, and all the glory of her dominion over the ſhades of night.

The Sun is placed exactly at a diſtance moſt commodious for us. Were he much nearer, ourſelves, and every produce of nature, would be ſcorched with heat; or much farther off, we ſhould be frigid as at the Poles; our rivers and ſeas, icy glaſs.

Our moon, the earth's only companion in her annual tour around the ſun, in a friendly manner, lends us thoſe beams herſelf had borrowed from the ſun, and receives a reciprocal favour in return, as in all probability, our earth is a moon to the inhabitants of that ſecondary planet.

All the planets, both primary and ſecondary, that compoſe our ſyſtem, are placed at ſuch proper diſtances, impreſſed with ſuch laws of motion, and powers of gravitation both attractive and repulſive, as completely anſwer all the intentions of their Maker. But in this grand piece of divine machinery, ſuch is the connexion with, and dependance of one part upon another, that it appears to

me,

me, That they all derive their birth from the ſame date; and that the funeral obſequies of the whole may be celebrated together. Yet this hinders not, but that the component parts of their *ſurfaces* may undergo great changes, either by water or fire, without diſſolving the whole machine, or, perhaps, without much diſordering it in any very material part.

Aſtronomers tell us, That the mean diſtance of the Sun from our earth is eighty millions of miles; notwithſtanding that vaſt diſtance, the rays of light emitted from that fiery globe, are ſaid to reach us in ſeven minutes and a half!!

Phil. Aſtoniſhing indeed! The vaſt *momentum* with which theſe rays muſt ſtrike the tender pupil of the eye, muſt neceſſarily be ſo great, that one would wonder that they do not ſtrike us blind in a moment.

Didas. True. But the contrary is the caſe, for "Truly the light is ſweet, and pleaſant for the eyes to behold the ſun," *Eccles.* xi. 7. It is ſaid, that our earth, to a ſpectator in the ſun, would appear no bigger than a ſmall ſtar.

Phil. No wonder, the diſtance is ſo great! But, my dear friend, what is the bulk of this vaſt fiery globe?

Didas. It is ſaid to be no leſs than one million, ninety eight thouſand, ſix hundred times larger than our earth; even Jupiter is ſaid to be three thouſand, four hundred, and ſeventy one times bigger. Yet theſe large bodies, whoſe magnitude confounds our conceptions, ſtrictly conform to the laws of their maker; while man, *a mite*, dares to tranſgreſs them! The planets, launched in the vaſt depths of Ether, run their aſtoniſhing rounds without fear of interrupting each others progreſs, and never miſs their paths in the almoſt immenſity of ſpace! But the Paths and Motions of Comets

Comets are ftill more furprifing. They take their flight beyond the limits of our fyftem, as if they would never vifit us more. Arrefted in their fwift career, as if by the immediate hand of their Maker, with a fhort Curve they return back once more into our fyftem, to be rekindled by the Solar heat to the moft intenfe degree, as they fly around him; then crofs the Orbits of our Planets, and launch beyond them again into unknown tracts of fpace. Their fiery tails, of an aftonifhing length, threaten to burn the earth, or fome other of our Planets as they crofs their Orbits in paffing and repaffing to and from the Sun in the mean time.

The moon ftrictly obferves her appointed feafons. Likewife the fun knows the time of his rifing up and going down. He enlivens whatever he enlightens; and his penetrating heat finds its way into the caverns, and below the furface of the earth; and nothing in our fyftem can fubfift without his vivifying influences.

Phil. "When I confider thy heavens, the work of thy fingers, the moon and the ftars which Thou haft ordained; what is man that THOU art mindful of him? and the Son of man that THOU doft Vifit him? Will my dear Didas, indulge me a few minutes, while, with David, I confider the moon, &c.? What a welcome fubftitute for the fun is this governefs of tides, this powerful agent in the vegetating world, during his nocturnal abfence! The moon and ftars fhare with the fun, in perfect harmony, the government of night and day over our opaque and lightlefs globe. How wonderfully glorious muft their Maker be! Who can paint out a thoufandth part of His glory, who can hang out fuch flaming torches from the windows of heaven, whofe fplendid brightnefs dazzles human fight with their created Glory? How exuberant his goodnefs, who lends fuch ufeful lights to mortals!

mortals! These grand mediums of vision discover thousands of beauties in nature, in the stupendous works of the God of nature; without which, our earth would be an inhospitable dreary dungeon. These deputy governors of God most punctually exercise their delegated authority, in the alternate government of day and night. They never interfere with each others government, or invade each others rights. The pale-faced moon never envies the superior lustre of the sun. These prophetic emblems of worldly Monarchs have set an example which have been very badly imitated by those they represented. Since their authority commenced, what numbers of earthly monarchs have they seen shed rivers of human blood to gratify ambition, and satiate unbounded avarice!! What Kings and Kingdoms have been overturned, with more than brutal rage, and savage cruelty!

Didas. What has the world in general been, but a large Aceldama? But, my dear Phil. Dominion was not the only use of those Deputy Governors under God, "Let them be for signs," said He who appointed the ordinances of heaven. Signs portentous of subverted and subverting kingdoms; Famines, Pestilences, and such-like dire calamities, that in every age afflict the world of mankind; but more especially those awful signs that will precede and usher in the advent of their great Creator. *Luk.* xxi. 25.

To distinguish *seasons*, summer, winter, spring, and autumn, was another office of these heavenly delegates, and obvious to every capacity. With what astonishing exactness do those vast time-keepers measure *days and years!* They never vary, they never go wrong one moment. He who made them, and first set them a going, has still maintained them in perfect order: He has hung them up under the canopy of heaven for all the world to see.

There

There they will remain, the ſtandards of time—the chronologer's guide—till they have run the length of their own and of the world's duration.

Phil. Surely the annual and diurnal motions of the earth are very inſtructing! It is by means of this double whirl on the earth's axis and in her orbit, that we are ever able to calculate time. And though in reality this is the fact, yet apparently it is otherwiſe. To us the ſun ſeems to riſe and ſet, as the earth performs its diurnal motion; and therefore pleaſe, my dear Didas, to permit me to ſing,

"Awake, my ſoul, and with the ſun,
"Thy daily ſtage of duty run;
"Shake off dull ſloth, and early riſe,
"To pay thy morning ſacrifice."

Didas. Go on, my friend, and let the riſing ſun ſtimulate your devotion, the morning breezes exhilarate your ſpirits, while I proceed to obſerve, That the fixed ſtars, beyond the limits of the ſolar ſyſtem, are juſtly ſuppoſed to be ſo many Suns, in the centres of planets that dance in circles round about them,

"For ever ſinging, as they ſhine,
"The Hand that made us *is divine*."

As moſt, if not all of theſe, exiſted prior to the Moſaical creation, they are only occaſionally mentioned, (*ver.* 16.) juſt to inform us, that God made them; and, among other uſes, to aſſiſt the moon in her nocturnal government, as above obſerved: That, therefore, they are only creatures, and conſequently by no means ought to be worſhiped. By the annual and diurnal revolutions of the earth, Time, as you have heard above, is meaſured to a tittle; a grateful and neceſſary variety of ſeaſons, ſpring, ſummer, autumn, and winter, are all pro-

 duced.

duced. These include the bleſſings of ſeed-time and harveſt, cold and heat, day and night, with all their benefits and beauties, which are the conſtant attendants of this aſtoniſhing Mechaniſm; and without which, no ſuch bleſſings would be produced, ſo far as we know, from all the machinery of earth and heaven.

And now, my dear Phil. we muſt pauſe a moment, being about to advance a large ſtep in the ſcale of creation.

Phil. Pray what ſtep is it? Shall I be able to mount it with you?

Didas. No doubt of that. But here the ſtrength of human reaſon, with all the aid of Revelation, will be found inadequate completely to comprehend the ſubject. From inanimate, we muſt now enter into a world of animated nature—a world of the greateſt wonders! For,

However ſurpriſing it may appear to ſee a world of matter ſpring, at a Word, out of nothing; light ſhine out of darkneſs; immenſe worlds ſuſpended in Ether, and flying regularly about in circles of aſtoniſhing dimenſions, &c. &c. Theſe are but a ſmall part of the works of God. The leaſt particle of matter, that has life beſtowed upon, tranſcends all other mechaniſm, however huge or curious they may otherwiſe be. Life! What is it? Who can explore its nature or eſſence? We ſee it in its effects—we feel it—we are replete with it—it ſurrounds us on every ſide: From the microſcopic *Animalculæ* floating in air or water, or feaſting themſelves upon herbage or foliage; to the huge Elephant roaming at pleaſure in the deſert; or the mountainous maſſy whale, ſporting in gambols, like floating Iſlands in the watery deep—We ſee millions of creatures in every ſhape, of every ſize, in every attitude, flying in the air, floating in the water, or boring into the bowels of the earth,

where

where Man in vain attempts to follow. "Every part of Nature is peopled, every green leaf ſwarms with Inhabitants. There is ſcarce a ſingle Humour in the body of Man, or of any other Animal, in which our glaſſes do not diſcover myriads of living creatures. The ſurface of Animals is covered with other Animals, which are in the ſame manner the baſis of other Animals that live upon it; nay, we find in the moſt ſolid bodies, as in Marble itſelf, innumerable Cells and Cavities, that are crowded with ſuch imperceptible inhabitants, as are too little for the naked eye to diſcover." Again, Thouſands of quadruped and biped animals, grazing upon herbage; catching the falling crumbs from our tables; or traverſing our yards, and attending our barns to pick up the offals and refuſe, that nothing be loſt: All theſe, poſſeſt of the keeneſt ſenſibility or moſt delicate feelings, exiſt longer or ſhorter, as their maker pleaſeth; and, no doubt, every Genus enjoys its felicities.

Among this vaſt variety, ſome are wild, others tame; ſome for our ſervice, but not ſuſtenance, as the horſe, the mule, the aſs; others for ſuſtenance, but not ſervice, as the pig, the ſheep, &c. Others, again, for both, as the ox; and finally, ſome for neither, as the tiger, &c. But what all theſe are, their actions, ends, and uſes, how ſmall a part do we know! But this we know, O Lord, "That in Wiſdom Thou haſt made them all!" Every living creature, from a mite to a man, is moſt exquiſitely made. Veſſels, conveying different circulating fluids in a thouſand directions, pervade the whole body, and carry matter in their currents, however minute, which nature aſſimulates, and thereby repairs its perpetual waſte. The noxious and ſuperfluous vapours gain an exit thro' the pores, by inſenſible perſpiration; the groſſer parts, by other paſſages, gain a diſcharge, and thus

thus relieve over-loaded nature. Bones, muſcles, ſinews, and different ſorts of teguments, from the Lady's ſkin to the hedge-hog's briſtles, give ſtrength, beauty, and afford defence to different animals, human and brutiſh; while the ſyſtem of the nerves afford the fineſt ſenſibility to the whole machine. By means of theſe, every animal, by reaſon or inſtinct, performs a thouſand volitions and actions, which, while they exite our aſtoniſhment, leave reaſon behind, in all her attempts, to account for them.

Nothing was ever brought forth by ſpontaneous generation. From the ſhrimp to the whale, this divine *fiat* produced them all, "Let the waters bring forth abundantly, &c." The leaſt particle of matter, being diviſible *ad infinitum*, confounds the human intellect! But how much more, when modified and formed into different kinds of animated creatures? 1 *Cor*. xv. 29. Both fiſh and fowl, God created, and formed them of matter properly prepared in the waters. To both fiſh and fowl, He gave a texture and form, moſt curiouſly adapted to the reſpective elements of air and water, in which they float and fly at large, the freeſt of all creatures.

The oviparous broods of fiſhes are innumerable. It is curious to obſerve how they ſcud and dive in the water: Their tails are natural helms, by which they ſteer their courſe at pleaſure; they dive into vaſt depths, or riſe to the ſurface to catch their prey, where human nature cannot follow. "Be fruitful and multiply," ſaid their Maker. What countleſs multitudes have thoſe words produced ſince firſt delivered! To this prolific word, all the innumerable ſhoals in every part of the ocean, or meandering in rivers, in every age, owe their exiſtence.

But

But it is obſervable, That fiſh are leſs perfect in kind and curious in their texture than land-animals: With theſe the Creator began peopling his new world. This ſeems to be the plan of *providence*, To proceed from the leſs to the more perfect; and alſo of grace, from the ſmalleſt beginnings to the higheſt attainments, both of holineſs and happineſs.

Air and ocean being now replenished with inhabitants, terreſtrial Animals muſt now follow.

Brutes, Moſes diſtributes into three claſſes. The *Behemoth*, or the larger kinds of creatures, whether terrene or amphibious; as in the water, the Rhinoceros and Whale; upon land, the Elephant, Dromedary, &c. The *Caijah*, or domeſtic animals, as the horſe, ox, ſheep, dog, &c. In this word he ſeems to include all the wild, fiery, and more *lively* animals, as the lion, bear, tiger, wolf, hyæna, &c. The *Remes*, all reptiles and creeping things, whether upon the ſurface of the earth, or within its bowels; as ſerpents, worms, and the innumerable tribes of inſects; all which appear to have been formed in the full perfection of their natures, and poſſeſſed of powers and inſtincts for ſelf-preſervation and propagating their kinds.

But the principal, and for whom all the reſt were made, was MAN. But he was not introduced into the world, until every thing was completely ready for his Comfortable Accommodation.

The ſolar heat and gentle breezes had ſufficiently clarified the air, and prepared it for human reſpiration. The water was purified from every degree of turbidneſs, and rendered fit to miniſter both to his neceſſities and delight. The dry land was drained and cruſted, and of ſufficient ſolidity to ſupport him: At the ſame time it was repleniſhed with herbs, flowers, fruits, &c. for ſuſtenance, when required.

The music of the feathered choirs would doubtless charm his ears; his olfactory nerves would be regaled with the richest perfumes and sweetest odours, conveyed from fruits, flowers, gums, &c. by every breeze. The vast theatre of earth, and bright luminaries of heaven, ready to invite his contemplating powers into exercise, shedding their benign influences upon him as soon as made.

The *Elohim*, or God, afterwards revealed as Father, Son, and Holy Ghost, consult in sacred Council. One of the sacred three proposed, "Let Us make man in Our image, after Our likeness." This proposal was agreed to, and immediately carried into execution. "So Elohim created man in His own image; in the image of Elohim created He him."

Phil. Is it not evident, That Elohim must include more persons than one? Otherwise, how can this greatest of all the divine transactions that we are acquainted withal, ever be reconciled to common sense? The proposal is made in the first person plural, *Us*: The execution is performed by One in the third person sing. masc. gender, *His*, *He*. This change of *number* and *person* is so obvious, that one would imagine it to be sufficient to silence all objections against the orthodox interpretation of *Elohim*, as including in it the three divine Persons in the unity of the Deity, or Father, Son, and Holy Ghost, into whose Name we are Baptized.

Didas. That there is a Trinity of Persons in the Unity of the Deity, is so plainly and frequently revealed in the New Testament, that it is surprising that any, who have been baptized into their sacred Name, should ever call the truth of it into question. And as Father, Son, and Holy Ghost, have each discovered their respective Persons and Works, in the redemption of mankind; is it any

wonder,

wonder, if they united in council when they were about to make man? Again,

In the *proposal*, (*ver.* 26.) the first person plural is three times used; and hence we are exhorted to remember our *Creators*, *Eccles.* xii. 1. For creation is ascribed to the Father, *Eph.* iii. 9. To the Son, *Heb.* i. 8, 10. And to the Spirit of God, *Job* xxxiii. 4. *Comp.* *Job* xxvi. 13. *Psa.* xxxiii. 6. civ. 30. Again, In the *execution* of that proposal, or in the history of it in *ver.* 27, the third pers. sing. is twice used, *His*, *He*.

Phil. What reason do you assign for this remarkable change in number and person?

Didas. First, Moses seems here *purposely* to explain the word *Elohim*, which word *alone* is used for Our Creators, as Solomon terms them, in the whole history of the Creation. This word *Elohim* or God, is used absolutely throughout the first Chapter of Genesis. This word is therefore put for the Trinity our Creators. But Moses. upon his beginning to treat upon the *Administration* of the affairs of the new created world, *Chap* ii. *ver.* 4. prefixes the word Jehovah; And from this verse *Jehovah-God* is used twenty times to the end of the third Chapter. This Jehovah appears plainly to be the *He* who is intended in *Chap.* i. 1. where we have the like form of speech, which is as literally and grammatically used in the second and third words of the bible. That which is rendered *God created*, in the Hebrew literally is, "The Gods *He* hath Created." The noun is plural, the verb is singular, and in the perfect tense. Now who can this He be, but the same *He* who created man, in the "Image of Elohim Created He him?" I look upon this He to be the same with that One in *Chap.* iii. 22. That *One* who was to *know evil*, viz: by experience, in the bruising of his heel; the evil of sin by imputation of guilt;

and

and of ſuffering for that guilt. Neither this evil, nor any other, in any ſenſe, neither the Father nor the Holy Spirit ever knew; conſequently it was the intended Seed of the woman who was to know evil. Secondly, Another reaſon may be aſſigned, which is, that "Theſe three are one." 1 *Joh.* v. 7. which accords with *Deut.* vi. 4, 5.

Phil. Does it not then ſeem probable, That He who propoſed the making of man in *ver.* 26. was He who actually made him in *ver.* 27. in his own image?

Didas. It looks very like it. If ſo, was it not the ſame with Him who is the "Image of the invisible God?" And was it not in the Image of this *divine* Image that man was originally created or made? Does not the Apoſtle tell us, that "By him were all things created that are in heaven, and that are in earth? and alſo that, By Him all things conſiſt; and He is the Head of his Body the Church," (*Col.* i. 15, 17.) now Reſtored by Redemption?

Phil. It ſeems that this Head was He who ſaid, "Let us make man;" and man multiplied by generation, ſeems to have been his *intended* Body, or a myſtical ſpouſe—Image of Himſelf; though defeated by the fall.

Didas. This appears to have been the caſe, ſeeing that all things were created for Him, as well as by him. The Church, his body, in this ſenſe, was mankind. If man, then, had never ſinned, being created for Him, of courſe mankind would have been his body by *creation*.

Phil. This is plain. But this firſt union of the head and body was diſſolved by ſin; and the body, on account of ſin, doomed to death. But the Head, unincarnated, could never die, though the body did.

Didas. True. But ſhall this ſame body for ever

ever perish, being cut off from the Head? Blessed be God, no. For though by Sin the created image was lost, and the body as actually died, as when a man is beheaded his dody dies, (and in this consists the essence of the fall) yet, nevertheless, our recovery is resolved upon. This St. Paul terms "The mystery of His Will, according to His good pleasure, which He hath purposed IN HIMSELF."

Phil. What he had purposed in Himself, must certainly remain an impenetrable mystery, till He himself reveals it; for "Who hath known the Mind of the Lord?"

Didas. But, blessed be His Name, He has revealed it. Though St. Paul seems to intimate, That it is the sum of all Wisdom and Prudence to understand it rightly, notwithstanding the discovery made of it.

Phil. And pray, my dear Didas. what is the sum of it?

Didas. Dr. Doddridge renders it thus:—"That in the Œconomy of the fulness of the Times, He might REUNITE UNDER ONE HEAD ALL THINGS IN CHRIST, both which are in Heaven, and which are on Earth, IN HIM." The Greek is properly to *Prehead*, or head over again. *Eph.* i. 8, 9, 10. The fact is this, "The Head of every man is Christ," 1 *Cor.* xi. 3. Christ was the Head of Mankind when created. Sin beheaded Him. And the mystery of God's will, and the purpose which He proposed in Himself, was, That in a series of future ages, He would REHEAD mankind with the same Head, though now Incarnated, which he had at his creation; and that this second Union would be indissoluble, by the Incarnation.

Phil. If I then understand you right, The HE, or divine Person in the Elohim, who created man, was

was the Head of man or mankind by creation: But, by sin, this headship was dissolved, and the body ruined: But God's secret purpose was, to Rehead them again with the same divine Head, with this farther addition—That as the Body consisted of both flesh and spirit, but the first head of spirit only, He, AS the HEAD, would take upon Himself flesh also; and so, *as God in Human Nature*, He would Rehead and Reunite them again unto Himself, by a vital union of both Flesh and Spirit.

Didas. That is my meaning. And this is the redemption which is in Jesus—A redemption of the soul from sin, satan, and the woeful miseries consequent upon slavery under them; and of the body from mortality and death. The whole of this grand plan, *in the fulness of Times*, being the same with *Christ's own proper Times*, (1 Tim. ii. 6.) will be most clearly exhibited; and this Reheading of all things in Christ will then be found to have such an universal extent, as will greatly surprise all who have believed and taught otherwise. To examine into these Times, and the extent of this Redemption, are two principal designs in the present undertaking, the execution of which will appear below.

DIALOGUE

DIALOGUE III.

Being a Continuation of the Creation, Formation of Man in God's Image, &c.

Philotheos. MY dear Didas. this subject appears to me of considerable importance: Shall therefore take it as a favour to pursue the same a little farther.

Didas. This you will meet with below, rather more at large, in our introduction to the Paraphrastical notes and observations upon *Rom.* v. 12, &c.

Phil. Pray then, as One of the divine persons in Elohim seems to have been the principal in actually Making man, as well as of Redeeming him; and in whose more immediate Image he was made; what are we to understand by that original Image, antecedent to his incarnation?

Didas. Christ is the Image of the invisible God; and, when he shall appear in glory, he will exhibit this Image in his humanity, so as, in a sense, to render God himself visible in it.—This Image Jehovah appeared in to Adam proleptically when he formed him out of the Dust, and breathed into him the breath of Lives. This was intended as an Image of his incarnation, or as the intended standard of human perfection. Regeneration renews the Soul in knowledge, righteousness, and true holiness, after the Image of him that created it, *Col* iii. 10. For " Man is the Image and Glory of God, 1 *Cor.* xi. 7. And in future ages, He will change our vile bodies, and fashion them like unto His glorious body: Then shall we bear the Image of the second Adam, the Lord from heaven, both in soul and body.

Man

Man is the great end and master-piece of all God's works in this earthly globe. The globe itself, and all its furniture, were created for Him. But then, man must be understood in the sense of David, (*Psa*. viii. 4, 8.) as explained by St. Paul, (*Heb*. ii. 5, 10.) which Man is collectively considered, as including both Head and Body, or Christ and Mankind. We are principally to note, That the world is the world after the "Times of the Restitution of all things," as well as the present evil one, (*Gal*. i. 4.) and intended by both David and his expositor, and expressly mentioned by the latter in *ver*. 5. Farther observe, that to make Man, or Mankind, was no less than to bring into a state of actual conscious existence an innumerable multitude of intellectual, rational, and immortal beings, candidates for endless happiness; or, if finally rebellious, of proportionable misery. Take but a very superficial view of the human frame, it will abundantly confirm that inspired remark, that we are fearfully and wonderfully made! The majestic gait, the erection of our bodies, the use of our tongue in conversation, &c. sufficiently evidence the human superiority over the brute. The Tongue is the interpreter of the heart—the instrument of conveying information, instruction—public, social, and reciprocal joy; as the Ear is the Organ of sounds; without which, the tongue would be of little use. The admirable construction and use of the Eye, the Casement of this earthly house, out at which the soul both shews itself, and beholds ten thousand beauteous objects in nature, as so many Indexes pointing to the Deity; how wonderful are these Organs in contemplation! But how much more wonderful in their different uses! The several Uses of the structure and position of each single Muscle, '*Galen* computed to be no less than ten in number.' '*De Form.*

Form. Fortus, page 81. And it is worth your while to obſerve, That Heaven and Earth, in a ſenſe, were united in our compoſition! Certainly no leſs than immortality, and the divine image, were infuſed into our frame by that divine afflatus (*Gen.* ii. 7.) or breath of *Lives*.

The capacities of our intellectual powers, in this lapſed condition, are truly wonderful! Underſtanding, judgment, volition or freedom of choice, memory or recollection, &c. in ſome perſons are very extraordinary; but the moral ſenſe, or conſciouſneſs of virtue and vice, as it proves us rational, ſo conſequently accountable creatures. By virtue of the image of Elohim, the firſt couple could ſuſtain a ſight of the divine glory, or unclouded Shechinah, with whom they were qualified to converſe, and actually poſſeſt the incomparable privilege.

Phil. The more perfect theſe endowments were, the greater would be the ſurpriſe of this new-made couple at the firſt appearance of the ſurrounding objects. But ſay, my dear Didas, did any thing intervene between the creation of Adam and formation of Eve?

Didas. Moſt certainly. But, obſerve, the woman, and probably all mankind, ſubſiſted in individual Adam at his creation. Of that One blood all the nations of men were made that have, or ever will be upon the face of the earth. The ſame holds goods both of animals, vegetables, &c. all previouſly ſubſiſting in their reſpective Seeds.

Adam was made of *Adamah*, or virgin earth, without the limits Paradiſe. This was the intended Capital and Palace of his Kingdom, which, as the Viceroy of his Maker, extended over the regions of Earth, Air, and Ocean. He was ſole Monarch over the inhabitants of thoſe three regions. Doubtleſs he was made in order to be inveſted with this

Dominion; but in this he was a type of Him that was to come, (*Psa.* viii.) as is evident in *Heb.* ii. 5. comp.

Phil. Do not many place the divine Image in this Dominion?

Didas. Certainly. But is it not rather the consequence of his being in the divine Image, than any essential part of the Image itself? When Adam was invested with this Dominion, no undue subordination was so much as hinted at, respecting either Eve or their Posterity. The Woman was equally invested with the same Dominion as himself before the Fall.

Phil. What was it that first introduced servile subordination into the world?

Didas. It was Sin; and obtained first between Man and Wife, and between man and man, *very different, both in kind and degree*, from what it otherwise would have been. Since which, Priority in birth seems to have laid the principal foundation of all inequality among mankind. This is to be understood of the latter days chiefly. Among the Patriarchs, the younger brother got the blessing, for the most part, as above observed, for a typical reason. Nevertheless, there seems to have been a degree of subordination between Man and Wife intended, though not at first expressed; the natural reason of which appears in the Apostle's remark, that "Adam was first formed, then Eve." Adam the glory of Christ—Eve the glory of Adam;—A holy and natural inequality!

The superior size, strength, and activity of terrene quadrupeds in lonely Adam, could excite no dread: So long as he bore the lovely Image of his maker, the Elephant, Dromedary, Camel, Rhinoceros, &c. could excite no timidity, or disagreeable sensation, in that mind that knew no conscious guilt. The dread was in the cattle, not in their

Lord

Lord and Proprietor. The gift of ſpeech, and knowledge of language, Adam firſt employed about his duty, *Ch.* ii. 15, 18. then, to ſhew his authority, in giving names to ſome of his inferior ſubjects; and at length to his Wife. But before this, obſerving the different ſexes coupled according to their kind, he would eaſily perceive his own want of a ſecond ſelf, to aſſiſt in propagation, *ver.* 20. This want, probably before perceived by himſelf, his indulgent maker had reſolved to ſupply, *ver.* 18. This was no ſooner done, and preſented, and given in Marriage, than the Father of all pronounced the ſuperiority of the marriage-union above the parental ties of nature. But this was not done, until Adam had obſerved an identity of nature in his bride, as fleſh of his fleſh, and bone of his bone— a ſecond ſelf, made out of him! Man being an intire dependent creature, rational, and therefore accountable for his conduct; his happineſs muſt ſpring from an union with the author and fountain of his Being, which union would continue ſo long as no diſobedience intervened on his part to interrupt it, for nothing elſe could; and ſo long his happineſs would be ſecure, and probably increaſing.

But his primeval created happineſs was neither the whole that his nature was capable of, nor that his indulgent Creator intended for him. Being no Machine, but an intelligent free agent, it comported both with his preſent ſtate, and his Maker's deſigns, that he ſhould give proof of his entire dependence upon, and voluntary ſubmiſſion to, his moſt ſacred will, in order to his future advancement.

With a view to this, what could be better adapted for the purpoſe of giving proof of his obedience, than a poſitive prohibition to abſtain from ſomething, which, while it put to the teſt all the powers

of

of his nature, ſhould nevertheleſs have nothing compulſive in it, but which ſhould leave his will in perfect *equilibrio*, without the leaſt bias to infringe upon his freedom?

Such, moſt certainly, was the forbidden fruit. But, query, would Adam ever have taſted it, if Eve had not led the way? And is it not another queſtion, whether Eve would have taſted it, if ſhe had not been Deceived by an enemy? The probability appears to me to lie on the negative ſide of the queſtion in both caſes. Theſe were circumſtances which might, in ſome degree, mitigate their guilt, heinous as it was. They were neither of them ſolely ſelf-tempted. The laſt, very probably, was the caſe with Devils. This, among others, might be one reaſon why we ſuppoſe that there is no mercy for them. But, be this as it may, we may juſtly ſuppoſe, that had he ſtood firm in his trial, his advancement to future happineſs, in due time, would have been a tranſlation into a better world, Enoch or Elijah-like; the fruit of the Tree of Life having immortalized his body in his primeval ſtate.

But as the caſe proved otherwiſe, degraded Adam loſt the divine Image, and with it his delegated Dominion, &c. A ſecond Adam was then appointed. This was no other than that divine Perſon in the Elohim, who, as above obſerved, ſeemed to have the moſt active hand in the formation of every thing. The deſign of this divine appointment was, among other things, to Rehead the human Race, by an incarnation or an aſſumption of the ſame nature: In this nature, to Do and Suffer the whole will of God—his ſufferings to be of a piacular kind, in order to make an Atonement for the firſt offence of the firſt Adam, and the abounding offences of his diſobedient Poſterity—To deſtroy the works of the Devil—and reſcue

Man

Man from the dreadful effects of sin, both original and actual, of which, God willing, much more below. Hence an union once more subsists between Man and his Maker, which, with regard to the body, is universal and indissoluble; in consequence of which, the wicked and righteous will all rise from the dead in their own Order, 1 *Cor.* xv. 23.

Phil. Do you suppose that the eternal *Logos* appeared in human shape, and in that shape conversed with Adam?

Didas. By all probability, and upon many occasions afterwards. The vehicle that He assumed, was an earnest of His future incarnation, as above noted. This vehicle was a visible prototype or pattern, after the *likeness* of which, man was originally formed. At this time, the future incarnation of the WORD was, doubtless, both foreseen and decreed. His intended body was the model: This was *the form* of a servant, which he put on, when he divested himself of the *form of God*. It is therefore to the man Christ Jesus we are to look for the likeness or conformity to his maker, in which the first Man was made, and unto which, in both body and mind, we are to be Restored.

Phil. Man appears to me to have had a faint reflection of some of his Maker's divine attributes imprest upon him, and that evidently, as in a mirror. His understanding being a faint reflection of divine wisdom—his dominion over the creatures, a shadow of divine authority—self-government and freedom of choice, a dull transcript of the power and will of his creator—the spirituality and immortality of his soul, evidencing him to be the offspring of Him who is an eternal spirit.

Didas. Every image ought to possess a striking likeness of its original; and this, no doubt, man originally did. These things are all very wonderful,

ful, but rendered much more ſo by the faculty of ſpeech. This noble faculty ſeems to be a god-like endowment. He, who made the human intellect, knows how to communicate knowledge unto it, as well as to bring a world into being by a word. Has *he* not imparted a degree of this power unto Man? Who can deſcribe the almoſt omnipotence of words—the communication of ideas conveyed in intelligent ſounds, and the aſtoniſhing impreſſions they make upon the mental powers? Nor is it leſs wonderful to obſerve, how, by arbitrary characters in different forms and in different languages, we can read the minds of perſons many thouſands of years ſince lodged in the houſe appointed for all living; and tranſmit our own ſentiments to the lateſt ages yet to come. Theſe are vehicles of knowledge, which neither diſtance of time nor place can prevent its conveyance. In a word, languages ſpoken and written, are the Keys by which we have acceſs to one another's hearts, which give, in a degree, that God-like property to ſearch them; to know and communicate Thoughts, Deſigns, &c. But the moſt excellent property belonging to this Microcoſm, called Man, the perfection and crown of all the reſt, is his capability of an *union unto*, and *communion with* the Deity, in whoſe image he was made; whom, ſavingly to know, fervently to love, reverentially to fear, ſpiritually to worſhip, and faithfully to ſerve, is at once his duty, privilege, honour, and happineſs. In theſe, the true dignity and ſuper-excellency of man conſiſt. Herein he vies and will vie with angels, in equality. In this reſpect, difference of ſex, time, or climate, make no difference at all.

Phil. In *Gen.* i. 27. the word *created* is three times uſed: Twice, reſpecting man's creation in the divine image; the third time is, " Male and Female

Female *created* He Them." Which mode of expression seems to me to import, That the female was not altogether created in that image. The distinction is still more obvious in *Ch.* v. 1, 2. Pray, my dear Didas, why, think you, did Moses make this obvious distinction?

Didas. The distinction is too plain to escape the notice of an attentive reader. But, perhaps, the reason of it is not so plain. 1st. Did not the woman derive her vitality, as well as substance, from the man? Did not God bless them, and call *their name Adam, in the day they were created?* What difference then subsisted between them except that of sex? And is not this difference the real reason of the distinction observable in the text? 2d. And is not the difference of sex very important? If the *male* was made in the *likeness* of that One in the *Elohim*, whose heel was to be bruised, by which He was *to know Evil*; certainly the *female* was not. That ONE incarnated was Christ, *a man*, and not *a woman*. Neverthelefs, a woman has an immortal soul as well as a man; and though not the honour to be of the same sex, yet she is of the same nature with her blessed redeemer, whose humanity was derived from hers. This observation sufficiently evidences, that when it was proposed to Make man, a compound creature, consisting of a Spirit united to Flesh, a two-fold Pattern was proposed, as Models after which to Make him. The first was *Betzalmenu, In our Image*. May not this refer to the "Spirit in man?" The second was *Cidmuthenu, after*, or *according to our Likeness*. *Gen.* i. 26. What *likeness* is there between the Body of man, and the Divine nature? But is not the Body *a part* of Man, and a principal Part that was *made?* Does not this *likeness* then Principally refer to the Body? And was not the original Pattern or Model of that body some how Potentially

tially in the Elohim? But ſuppoſing the ſacred Trinity to be intended by that word, which of the Trinity ever had a body except the ſecond Perſon? And is not this that divine Perſon ſo eminently diſtinguiſhed, under the appellation of *Jehovah-Elohim*, in the ſecond, third, and fourth chapters? What can be plainer than the words of Eve, (*Ch.* iv. 1.) in the Heb. *Kanithi Iſh eth Jehovah*, "*I have Gotten a Man, The Jehovah.*" It is hence evident, that ſhe ſuppoſed her Firſt Son was the promiſed Seed, and that Seed Jehovah. Therefore Jeſus is Jehovah.

The ſexes being diſtinguiſhed and adapted to procreation, the Father of the ſpirits of all fleſh iſſued out this fecundating mandate, "Be ye fruitful and multiply," by conjugal union. What a prolifical word was here! What countleſs millions have and will derive, in ſucceſſion, an intelligent being, by its influence! It appears, by the ſtanding uniform laws of nature, that man propagates man, as inferior animals do their kinds, ſoul as well as body. Who can find a difference, in this reſpect, between *ver.* 22 and 28? Had there been any in nature, might we not reaſonably have expected here to have found it, where divine Inſpiration profeſſedly treats of the original of all things, communicating the knowledge of every neceſſary and uſeful ſubject of this kind?

The degree of this multiplication of mankind, was "To repleniſh or fill the earth." A degree that has in no age hitherto taken place, any more than the following, to "Subdue it." The undiſcovered and uncultivated millions of known tracts of land, inhabited by ſavages, or brutes only, prove to demonſtration, That this earth is as far from being ſubdued as it is from being completely peopled. But God's purpoſe, and the extent of this bleſſed command, will not fall to the ground; the

the "Ages to come" will abundantly fulfil them; both as to population and subduction.

The charter for food for man and beast, you may read in *Chap.* i. 29. 30. What divine bounty had before provided, beneficence now bestowed. The luxuriant juicy herb, the delicious life-supporting fruit, to gratify the appetite, supply the lamp of life, and repair all the wasting fibres of the human frame, and every other animal.

Phil. But, if the human body thus stood in need of nourishment in the state of innocence, does it not seem to suppose, if not to prove its natural mortality? A thing immortal admits of no decay.

Didas. True. There is no need to supply nourishment, where there is no possible waste. But may it not be supposed, that though the bodies of saints will rise immortal and incorruptible, that is, that they shall never die nor corrupt more, yet, that this will not be from a *necessity of nature*, at the least in the first stages of its future advancement, but by the mediums of the fruit of the Tree of Life, and of the water of life? This is the more probable, as it is certain, that this actually was the case with Adam in a state of innocence. But of this D. V. more hereafter.

The world being thus made; replenished with inhabitants; with ample provision for its continuance, by procreation; with proper nourishment for every creature requiring it; the clock of Time having measured six days and nights; every wheel and spring in the vast machine set a going; the omniscient architect, at one penetrating glance, surveyed the whole, and pronounced them all to be VERY GOOD.

Phil. As EVIL of no kind, whether moral, spiritual, or natural, had as yet any being in this new creation; and as man and woman were the principal creatures in it; and man the deputy-

governor

governor of the animal world, for whose accommodation, chiefly, all other things were made; in what point of light must we view this divine approbation? Must we not consider it as chiefly referring to mankind, in whom all the rest centre?

Didas. Certainly we must.

Phil. I ask then, was the divine approbation limitted to Adam and Eve, personally considered, and that in a state of innocence; or did it include their posterity, contained virtually in themselves?

Didas. No doubt but that it included their posterity, if their posterity were included in them.

Phil. Adam and Eve were the only intended parents of mankind. But if so, and mankind existed then *in them*, how could it be said of them, that they, as well as other things, were *very good*; if, as many have supposed, the far greatest part of mankind will be for ever miserable?

Didas. We must either suppose, That Adam and Eve were then considered personally, and that without any regard to their posterity; or, that the supposition of so many future miserable beings, then contained in the first pair, is a groundless hypothesis, and altogether unworthy of a God, whose tender mercies are over all his works.

But once more observe—If the plans of grace and providence, when completed, will advance by far the greatest part of Adam's race to happiness and endless glory, then, indeed, the divine Judgment past upon all His Works, That they were *very Good*, will be abundantly confirmed by the issue, and obtain a brilliancy, that will again make the morning stars sing together, and all the Sons of God shout for Joy!

Phil. If this be so, what becomes of the Horrible Decree?

Didas. It is a *non entity*, having no existence but in the mistaken Judgments of a few Mortals.

DIALOGUE

DIALOGUE IV.

The Continuation of the Subject, with a vast Variety of particular Observations.

Didascalos. YOU have heard, my dear friend, above, how that Adam, as the son of God, was the heir of the primitive world, God's Deputy-Governor, invested with a Right of Authority to use every thing in it to the Good of his Subjects, the Glory of his Sovereign, and his own Comfort and Satisfaction. And so long as his obedience continued as Son, and Subject to his Father and Sovereign, his Title was indefeasible, his honour and happiness great and secure. Being the offspring of God, his mental powers abundantly evidenced their divine original. What is it that the spirit which is in man, is not capable of, when the inspiration of the Almighty giveth understanding? But if its powers and operations are so wonderful while confined in a house of clay, how much more active and perfect may we justly suppose them to be, when freed from these fetters, and united to a spiritual body, more homogeneous to its own nature? Eternity, and the vast objects of eternity alone, are adequate to the vast capacities of the human mind!

The self determining power of the will alone, renders man an accountable creature. It is true, there are motions in the body altogether involuntary; such are the beating of the heart and pulse, &c. yet it does not appear, that, in an ordinary way, there are any such absolute impulsive motions impress upon the mind. If any superior power, independent of the mind, absolutely determines human

human choice, there is an end of all freedom, and consequently of all virtue and vice, strictly considered. For so far as the will is compelled by any foreign force, virtue and vice abate, in the goodness of the one, and malignity of the other.

It is highly reasonable, and, no doubt, originally intended, that the will of man should be wholly subordinate unto, and subserve the will of his maker, and that in all things. But, by what criterion, in the then circumstances of the world, could such an obedience of Adam to his maker be fairly tried? The genuine simple obedience of the heart, can only be known to Him who made it. Was it not then quite necessary, that there should be some external Test, to afford some visible proof of the obedience or disobedience of the first Father of mankind to the will of his Maker, and that for the satisfaction of posterity, so eminently concerned therein?

Phil. Most certainly so. If it was necessary for Abraham to shew his faith by such an heroic act of obedience, as the sacrificing his only son for an example to believers, (for God knew his heart without any external evidence) how much more needful in the case of Adam, for his posterity to know the issue of his trial!

Didas. True. Adam's duty was totally to abstain from tasting the forbidden fruit. Death was the awful penalty, in case of disobedience. But the case of Adam was as peculiar as the issue was important.

He was the seminal root and federal head of mankind: To complete his probation, and assist in propagating his posterity, a second self was extracted from his side, as a social companion and certain partaker of his happiness or misery in this life. Upon trial, had Adam proved obedient, Paradise would have been his royal residence; all its

 delicious

delicious fruits his food; and the tree of life the certain pledge of his immortality. We have reason to believe, that every element would have been friendly to his constitution, and every animal paid him homage as to the Viceroy of their maker. There would have been neither curse, nor any malignant property in nature; but an universal harmony, without one discordant string. The praises of their Maker, and the happiness of Mankind, would have been the burden of every song. Thus would the happiness of Time have anticipated the joys of Eternity; and Paradise on earth would have been a sure pledge of a still more glorious Paradise in the future world.

For Adam to have retained his innocence, must certainly have been no very difficult thing. He had nothing to do, and nothing to suffer: His duty was self-denial—to deny himself the eating the forbidden fruit only.

Phil. The prohibition not to eat, being attended with a threatening that seemed to import no less than the very loss of his existence, was a fence sufficient, one would imagine, to have deterred him from touching it, however drawn by inclination, or driven by the force of temptation.

Didas. True, it no doubt was sufficient, and therefore the more heinous his offence in daring to sin notwithstanding.

Phil. Do you suppose that Adam ever tasted of the fruit of the Tree of Life?

Didas. It seems to be very uncertain; but to be more probable that he never did. That fruit appears to have been possessed of such an invigorating virtue, either natural or sacramental, as would have maintained all the organs of the human body without decay, until man should, if he had not sinned, have been translated, Enoch-like, into a celestial Paradise. And this is the more probable,

 not

not only from its name, its opposition to the other tree, the tasting of which brought certain death, its typical use as appears from *Rev.* xxii. but above all, from this fact, That after Adam's expulsion from Paradise, an angelical guard was necessary to prevent his returning, lest he should have eat of it *after* he was doomed to mortality; which, on the contrary, it is plain, that, had he been permitted to have eat of it then, he would have Lived for Ever, *Gen.* iii. 22. From which we may observe its superior property to continue Life, above the malignant juice of the other Tree to inflict inevitable death.

But the criminal was sentenced, and the sentence must take place, "Unto Dust thou shalt return." The world was now his prison, that was lately his kingdom—himself only a prisoner at large, though lately the Viceroy of Heaven. How was the mighty fallen! a fall, only exceeded by that of Lucifer, son of the morning!

Phil. Unspeakable, then, was the mercy and goodness of God in preventing Adam's returning to eat of the Tree of Life after his fall! For in that case, he would have Lived for Ever under the displeasure of his Maker, devil-like: and subject to all the miseries of this present evil world, which would have been a kind of Hell unto him of his own making.

Didas. This is all true. But observe farther, the counsel of God shall stand. This counsel was to Restore all Things by a second Adam; in which, as above intimated, would appear the most glorious displays of infinite wisdom and goodness; the whole of which being to be executed by the Lord from heaven, would stamp it with the greater brilliancy.

Phil. To Adam then, it seems, That innocent or criminal, his immortality depended upon his eating

eating of the fruit of the Tree of Life. Indulged as he was with an unlimitted liberty to gratify himſelf with the richeſt productions of terreſtrial Paradiſe, a Planting of the Lord, with only one exception; his abuſing this indulgence, in that ſingle inſtance, muſt neceſſarily enhance the magnitude of his crime in proportion to his obligations to obedience, the eaſineſs of performing his duty, and the dreadfulneſs of the threatened puniſhment. But is it not ſuppoſed by many, That Adam's offence was a very trivial affair—only the indulging himſelf in eating an apple, &c.?

Didas. It is ſo. But this ſuppoſition muſt proceed, either from no ſmall degree of ignorance, or inattention. For, in fact, how can we view it in any better light than that of wilful diſobedience to a moſt indulgent Father—open rebellion againſt his only rightful Sovereign—renouncing all dependance upon his Maker, for whom he evidently caſt off all due reverence, love, and regard: At the ſame time, voluntarily enliſting himſelf under the banners of his Maker's enemy, and ſurrendering himſelf up unto him as his entire ſervant and vaſſal, and with himſelf all his delegated dominion, *Luk.* iv. 5, 6. Hereby he ſubverted the very end of his creation, forfeited his own life, and virtually murdered a whole world, at a ſtroke, which was ſeminally contained in his loins; and, for any thing that he knew to the contrary, defeated all the deſigns of Providence in both creating the world, and himſelf, with every other creature.

By this important apoſtaſy of the viſible Head of Mankind, the whole œconomy of Providence, in the primitive ſtate of things, ſeemed to be confounded; and not only liable to be reduced to a ſtate of miſery and ruin, but actually ſubjected by man's ſin under the Ban of its Maker, and ſubjugated under the Dominion of Satan; who, to the

the present, has maintained a kind of Diabolical Sovereignty, as both Prince and God of this world, in a very awful degree, and to a very great extent.

But, behold! infinite Wisdom cannot be defeated—infinite goodness cannot be exhausted! The œconomy is varied; a second Adam is substituted in the room of the first; and an intire new dispensation takes place, to be administered by the Woman's Seed, being now Appointed Heir of all things.

It may not be amiss here to observe, The woman was deceived, the man was not. This was the greatest aggravation of his crime. Neither the entreaty nor example of Eve, nor any other being, ought to have had any weight with him, however tempting they might be; for force him they could not.

Phil. But is it not rational to suppose, that his natural and conjugal attachments to Eve might principally influence his conduct in that deadly affair?

Didas. The social passions were, without doubt, his weakest side. The subtle enemy knew this, and where and how to make his attack with the greatest advantage. We cannot suppose, that the Devil was a stranger to the woman's extraction; nor of the natural and social ties subsisting between them. Hence he would rationally infer, that the woman was the weaker vessel, and therefore the more proper subject first to attack.

As the understanding often influences the judgment, and passion and imagination often impose upon the understanding; the enemy thought, that if he could but work upon her passions and imaginations, so as to blind her understanding and corrupt her judgment, by the apparent properties of the forbidden fruit, he should easily so bias her will

as

as to give credit to his infinuations, and thereby the more readily fucceed.

This he attempted. And from the attracting and engaging beauty of the fruit; its fuperexcellency for food; and above all, from its apparent ufefulnefs to increafe wifdom in thofe who eat of it, fo as even to exalt them to an equality with Elohim, or God, in knowledge, &c. he at length prevailed: She took and eat, probably in imitation of the Serpent. No doubt the cunning enemy now thought that the better half of the work was well done; as he might judge, very probably, that the man would follow the fate of his wife. Her conduct formed a precedent; fhe believed the Serpent before her Maker. At length, *perfuafion*, *example*, and *love*, prevailed. Thefe were the weights that preponderated the fcale—that deftroyed the *equilibrio* in his will, and he dared to eat alfo, at all events.

Now Adam being in a ftate of probation for life or death, the point in proof was, Whether he would believe and obey his Maker, in abftaining from the forbidden fruit, however tempted to the contrary; or yield to his animal paffions, however excited, in direct difobedience to God's command, and in difbelief and contempt of his folemn and awful threat'ning.

Adam probably was *afleep* when the enemy firft fowed his Tares, as the parable feems to import, *Matth* xiii. 24, 25. No fooner had Eve tafted the fruit, than with her it was a loft game: Adam's fecond felf muft certainly die. Well, now was the grand crifis, the critical moment: The life of the whole world, contained in a fingle individual, is now in the utmoft fufpenfe.

Adam could not be infenfible that his beloved Eve muft return to that Duft of which himfelf had been made, for Death could import no lefs.

 Confidering

Considering that he must be left once more *alone*, when she died; But not considering how easily his Maker could have made him another helpmate; from existing circumstances, and his present attachments, at her solicitation, he daringly resolved upon the dreadful sin—Partners in sin and partners in punishment he seemed resolved to be. Thus, through the enemy's subtility, instead of being a helper to his happiness, she became the grand occasion of his ruin.

Phil. Shall be happy to hear a hint from you, how matters then stood at this important moment.

Didas. Matters then *stood!* They all *hung* in solemn suspense. The world was created—paradise planted—the new earth enriched with animals and plants of every genus and species—the air with fowls—and the ocean with fishes—The secret springs of nature, whether animal, vegetable, or mineral, were all at work—the Planets, each whirling about upon their respective axis—and attempting to find their way, for the first time, as is usually supposed, through the vast expanse of yielding ether:* While man—man, originally made the bright Image of his maker—the mirror of His communicable perfections—little less than the angels—and God's Deputy-Governor of the world—Alas! this man, by voluntary rebellion, degraded himself, in a sense, below the brutes, and introduced universal death, both into himself and all the world around him!!

Phil. Astonishing above measure! What shall we say? Shall Hell overturn the vast designs—nullify the schemes—and render abortive the glorious works of the great *Elohim?* Or, shall the great Architect of heaven unmake what He had made,

* This is agreeable to the common hypothesis. At the same time, the Author is inclined to think, That the six days of the creation were Polar Days or Years.

made, and reduce into a second chaos the beautiful system? Or abandon them to the power and pleasure of a diabolical usurper? Shall the whole human race perish in the root—wither and die in the bud by a hellish blast? In one word, must earth be unpeopled, or if not, be made a habitation for infernals, by the subtility of an enemy gaining an usurped authority over God's work, by the conquest of one man?

Didas. No, my dear Phil. no: God forbid. Infinite wisdom can never be out-witted—infinite power can never be defeated. But such is that wisdom and that power, that made the world and man.

If a created spirit, embodied in moulded animated clay, be foiled and driven from the field; One of the *Elohim*, by whom and for whom all things were made, Himself will come in the likeness of sinful flesh; enter the lists with the grand deceiver and usurper; rescue man from his hellish vassalage; and, in due time, advance the world itself to glory and happiness, far superior to its primitive state and condition.

But, in the mean time, observe, The sin being committed, the guilty criminals fly; but Fear could not supply wings sufficient to waft them beyond the ken of an all-seeing eye! nor could all the foliage of Paradise supply a retreat from the presence of Him whom the heaven of heavens cannot contain! whose Eyes, at a glance, pierce through all the universe!

Their indulgent creator must now become their Judge. At this solemn Assize, the world of Mankind was Representatively Judged; and at this time, being first Constituted Sinners, a sentence of Death pass upon all men, or Judgment passed to condemnation, and all die in consequence. At this time also, the whole Creation was made subject

ſubject to Vanity for the guilt of Adam's Offence, *Rom.* viii. 20.

Phil. But who was the Judge upon this weighty occaſion?

Didas. *Jehovah-Elohim*, or One of the Elohim, *Gen.* iii. 9, 23. This One was the ſon of God, as was afterwards Revealed. For the "Father Judgeth no man, but hath committed all Judgment unto the Son;" with "Authority to Execute Judgment, BECAUSE HE IS THE SON OF MAN." This is the ſame *intended* by Eve under the name of A MAN, "THE JEHOVAH." *Comp. Gen.* iv. 1. with *Joh.* v. 22, 27.

Phil. But, my dear Didas. was it the voice of Judgment, or of Mercy, that ſwift purſued the criminals, to ſummon them to the Bar?

Didas. Doubtleſs of both. The compaſſionate Judge in the midſt of wrath remembered mercy. While Juſtice held the Scales, to paſs a ſentence equivalent to their crime, Mercy erected a Throne of grace, that, in the iſſue, will ſoon triumph over Judgment: By this, the honour of the Lawgiver will be ſecured, and the caſe of the guilty rendered ſalvable. An inſtance of this will appear in the following proceſs. Where you may obſerve,

Firſt. The judge himſelf gives the ſummons, with an "Adam! where art thou?" The judge was neither ignorant of the offence, nor where the offenders were. This was the language of a parental ſovereign, in purſuit of a rebellious ſon—a ſummons to the bar, where juſtice, compounded with mercy, will paſs a ſentence, at once exhibiting the heinouſneſs of the offence, the juſtice of the puniſhment, and the exuberant goodneſs of the judge. This proceſs will point out ſuch a method of ſalvation for man, as will properly diſplay a wonder of wonders! It will aſtoniſh angels, confound devils, and afford ſubjects for the ſongs of the Redeemed in future ages and future worlds!

Phil. At the summons of the judge, methinks I see the guilty couple advance with reluctance from the Thicket, as from a self-made prison. Behold! trembling they stand empannelled at the awful Bar! Guilt reddens their countenance—with appalled hearts and trembling limbs, they listen for the voice that will fix their doom. Please permit me to attend that solemn assize, where all the world was sentenced for Adam's sin—sentenced to suffer—to die!

Didas. Second. Solemn indeed! and probably attended by thousands of invisible spectators, waiting to hear the issue. And first, the man is summoned, and examined at the dread tribunal. Thus the Judge proceeds, "Hast thou eaten of the Tree of which I commanded thee, saying, Thou shalt not eat of it?" The trembling culprit circumstantially confesses his crime, "The woman which Thou gavest to be with me, She gave me of the Tree, AND I DID EAT." Second, The woman is then examined, being by her husband accused as a principal in the action: Thus the Judge proceeds, "What is This that Thou hast done?" She confesses her guilt, but pleads deception in mitigation of it, "The Serpent beguiled me, AND I DID EAT." Here the judge suspends their sentence until He had condemned the Serpent, being the first grand offender.

Third. The Serpent neither denied nor replied to the woman's allegation.

The Judge immediately proceeds to pass sentence upon the Serpent. This sentence contained, 1st. a Curse; 2d. Degradation in his body and in his food; 3d. in the issue, the bruising of his Head.

Phil. Have you not intimated above, That both Adam and Eve *penitently* confessed their crime unto the Judge?

Didas.

Didas. Moſt certainly I have, and ſo I think both of them did.

Phil. But the current of Commentators and Divines, with *Mr. Pool*, ſay, that Adam "Excuſed *himſelf*, and charged God fooliſhly with his ſin." Pray why do you ſeem to think otherwiſe?

Didas. If *Mr. Pool*, &c. were preſent, I would beg leave humbly to propoſe a few queſtions, out of many more that might be aſked, not by way of litigation, which I always decline, but of information. I would beg leave to enquire

1ſt. Do his words neceſſarily infer ſuch a conſequence? Is it impoſſible fairly to conſtrue them in a more amiable light, and leſs offenſive?

2d. May not his caſe be rather conſidered, in ſome degree, like that of a *legal* penitent, under the terrors of a guilty conſcience and the fears of deſerved puniſhment? Fears which a Deiſt may and ought to feel?

3d. If the charging God with his ſin, appeared to him a ſufficient excuſe for his crime, why did his fears make him fly from his Maker? Why endeavour to hide himſelf at all, being poſſeſt of ſo good an excuſe, or at leaſt a palliation for his crime?

4th. If Adam did not *now* humbly confeſs his ſin, I beg to be informed, where do we read that he ever did? Did Adam never repent at all? Or did Moſes, who recorded his crime, forget or neglect to record his repentance?

5th. Is not repentance a prerequiſite for pardon? Is not to charge God fooliſhly with a ſin, a moſt diabolical preſumptuous ſin in itſelf? Could any thing aggravate his firſt ſin more than ſuch a charge?

6th. Before ever the Judge paſſed a word of the ſentence upon the human culprits, did he not firſt publiſh the glad tidings of pardon and ſalvation

tion *in their hearing*, while he gave out his divine Oracle in *ver.* 15?

7th. Did not Adam believe that gracious Oracle, in which it was Promised, that the woman—the woman, his wife, should have a Seed, whose name he changed, upon the authority of this very oracle, from *Ishah* to *Chevah*, because she was, or was to be, the Mother of all living of Mankind?

8th. If Adam *then* believed this evangelical oracle, was he not then pardoned, or justified by faith? And now, did not his maker discover his present reconciliation unto both, by cloathing them, &c. as Adam did his faith by changing and giving a new Name to his wife? The pardon that Adam received, like that of ours, was partial—a pardon for his sin *as to the eternal penal sentence due to him*, but not to exempt his body from sufferings and death. This is the true reason, that in his sentence, there is no mention made of either curse or, of sufferings in another world. Can this remark be fairly denied? If it cannot, the consequence is evident, namely, That no one will be finally condemned to hell solely for the Sin of Adam?

9th. Is not this supposition exactly agreeable to the tenor and scope of divine Revelation, touching the important doctrine of Justification by faith? A doctrine which is the same in all ages, and under all dispensations, whatever many mistaken good and great men have or do believe to the contrary.

10th. I ask, was it not at one and the same time, that the culprits were examined, the oracle (*ver.* 15.) delivered, and the sentence passed both upon the Serpent—the Earth—Adam—and Eve? If so, and if Adam believed that oracle *then* upon its delivery, what can equal the absurdity, which supposes that Adam both excused himself, and charged God foolishly with his sin, at the very moment his Judge most mercifully forgave his sin?

Phil.

Phil. You say, that Adam made a circumstantial confession of his sin.

Didas. I do. And is it not both true and plain? Did not God give the woman, and the woman the fruit to Adam? It was to these historical facts, beyond doubt, that Adam referred, and that without any malignant reflection upon either his Maker or beloved Bride. Could he have confessed his sin without mentioning these circumstances? On the contrary, they appear to me rather to aggravate than extenuate his sin in his own sight. Did he not know that it was his Maker's love to him, as well as other reasons, that made her and married them? What but love to her could induce him to listen to her persuasive arguments, when he "Hearkened to her voice," and took and eat at all hazards? What ingratitude was this to his Maker, he would naturally reflect! He gave her—himself had abused the gift, by too fondly attending to her persuasions instead of his duty to his God! He loved her—Love listened to her—alas! "I did eat." Thoughtless, rebellious, ungrateful, to the last degree!

Phil. Indeed, my dear Didas. I thank you for these Remarks; in which you have rescued an important passage from the ridicule of Deists; the conduct of Adam from the misconstructions of the friends of Revelation; and resolved, I hope satisfactorily, the doubts of thousands concerning the repentance, faith, and consequent salvation, of the common Parents of Mankind.

Didas. Now, my dear Phil. we are arrived at a very important period of Providence, which demands our attention.

First. The primitive state of the world, in which every thing was *very good*, is now at an end. Paradise, destitute of human inhabitants, becomes an habitation of devils. The immortalizing fruit of the

the Tree of Life must never be tasted; but, as it created and planted in vain, must be left to perish, until it springs and grows up again in Paradise Restored.

Secondly. The ground, however originally *very good*, is now subjected under the curse of its maker; producing noxious briers, thorns, furze, &c. and all animals, &c. reduced to a groaning condition of misery and mortality, not indeed for any fault; but it is their misfortune, at the present. However, a happy deliverance awaits them in future!

Thirdly. A mixed state of good and evil took place in every thing. The evil usually predominates; owing, probably, to the abounding offences of mankind. Hence a state of the world took place, so very different from the primitive, that it may justly be deemed a new world. The same, indeed, in substance, but its qualities are so vastly changed for the worse. And here a very important question, "*Pothen ton Kakon*," *whence came evil?* is answered.

Fourthly. Indeed, Why an infinitely wise and good God should ever have permitted either moral or natural Evil to invade his creation, and make such inroads and depredations therein, as universal experience and observation fully demonstrate, is and ever has been the most difficult problem to resolve. And, without a supposition founded upon human Redemption, and a Restoration of every other creature, must for ever remain such. But when once the last link of the golden chain of Providence and Grace is exhibited to view, every difficulty will vanish like the shades of the night; and the rising Son of Righteousness will display an increasing glory more brilliant than diamonds; and, at different periods, reinstate the world far superior to the primitive Paradise, under the care

 and

and conduct of the second Adam, the Lord from Heaven; He being now the appointed Heir of all Things in these future ages.

Fifthly. Does not *Kosmos*, when it stands for the *natural World*, which it very rarely does, though used in the New Testament at least 144 Times, and 94 of them by St. John, if I mistake not: Out of those 94, he intends Adam's fallen Race exclusive of the natural world, at the least 64 Times: And they are often included in other places; and therefore, when put for the natural world, must it not mean the *present evil world* in its *fallen accursed state?* And may not this be the true reason why it is so often put, either for the whole fallen Race of Mankind, or for the wicked as distinguished from the converted few who believe in Jesus? *Read Joh.* iii. 16. *Eph.* ii. 2. *Joh.* xvii. 6, 9, 11, 12, 13, 14, 15, 16, 18, 21, 23. And if this be its meaning, "*Pro kataboles kosmou,*" *Eph.* i. 4, &c. and "*Pro chronon aionion,*" *Before the foundation of the world*, and *Before the Times of the Ages*, may mean the same date. Not *before* the Mosaic Creation, but in that period, when, *after* the Fall of Adam, yet *before* the Promise was given, and before the curse took place; that is, in the interval between the Commission of the sin, and the Pardon of the sinners. This was an important interval, of what continuance we know not. But this is plain and not to be disputed,

First, That Adam, the moment he sinned, *forfeited his life* and kingdom together. From that moment, he became *legally dead* at least.

Secondly. That although he was reprieved, in order to propagate a posterity; yet, that posterity, then contained in his loins, like himself, then was, and still is, by the just sentence of the Judge, doomed to the Dust.

Thirdly.

Thirdly. Of consequence, though Adam could propagate man, yet he could neither propagate nor promote man's happiness, either of body or soul, either in this or in any future world. Therefore, with respect to Adam personally, and his posterity, dominion, &c. yea every thing was lost, forfeited, and fallen into the utmost confusion and ruin. Neither himself nor his posterity, considered *in him* or as descending from him, were Heirs of any thing whatever; all heirship had the Entail cut off by his disobedience and rebellion; only sin, misery, and death, must henceforth be the certain and inevitable Portion both of himself and posterity, as DERIVED from him.

Phil. It appears, then, very plain, That there must be an entire new Appointment or Constitution of Things, or the Creation itself be rendered null—the gracious designs of the Creator defeated—while hell triumphs over heaven; and mankind, if generated, for ever wretched!

Didas. True. But, blessed be God, the case, in the issue, will be far otherwise, as we have already hinted, and which I hope hereafter to demonstrate with sufficient evidence. In the mean time, observe, Adam was the first Human Head of Mankind, and Heir of the Primitive World. This heirship was forfeited by his Rebellion. *Immediately* upon which, the Second Adam was appointed the Second Head of Mankind, to be by Him Raised from the Dead in another World. Of this new World, (or future Ages) and all its Glories, He was *then*, and in Fact not *before then*, Constituted the proper Heir and Sovereign, *Heb.* i. 2, 8. Hence he confessed before Pilate, That he was a King, but that his Kingdom was not *Ektou Kosmou Toutou* of this Kosmos or World, *Joh.* xviii. 36. So far from that, That He Himself stiles the Devil the Archon or despotic Prince *Ho tou Kosmou*

Toutou

Toutou of this Kofmos or World, *Ibid.* xiv. 30. and xvi. 11. They were the kingdoms of Kofmos, or this World, that Satan propofed to *refign* to our Saviour for a fingle act of Adoration, *Matt.* iv. 8, 9. According to St. Luke, the Devil claimed an undeniable property in the Power and Glory of the Kingdoms of the Inhabited World, being *Delivered* unto him; which claim our Saviour never once pretended to difpute; which, if ill founded, no doubt but he would.

Phil. It appears to me, that there was no probability that he fhould. For if the Devil had not been the Defpotic Prince of them, our Saviour would never have declared him to be the *Archon* or *Defpot* of *Kofmos*, *Joh.* xii. 31. Befides, as our Saviour pofitively declared that *This Kofmos* or world was not His Kingdom, whofe elfe could the Kingdoms of Kofmos be but the Devil's, as he told our Lord plainly, after the Jewifh Kingdom had failed?

Didas. Very true. And this is the true ground of that Petition, "Thy Kingdom come." For in a worldly or civil fenfe, this kingdom is not yet come; neither will it, until it is Reftored unto Ifrael, when Chrift fhall defcend from heaven in clouds, in like manner as he afcended: Then, and not till then, will the "Kingdoms of *Kofmos* or of the World, become the Lord's," *Rev.* xi. 15.

Now the Primitive World, before the Rebellion of Adam, was Very Good. This world, in its *very good* condition, would have continued fuch, and would have been the Property and Dominion of Adam and Mankind, as a Kingdom of Saints, had Sin never entered into it. This will be in fact the cafe, in its perfectly Reftored ftate, fo far as Paradife will extend. But its fallen accurfed ftate, (*Gen.* iii. 17, 18.) which is the prefent, you have already heard, is not under any other Providential Government,

Government, but that of Rebels in a Probationary ſtate for happineſs.

As it ſeems plain from what has been ſaid, (and much more might be ſaid) That Koſmos properly means this World in its Accurſed condition, ſo "Before the Foundation of Koſmos," may mean *before* the divine malediction was paſt upon it by the Judge, as above obſerved, not extending to its Primeval ſtate. The moment Adam ſinned, is one point—the moment the Curſe took place, is the other point; the interval between theſe points was very important, in which, *Koſmos was founded* as the Preſent evil World, and that by the Sentence of the Judge, *Gen.* iii. 17, 18.

DIALOGUE V.

The same Subject continued.

Didascales. MY dear Philotheos, St. Paul, the greatest and best Expositor of the Old Testament, begins his Epistle to the Hebrews with the very subject now before us. In *ver.* 2. he lays down two Foundation-truths, upon which the whole fabric of Christianity stands erected. They are these, first, That God hath "Appointed His Son the HEIR *of all Things.*" Second, That "By Him He constituted the *Ages,*" not the Worlds, as in our version.

1. Christ, then, is the Appointed heir of all things in the *future Ages.*"

Phil. And when do you suppose that this *appointment* took place, *de jure*, or by legal Right?

Didas. Christ, you know, is the second Adam and the second Head of mankind, and in point of *dignity* ought to have been the first; but in point of *time*, infinite wisdom appointed him the second. This order of things, in fact, we see has taken place. Now in the nature of things, Christ could not be a *second* Adam, or a *second* Head of Mankind, so long as the *first* continued such. But when the first fell – cut off by *legal death*, then the second was substituted in the room of the first.

Now the first fell, and became legally dead the very moment that he sinned. Consequently, the second immediately succeeded him in Order, as the Heir Apparent does the King by Law. The time, then, when Christ became a second Adam, and a second Head, *de jure*, was the moment that Adam sinned. The time when Christ became a second

second Adam, and a second Head, *de facto*, commenced at his incarnation and resurrection inchoately, but will Perfectly at his next advent, and certainly not before. Christ was Appointed the Heir of all things, *as the second Adam*, and *as the second Head* of Mankind; therefore he commenced Heir, according to the Father's Appointment, when He commenced the second Adam and Head of Mankind, and in all reason not before.

2. "By Him He Constituted the *Ages*."

Phil. But what Ages, I pray? and when did he Constitute them?

Didas. 1st. These ages take in the whole duration of Christ's Mediatorship, or from the Time that He commenced the second Adam and Head of Mankind, until He shall Deliver up the Kingdoms to the Father at the end of the Ages of Ages. Now, as the Time of His commencing the second Head of Mankind, and appointment as Heir of all things, is dated from the moment of Adam's Fall; and as Adam, and all Mankind in his loins, seminally contained, certainly at that very moment died, at the least in a legal sense; so *all the Ages* intervening between the Moment that Adam believed the Promise, (*Gen.* iii. 15.) even to the End of the Ages of Ages, were then constituted. For it was at the Time that Adam believed, that he began Again properly to live. Now of course the Promise was made, *before* Adam could believe it: And Adam must believe it *before* his life was restored to him, or before his Age commenced under the Œconomy of the Son of God. The Ages of Adam and Eve, then, must properly commence and be dated from the Time of their Conversion through faith in the Promise, their created life having been forfeited by sin.

Phil. Adam and Eve, then, received a two-fold life with a two-fold date. First, a Created natural life:

life: This had been legally loſt—But I ſuppoſe no perſon knows how long this life had laſted. Second, a Supernatural life in the ſoul, and a moſt gracious Continuation of the life of the body, in conſequence of believing in the Promiſed Seed, being the Second Adam.

Didas. Exactly ſo. Here, then, farther obſerve, Whatever took place between the Tranſgreſſion and Converſion of Adam, was, in fact, *before the Times of the Ages*, ſeeing that thoſe Ages did not begin till that Converſion took place.

Phil. And pray what things did take place in that very important interval?

Didas. 1ſt. Chriſt was *ſet up* a ſecond Adam and a ſecond Head of Mankind. This lays the foundation of Redemption and Salvation by Him.

2d. According to God's Purpoſe, Grace was *then given to us in Chriſt Jeſus*, (1 *Tim.* i. 9.) without which Grace, no one can ever get to heaven; but it hath pleaſed the Father, that in Him all fulneſs ſhould dwell, that out of His fulneſs we all ſhould receive grace for grace.

3d. God, that cannot lie, *then* Promiſed unto us eternal life, &c. *Tit.* i. 2.

Phil. But both the texts laſt quoted, ſay, that the grace was given unto us, and the Promiſe of eternal Life made, " Before the world began."

Didas. Our Tranſlators ſay ſo, but St. Paul never did. His words are, " *Pro chronon aionion*," literally and properly, " Before the Times of the Ages." That is, When Chriſt was ſet up a ſecond Adam and a ſecond Head to Mankind, as I ſaid juſt now; or *before* Adam was pardoned.

4th. Then, properly, was Chriſt appointed the " Heir of all things," the former heir having rebelled and forfeited his life and dominion together.

5th. Then alſo were (not the worlds) but the Ages *made* or conſtituted. He who calls the *end* from

from the *beginning*, and thoſe things that are not, as though they were then, formed the grand plans of His own Providence and our Redemption, which all the Art of Hell ſhall never defeat. All this, divine preſcience had foreſeen, but not formed into actual exiſtence until now, in the proper Time and Order of Things.

Again, the Enmity mentioned in the firſt promiſe is reciprocal or mutual, ſubſiſting between the Serpent and the Woman, and between their reſpective Seeds. But on the part of Chriſt and his Church, Love is the prominent feature in his Religion—Love your enemies, &c. So that the Enmity which God *puts* into his ſeed, againſt the ſeed of the ſerpent, can be no other than a gracious abhorrence of ſin and ſatan; by which, ſin is hated, and ſatan as the grand tempter unto it. Now this hatred to ſin can proceed from no other than a gracious principle which the ſpirit of God inſpires into the hearts of God-fearing people. No other enmity in Chriſt and Chriſtians can poſſibly exiſt at all.

Phil. It ſeems, then, that the holy ſpirit alſo was implicitly promiſed before the times of the ages commenced, by the Converſion of Adam.

Didas. Moſt certainly. For what leſs can be intended by the "Grace which was given unto us?" Is it not the grace of the ſpirit of Chriſt? So that both eternal Life, and the means of obtaining it, were "Given unto us in Chriſt *before* the Times of the Ages" commenced. It was by this grace that Adam himſelf both Repented and Believed the Promiſe. Then was the time when the Son of God, now appointed heir of all things, firſt began to act the glorious and friendly part of a Mediator. Indeed, all things were created by Him and for Him. Adam, in a ſenſe, was only His Deputy or Viceroy. How congruous was it for him, by *whom*

are

are all things, and for whom are all things, to come to the rescue of a captivated race—to undertake the destruction of the Devil's works—and to effect a glorious Restoration of all things—a Restoration worthy of the glorious undertaker—and, indeed, which none but Himself had either a right or ability to perform; but, in which He will not fail.

Phil. You have already observed above, that our first Parents, upon hearing and believing the glorious Promise of the Woman's Seed and the serpent's bruiser, obtained a pardon for their sin, by which they were exempted from punishment in a future life; but what were the temporary sufferings they were subjected unto in the time they were reprieved from death?

Didas. The Tree of the knowledge of Good and Evil, in its very name, sufficiently implied the *mixed* state that tasting it would introduce into the world, which before was all *very good.* But ever since the Fall, the case has been far otherwise. Evil, moral, spiritual, and natural, according to the nature of the subject, has ever, more or less, invaded every person and thing; generally gained the ascendant; and, in most cases, almost leavened the whole lump, not only of Mankind, but of the whole world, *Rom.* viii. 20.

Indeed, what is the Redemption of the world, by our blessed Saviour; or what the great end of His glorious undertaking; but to rescue mankind, with the rest of the creatures, from the ruins of the fall? and from the dignity of his person, and the execution of his plan, advance the whole to far superior degrees of bliss in the issue—defeating Satan's designs—illustrating the glories of his own perfections, human and divine—and, by enhancing the creatures' happiness, secure and promote his own honour and glory, as Emmanuel and that of the Deity.

As to the temporary sufferings the first sin introduced, they are numberless; but abundantly both multiplied and magnified, by the abounding offences of Mankind. As the Female first Tasted the forbidden fruit, she was first sentenced to suffer, a multiplication of conceptions, as in the case of abortion—of sorrows in the time of gestation and child-birth—a kind of abject submission to the will of her husband, under whose control she was greatly reduced; which, in millions of cases, have proved most irksome and mortifying to the sex, as experience abundantly evidences.

As the man was so strictly connected with the ground out of which he was taken, and from which he was henceforth to derive his principal support, his sentence commenced, 1st. With a Curse upon the ground, for his sake. Under this curse it groans to this day. 2d. "In sorrow shalt thou eat of it all the days of thy life." 3d. "Briers and Thorns shall it bring forth unto thee, and thou shalt eat the herb of the field:" i. e. instead of the more delicious fruits of Paradise. 4th. "In the sweat of thy face shalt thou eat bread"—both earn and eat it in toil and sorrow, and that until thou shalt return to dust. This, in old age especially, is very often a sore affliction. "For dust thou art" (in thy first principles) "and unto dust shalt thou return;" yet not without hope of a Resurrection by the Seed of the Woman, to a much happier life.

And thus the Judge reduced them into a situation, in which their own experience would teach them the knowledge of both Good and Evil to an extensive degree.

And now let my dear Phil. observe, That as the root of a tree affects its branches--a fountain its streams—or as the head affects the body—so were all the posterity of Adam affected by him. In him

they

they ſinned—in him they ſuffer, and the whole creation with them, though only for a ſeaſon.

Phil. But how is ſuch a procedure conſiſtent with the divine attributes of Juſtice, Goodneſs, and Love?

Didas. In anſwer to this, it highly becomes us to be humble and modeſt. For the moſt exalted Reaſon, without Revelation, could never have formed a ſatisfactory anſwer. Even Revelation itſelf unfolds it very gradually. Promiſes and Prophecies, like two heavenly torches, in a meaſure ſhine upon our path, and will lead us through the intricate mazes of this complicated ſubject.

But their certain accompliſhment, by the ſpirit and providence of God, can alone reſolve every difficulty, and ſatisfy every critical enquiry. The better to underſtand it, ſo far as falls within the compaſs of our deſign, we muſt go retrogade a little, and make a few more obſervations upon the ſtate of Adam, and his Relation to others, when firſt created.

1. Adam was a probationer. As ſuch, doubtleſs, his condition was precarious. As the hinge turned in his trial, his exaltation or degradation muſt certainly follow.

2. Hence it is plain, That he was a free-agent, poſſeſſed of a ſelf-determining will, and therefore of an innate power of chuſing or refuſing. Now choice, where evil and good are in the caſe, implies a power of abuſe, otherwiſe it could not be Liberty. And if not free, then not accountable, and ſo not reaſonable; and if not reaſonable, then not capable of a covenant or a law, with ſanctions of life or death; that is, no ſubject of Moral Government.

3. Adam was a compounded creature. His mind was related to the inviſible and intellectual world; endued with underſtanding, judgment, free choice,

choice, and reafoning powers; to which may be added, a moral fenfe or confcioufnefs of good and evil. His body was endued with the organs of fenfe in their greateft perfection. This compound afforded a vaft variety of Paffions; all indeed innocent, yet exceeding active, related to, fitted for, and communicating with, a vaft variety of external objects, to awaken their active powers, and exercife themfelves upon.

4. Whatever he was, he was by creation. He therefore entirely ftood by his own native original ftrength, or fell by his own fault. Grace, Gofpel Grace, had not yet erected her Throne within him; nor had he any Mediator, from whom to receive additional fupplies. He was a kind of a moral *Automaton*, or felf-moving agent.

"Able to ftand, though free to fall."

5. Had he ftood, the fruit of the Tree of Life would have immortalized his body. In that cafe, with Chrift he might have walked upon the water, as on a cryftal pavement—with Daniel, took up his lodgings with lions—or with Daniel's Companions, walked, without being fcorched, in the glowing Furnace. Immortality bids defiance to all the rage of elements, and would pafs unhurt in the midft of burning worlds. Such would have been the cafe with the bodies of our firft parents, had they never finned, whether in Paradife, or without the bounds of the facred inclofure.

6. With regard to his mortal ftate, he moft certainly poffeffed innocence and uprightnefs in perfection; entirely free from every criminal principle or paffion, though capable of both, as the event proved. So long as his innocence lafted, he had the happinefs both of felf and divine approbation; open to farther and greater communications from heaven; to a free and conftant intercourfe with God and his Angels; perfectly free

 from

from uneasy perturbations of jarring passions; and stings of conscious guilt. In a word, he was a mirror of his maker, and an endeared object of his love, as well as his delegated Sovereign over the world.

At the same time, had he, by creation, been placed in such heights of *positive* holiness and perfection, as some polemical writers have imagined, they would most certainly have been inconsistent with a state of probation, and precluded the possibility of his fall, by infringing upon his free-agency, and firmly fixing him in his Primeval state.

7. Adam's relative state was singular and very remarkable. He stood as the creature, son, subject, and servant, to Almighty God—His viceroy and deputy governor upon earth. To Eve he was related by natural consanguinity, as she derived her substance from his, who was of course her head; and, by matrimonial ties, her husband. He was also both natural and federal Head of his posterity. As to the rest of the creatures, God put all things under his feet. Earth, air, and ocean, were the limits of his kingdom, and their various inhabitants his subjects. He had Paradise for his Palace, fitted up and furnished by his Maker.

8. If, upon his trial, he had maintained his integrity—begotten a posterity to succeed him—the time of his probation finished to the satisfaction of his maker and sovereign—dwelt upon earth during his maker's pleasure, probably as long as the millennium will last—He at length would have had the clouds for his chariot; and, taking his flight upon the wings of the wind, he would have measured the vast tracts of ether by his passage in the midst of a convoy of angels; and arriving at the Court of his Maker, all heaven would have welcomed him with shouts of applause, and hailed him as the conqueror of the Prince of Hell!

Phil.

Phil. And how would it have fared, do you ſuppoſe, with his poſterity, after this glorious farewel of their firſt Father?

Didas. Earth would have been a kind of heaven; that which we now daily pray for, would have been actually realized, viz. "Thy will be done on earth, as it is in heaven." But ſo much will be ſaid upon this ſubject when we come to the Times of the Reſtitution of all Things, that we need ſay nothing more upon the ſubject in this place.

Phil. The fate of Adam's poſterity was wrapt up in his own. But ſuppoſe it had been otherwiſe, and that every perſon born into the world had been neither better nor worſe than Adam was when created, how, think you, would matters have gone on then?

Didas. Every individual perſon, like him, muſt have ſtood or fallen, by their own conduct. Laws would have been made according to exiſting circumſtances, which would have been the Teſt of every one's Trial. But in this caſe, as mankind multiplied, laws muſt neceſſarily multiply with them. The more laws, the greater danger of tranſgreſſion. The more people, the more objects of temptation, and in proportion the greater danger of falling. And to every individual perſon, one ſingle offence muſt bring certain ruin—ſubjects worthy the Deiſts' conſideration.

If, then, our firſt Parents fell in the leſſer danger, what reaſon is there to ſuppoſe that their children would have ſtood in the greater? In this caſe, all would have ſinned, and all muſt have periſhed in their ſin. Nor does it appear, that any divine interpoſition could have prevented it, conſiſtent with the ſtate of the world, and of human liberty.

Phil. Had this been the caſe, and Death the penalty

penalty of every crime; what would have become of fuch a world of criminals?

Didas. As to the body, certain death, without a poffibility of a Refurrection: The foul, deprived for ever of that vehicle, in the *mundus animarum*, would have been a kind of devil or demon, under the difpleafure of God, and a companion for the worft of beings for ever in *Tartaros*.

Phil. But could not God raife their bodies up again?

Didas. No doubt but he could. But why rife again to be for ever miferable? Would not the re-union of body and foul have been an augmentation of their fufferings? Befides, what God could do, is not the queftion; but what he would do. When the threatening was given to Adam, what ground had he to fuppofe, That if he finned and died, that his Maker would raife him up again? Or what better ground to this day, fetting Revelation afide?

Phil. Not the leaft that I can fee; for God had not, upon any condition whatever, promifed or in the leaft intimated fuch a defign.

Didas. Very true. And upon the above fuppofition, would not a world of wretches have been in the very fame fituation?

Phil. No doubt. But then, He who iffued out the folemn threatening, could not he have reverfed it; and pardon the finner, without ever inflicting the denounced punifhment?

Didas. Here, again, what God can do is one thing, and what he will do is another. Where did he promife this to Adam *before* he finned? Who fhall prefcribe laws of Government, or terms of Pardon for offenders, to the Maker and Governor of the Univerfe? Has not He a right to do what he will with his own? Who fhall fay unto Him, why doft Thou this? To deny this, is to deny

deny His Sovereignty—To allow this, is to leave Him to do what He pleafes, and who will difpute His Right?

Whether God *could* or *could not* have abfolutely forgiven the fin of Adam and his finning pofterity, confiftent with his divine attributes, is a queftion above the folution of mortals. But this we know, that he *would not* without an Atonement, if the Bible be true. Is it not then the height of prefumptuous folly, to reft the hope of our Salvation upon fuch a precarious foundation? But if the malignity of fin be fo great, that an atonement is abfolutely neceffary, according to the Bible, he who believes in that atonement is fafe, but woe to the wilful unbeliever!

If then God has a right to prefcribe Laws, with fanctions, to His rational creatures—terms of acceptance to offenders, and of Reftoration to the fallen; let us leave both the one and the other to Himfelf, and take him at his word.

Phil. But who hath known the mind of the Lord? Who, by fearching, can find out God, or the Almighty, to perfection?

Didas. Moft certainly no created being. We may as well pretend to fpan the heavens, or embrace the globe of the earth in our arms, as to penetrate His Counfels—the purpofes which He hath purpofed in Himfelf, until He is pleafed to make them known: And hence we fee the neceffity of a divine Revelation.

Phil. All this is infallibly true, and the facred Scriptures afford us one.

Didas. But if fo, it becomes us humbly to enquire into the Scriptural PLAN of Human Redemption, in which we are all fo greatly concerned, as there is no other poffible way ever to come at the knowledge of it.

Phil. Very true. But when I reflect for a moment upon the very different principles and opinions held and maintained by many of the most learned and even best of men, upon that important subject, it fully convinces me, that it is involved in considerable obscurity, and attended with such difficulties, as cannot be easily surmounted by human reason only.

Didas. Such a supposition by no means derogates from the excellency of that Revelation which contains it. It rather evidences the divinity of its original; seeing that the spirit that Revealed it searches even the deep things of God, which still remain inscrutable to all to whom that spirit does not reveal them. Utterly abandoning all human schemes and prejudices of Education whatever, with perfect freedom of thought, both allowed to others and assumed by ourselves, let us go in search of the Scriptural Plan of Human Redemption; to inform us of which, the Scriptures alone will be sufficient, with divine assistance.

This Plan, if I mistake not, my dear Phil. will lead us to Him in whom dwells all the Treasures of Wisdom and Divine Knowledge—and will include in it some of the Unsearchable Riches of Christ—point out a most glorious issue of all things—exhibit such a display of divine grace and philantropy, as nothing but the length, and breadth, and depth, and height, of the Love of Christ can equal. This plan will point out a happy Restoration from the ruins of the world of mankind, into which the conduct of Adam had hurled it—reunite man once more to his God, by the medium of Emmanuel; through whom, a communication with heaven is again opened—a divine nature imparted to the human, until the last will be filled with all the communicable fulness of God; and advanced

to

to a degree of holineſs and happineſs, as much ſuperior to the Adamical ſtate, as the heaven is high above the earth.

May he, who giveth Wiſdom to the ſimple honeſt enquirer after Truth, anoint our eyes with His eye-ſalve—give us to ſee light in His light—diſcover the unſearchable Riches of Chriſt—exhibit to our view His Plans of Grace and Providence ſo far as He has been pleaſed to Reveal them—and accompany, with His Bleſſing, our honeſt endeavours to lay them before the Public.

DIALOGUE VI.

Upon the Imputation of Sin, and of Righteousness for our Justification from Personal Guilt, &c.

Didascalos. LET us, my friend, lay the foundation of our following Essay upon two propositions, and never lose sight of the momentous truths they contain, however extensive our Plan may lead us, both as to Time, Place, or Person.

I. There is no other Name given under Heaven among men whereby we can be Saved, but the Name of JESUS CHRIST. Unto which I beg leave to subjoin,

II. Who gave Himself a Ransome FOR ALL, to be Testified in His Own Times. *Comp. Acts* iv. 12. with 1 *Tim.* ii. 6. *Gr.*

Phil. Pray, my dear Didas. do you intend a formal discourse upon these two scriptures?

Didas. By no means. We shall quickly lose sight of the words, but I hope never of their meaning.

Phil. I beg leave to attend you wherever your thoughts may travel, to select a few passages, out of the most fruitful field of God's divine Revelation, with a view to illustrate the meaning of the above Propositions. And as the Salvation of Man is the most important subject in the world, it will afford me the greatest pleasure to hear unfolded that Mystery of Godliness in its extent—The Imputation of Adam's sin to his Posterity—and the Deliverance of that Posterity from the effects of that Imputation, as well as from personal guilt.

Didas. The necessity of Salvation by Jesus Christ partly originates from that Imputation. Let us therefore speak a word or two upon imputation in general.

1. To impute, in fcripture, is to lay to the account of a perfon his *own* doings, whether Good, as *Pfa*. cvi. 31. Or Bad, as *Levit*. xvii. 4.

2. To impute is ufed in an evil fenfe, 1 *Sam*. xxii. 15. and in a good fenfe, 2 *Sam*. xix. 19. *Pfa*. xxxii. 2.

3. To impute, is to afcribe the benefit or good effect of fome laudable action to a perfon who has not deferved it, from confiderations arifing entirely from other caufes than can be found in him who receives the benefit, *Rom*. iv. 6.

4. Imputation in the Old Teftament, is ufually expreft by the word *Hhafhab*; and in the New Teftament by *Logigomai*, in its varied grammatical Forms. It is ufed with refpect to the Subjects of Sin, and Righteoufnefs. The Perfons concerned are Adam, and Chrift, as Principals and Heads of Mankind. Imputation, with refpect to Adam, is ufually termed Original fin. To which it is objected, as unjuft in the Divine Being, to punifh an innocent offspring, for the guilt of the Parent; and alfo cruel, to deal with harmlefs Infants, as if adult Offenders; the objectors fuppofing, That it is irrational and abfurd, it being impoffible to make a transfer of Guilt from one to another. It is therefore fuppofed to be both unfcriptural and attended with dangerous confequences.

The important Subject of Man's Redemption; or in other words, The Ruin of the World by the firft Adam, and the Reftoration of it by the fecond Adam, have always, and ever will be, fubjects of ridicule to unenlightened Reafon. But is it not the higheft reafon to allow, That God fhould execute all his Works after the counfel of His own Will? His will is certainly influenced, in all its volitions, by infinite goodnefs, love, and mercy; and being directed by infinite wifdom and forefight, can reafon fuppofe any other, Than that He

will

will uniformly compaſs the beſt ends, by the beſt means? Or that thoſe ends can ever be defeated?

Phil. Surely no. Therefore, our reaſon at all times, and in all things, ought to be guided by, and be entirely obſequious to this will, whenever or in whatever ſubject He is pleaſed to Reveal it. More eſpecially in thoſe that concern our great Salvation.

Didas. True. And, bleſſed be His name, This His Will is Revealed in His moſt holy Word. By this Rule we muſt form our judgment, and by this alone, as well as direct our practice; all others are fallible and deluſive.

Phil. Doubtleſs, this will be our wiſdom. I have often thought, That the great Apoſtle treats upon this ſubject *profeſſedly* in *Rom.* v. 12—21. incluſively. And if you judge it agreeable, you will not a little oblige me by giving a few thoughts upon the paſſage; more eſpecially, as it appears to me to be directly in point upon the ſubject of Imputation, &c.

Didas. To me it appears in the ſame light. Am willing to afford you what aſſiſtance I can, to remove, or leſſen the Herculian difficulties attending it, upon every hypotheſis hitherto advanced, ſo far as I know.

The following Remarks I freely propoſe to your candid conſideration, without the leaſt dogmatizing; but leave every one perfectly free to Judge for themſelves. With your Bible before you, and your eye upon the paſſage, pleaſe to give due attention with candour, and free from preconceived prejudices, the bane of rational enquiries.

I. The great Apoſtle informs us here of two *Adams*; in ſome reſpects, type and antitype—Of two *Laws*; one given to Adam, which was literally poſſitive, but implicitly moral; the other long afterwards came by Moſes—Of two *Offences* againſt theſe laws reſpectively, or the One offence of of Adam, and the abounding offences of his posterity—Of two *just sentences to condemnation* for those offences; the first for Adam's, the second for our own—Of two *Deaths* which those sentences doom unto; the death of this body, and the second death—Two Justifications; one from the *imputed* guilt of Adam's sin, the other from the real guilt of our own, upon gospel-terms—Two *Lives*; the present life, and a life after the Resurrection, to be absolutely restored unto all mankind—A *two-fold Grace*; the former bestowed, like a Talent, for improvement; the latter is abounding grace given to all who improve their Talents—A *two-fold Righteousness*; the first is the Righteousness of Christ, called the righteousness of One; by this we are justified from Adam's imputed guilt; the other is termed the Gift of righteousness; this is received by faith: By this, genuine believers are justified from their own personal guilt, freely by grace, through faith.

It has been above observed, that the two Adams, in some things, were type and antitype. With regard to the extent of their undertakings, in this respect they both represented all Mankind; 1st. In that Adam brought the poison of sin *into all*, *ver.* 12. but Christ the grace of God as its antidote, *ver.* 15. 2nd. Adam brought guilt; insomuch, that all mankind, *in him*, are Constituted sinners; but Christ brought Righteousness, that justifies all from that guilt. Both this guilt and righteousness are ours by *imputation*. 3rd. Adam brought condemnation unto death upon all; but Christ brought a justification of life upon all, *ver.* 18. Hence, as in Adam all die, even so in Christ shall all be made alive, (1 *Cor.* xv. 22.) whether Righteous or Wicked.

On the other hand, those two Heads of Mankind differ, 1st. in their Persons. Adam was of the earth,

earth, and therefore earthy; Christ is the Lord from heaven. 2nd. In their undertakings, and the effects thereof. With respect to duration, as public Representatives; Adam stood no longer the Representative of mankind than till he had sinned; but while he was reprieved from his sentence of death, in order to propagate a sinful mortal race like himself: The second Adam, as Mediator and Governor, began to administer the whole œconomy of Grace and Providence, as the principal Actor in the *Elohim*, as the whole history of the old Testament evidences. Upon this incarnation, which capacitated him for death, and a resurrection; having overcome death, and the devil, who till then had exercised the *power of it*, His august authority was exceedingly extended, and heaven and earth ever since have been His proper Domain. Notwithstanding this, His enemies are yet very far from being His footstool; but *in his own Times* they most certainly will be made such.

He now disposes, superintends, and brings about such events, whoever or whatever may be His agents and instruments, in heaven, earth, or hell, as will in the issue destroy the works of the devil—afford a glorious triumph over sin, death, and *hades*—restore the whole creation from its ruinous state—and to worlds, to us, visible or invisible, exibit the perfections and glorious attributes of Deity, now made manifest in Flesh, in such a splendid illustrious manner, as will mightily contribute unto the praise of the glory of His grace—promote and secure the holiness, happiness, and honour of human nature—dignifying it with an indissoluble union with Himself, diffusing His own glories throughout the whole, AS GOD IN HUMAN NATURE, or the mysterious Emmanuel.

As this grand Design necessarily involved a variety of circumstances in it; for which, in the nature

nature of things, it was impoſſible to find any thing anſwerable in the Headſhip of Adam; therefore, of courſe, the type and antitype muſt differ in many things: As,

1. Death, without a poſſibility of a Reſurrection, was the penal ſanction of the Adamic Law: The ſecond Death, after a Reſurrection, is the penal ſanction of the Law of Faith. 2. The Adamic Law neither afforded promiſe nor proſpect of pardon, if once tranſgreſſed; but left the offender neither help nor hope: The Goſpel Œconomy brings ſufficient help, and affords a broad baſis for hope to build up deſire and expectation upon, even to the higheſt degrees of holineſs and happineſs, here and hereafter. 3. The pardon of Adam's ſin, both to himſelf and poſterity, was imperfect; tho' his ſin was ſo far forgiven as not to be puniſhed hereafter, yet the threatened death, after a reſpite of nine hundred and thirty years, was executed upon himſelf: And all that time, he was a priſoner at large, with reſpect to his body. His poſterity have hitherto, and ſtill are, in the ſame caſe, with only two typical exceptions. 4. Temporal Death was not to be avoided; the ſecond Death may. Therefore the goſpel brings a complete pardon and an eternal ſalvation. 5. Adam's Offence, as we have obſerved above, put a period to his Œconomy; the Goſpel Œconomy ſuppoſes many offences, but upon repentance towards God, and faith in our Lord Jeſus Chriſt, completely pardons them all. From theſe conſiderations, you ſee the difference between the type and antitype. But farther,

The following obſervations may be very uſeful in our endeavours to underſtand this important paſſage. Keep your eye upon the text.

(1) Throughout this paſſage, the One Offence always means the ſingle ſin of Adam. This is

 termed

termed *Tranſgreſſion*, *ver.* 14. *Diſobedience*, *ver.* 19.

(2) The many offences, (*ver.* 16) are the ſame with the abounding offence, *ver.* 20. Both mean all the ſins of Mankind, as diſtinguiſhed from the one offence of Adam. And here carefully obſerve the following antitheſis.

1. The Offence of One is contraſted with the Righteouſneſs of One, *ver.* 18.

2. One Man's Diſobedience is contraſted with the Obedience of One, *ver.* 19.

3. The condemnation of all men, viz. unto death, is contraſted with the juſtification of life, viz. of all men, *ver.* 18.

4. The One man by whom ſin entered into the world (*ver*, 12) is contraſted with the One man by whom grace, and the gift by grace, entered, *ver.* 15.

5. The many dead are the ſame many to whom the grace of God, and the gift by grace, hath abounded, *ibid.* And *the many* in both places mean all mankind.

6. Many made ſinners is contraſted with many made righteous, *ver.* 19. Here, again, many is put for all. Farther obſerve,

7. By Adam, ſin entered into the world; by Chriſt, grace entered and abounded.

8. Death entered through ſin, but life through grace and righteouſneſs.

9. Sin reigned, by One Offence, to condemnation; but grace reigned, through One Righteouſneſs, to Juſtification, viz. from that condemnation.

10. Through the entrance of the Moſaic Law, ſin hath abounded; but where ſin abounded, grace hath much more abounded.

Juſtification and condemnation are here contraſted; but carefully obſerve, as above noticed, that there are two Juſtifications, but very different.

The

The Justification *of life*, (*ver.* 18) acquits mankind from condemnation for the sin of Adam; that is, both infants and adults, with regard to *future sufferings*. But the Justification in *ver.* 16, directly refers to our many personal offences, and the pardon of them upon gospel terms: The former is absolute and unconditional; but the latter is peculiar to believers, and to no others.

(3) The gift of Righteousness *received*, is very different from being *made* Righteous, *ver.* 19. Being made Righteous, is opposed to being made Sinners, and only justifies us from Adam's imputed guilt. This imputation of guilt and of righteousness are unconditional and universal. And certain it is, that in what sense soever we are condemned for the sin of Adam, in the same sense we are acquitted from that condemnation, by the righteousness of Christ. Or in other words, in whatever sense we are absolutely made sinners by the one, we are as absolutely made righteous by the other. And though our nature be sinful that we derive from the one, this is counterbalanced by the abounding grace which we derive from the other; and both are universally derived from these common Heads.

(4) For this abounding grace is given to all, like the Talents, for improvement. God's invariable rule is this—To give a stock like a capital; he who improves it the best, in a way of duty, shall receive more abundantly, as a reward of grace, but not of debt. For want of due improvement, too many, either like the Prodigal, waste it, or the wicked Servant, hide it, till God in justice takes away that which they had, and the dreadful issue is, that they die graceless.

(5) Before we proceed to give a few paraphrastical notes upon the passage, we will premise as follows—1st. The universal corruption of both the minds

minds and morals of Jew and Gentile, the Apoſtle had laid open at large in the three firſt Chapters of this Epiſtle. 2nd. Not only in point of guilt, but alſo in the method of acceptance with God, he put them upon a level, and boldly aſſerted, That there was no difference. This method of acceptance, 3rd. he aſſerts to be "Freely by grace, through the Redemption that is in Jeſus." But then, 4th. this Jeſus, he tells us, God hath ſet up a Propitiation through faith in His Blood. And that in conſequence of this divine plan, God evidences himſelf to be juſt, at the ſame time that He is the Juſtifier of him that believeth in Jeſus. Now, where is *the fountain* from whence theſe univerſal torrents of vice and wickedneſs flow, that thus deluge the whole world? Where is *the origin* of that free grace, and method of Juſtification, by which God can juſtly pardon and ſave the guilty? Theſe two grand and difficult queſtions the Apoſtle here profeſſedly anſwers. This accounts, implicitly and expreſsly, for the origin of Evil, and points out its only infallible Remedy, preſcribed by God Himſelf. Here both ancient and modern Sophiſts have been foiled; but to Moſes, and St. Paul his Expoſitor, we owe the important diſcovery.

Nevertheleſs, before we enter any farther upon the ſubject as explained by the Apoſtle—a ſubject, in which Revelation and the eſſential Doctrines of Chriſtianity are ſo nearly concerned; it may be proper to conſider what grounds the Apoſtle builds his Doctrine of Juſtification upon. *See Rom.* iii. 24, 25, 26. The Apoſtle here exhibits a golden chain of our Juſtification from *our own perſonal Guilt*, being preparatory to what we find on the ſubject under conſideration concerning our Juſtification from the *imputed* guilt of Adam's ſin. But I ſeldom reflect upon this paſſage without ſenſible

concern.

concern. It excites in me very great and different emotions; such as compassion for the Deist—Joy and satisfaction in the Christian Believer. Here 1st. both confess, that "All have sinned." 2nd. both hope [illegible] believe to be "Justified freely by God's Grace." Thus far they go hand in hand, but no farther. Upon what does the Deist found his hope of Justification or Pardon? Upon God's *free* Grace only, but has no certain ground for his hope; a *peradventure* is the sole foundation of his comfort. All God's Attributes are infinite; this he allows. If He be infinitely Good, He is infinitely Just and Holy. Does not Sin also Contaminate the Guilty Subject? If so, what ground from the divine Attributes have such to expect Purity any more than Pardon? Allowing Christianity to be a cunningly devised Fable, the christian, who did not devise it, is upon a level with the Deist, and has as good Grounds to hope for Pardon and Purity. But if the Gospel be the Wisdom of God, and the Power of God unto Salvation, unto every genuine Believer—-if it discovers the *only way* of Salvation; is the Deist then upon a level with the believing Christian? Where Deism halts, Christianity boldly advances in a Path where Reason, without Revelation, in vain attempts to follow. St. Paul, a converted Deist in some sense, leaving the Principles of Deism behind, proceeds to inform the World by what Mediums God has determined to Justify the sinner by his free Grace. He points us to the only channels in which this free Grace can find its way to save a guilty world. The grand medium or channel which comprehends all the rest is this, "Through the Redemption that is in Jesus Christ." But by what method was this Redemption accomplished by Christ Jesus? he answers, "God hath set him forth a Propitiation," or a *covering* for sin,

 as

as the Mercy-Seat covered the ark. By what means do the guilty receive the Benefit of that Propitiation? "Through Faith in His Blood." His blood alone being the atoning Sacrifice, and faith in his blood being the only mean of applying that atonement to the guilty conſcience. Hence it is evident, that upon the Goſpel Plan, Chriſt's Propitiatory ſacrifice, in which he ſhed his Blood, and Faith in that Blood, are eſſential parts of that Plan, and abſolutely neceſſary to Salvation. If ſo, what ſhall we think of obſtinate Unbelievers?

Upon this Plan, and no other, the Believer, once guilty, can face the Judge with boldneſs, and will ſtand *Juſtly* acquitted at that holy Tribunal, conſiſtent with every Attribute in the Deity.

Phil. Glorious Plan indeed! But how can the guilty be *juſtly* acquitted, when Perſonal Guilt will be proved againſt the Perſon?

Didas. Becauſe a Juſtifying Righteouſneſs is, by this ſcheme, provided by Deity itſelf; which Righteouſneſs is declared or ſet forth for the Remiſſion of ſins. On account of this Righteouſneſs, God is the Juſtifier of him that believeth in Jeſus, altogether conſiſtent with his moral or eſſential Juſtice. 'Tis true, Moral Juſtice demanded ſatiſfaction for moral offences, but this ſatisfaction was made and accepted by Deity, in behalf of the ſinner.

Phil. How or by what means?

Didas. He, againſt whom the offence was committed, who knew both its nature and extent, and who had authority to fix what penalty he pleaſed, and inflict that penalty where and as he pleaſed, choſe this gracious method, To Subſtitute his own Son, when incarnated, in the room of a guilty World; and, with his own Voluntary conſent, to transfer the guilt of that world upon him. Becauſe,

1. It

1. It was an axiom with Deity, but the reason who can tell? namely, That without shedding of blood, sin *could not* be remitted. And notwithstanding the universality of the practice all the world over, yet Reason gives her suffrage to this axiom, "That the blood of Bulls or Brutes could not take away sin," for this plain reason, Because Mankind, who are the sinners, are a kind of Beings far superior to brutes. Therefore commutative Justice will not admit of such an unworthy and inferior Substitution.

2. Man, the offender, could not atone by his own blood for his own offences. The reason is, because, by a prior Appointment of God, the life of all Mankind, in one aggregate mass, was forfeited by the Rebellion of the first of the kind. For as that One Blood contained in it the blood of his Whole Posterity, the forfeiture of that one was the forfeiture of the whole. Hence in Adam all justly died; and to object against this appointment of the all-wise God, is to object against that infinite Wisdom which gave a seminal existence to all mankind in that One Blood, for the one is the natural consequence of the other.

Thus the *natural head* of mankind, and the whole *body*, are doomed to die for the Rebellion of that head. Now the Logos, or Jehovah-Elohim, being made Flesh, or incarnated,

3. His blood, and his alone, remained as the only sacrifice to take away sin. He is the Second Adam, and the *second head of mankind*, who are his Body. And it is in this Capacity as He is the *Head of Mankind*, that he is the Propitiation for the sins of the *whole of the world*, (1 *Joh.* ii. 2.) and His Atonement Accepted.

Now the world of Mankind, and every individual, consist of Soul and Body. The soul was the immediate offspring of Jehovah-Elohim. And who

who can doubt, but that He was the *myſtical* Head of all the *ſouls* that he had created, and which were now all depoſited in that One Blood of Adam, who was the natural Head of the whole Race, body and ſoul, and poſſeſt of a power to propagate both, as well as to deſtroy the Body by ſin?

Though Jehovah-Elohim was the myſtical Head of the Souls of all Mankind, who, ſo long as Adam continued obedient, (that union being natural and flowing from Creation) would of courſe continue; yet He was not the Head of the bodies of mankind, becauſe the body of Adam, (the fountain of them all) was formed out of the Duſt; which kind of body he was not yet poſſeſſed of.

The vital union between Elohim and Adam's Soul, as a fountain and repreſentative of mankind, was diſſolved by the ſin of Adam. The conſequences of this were, 1ſt. By the diſſolution of this union, Mankind, with Adam, loſt all vital union and headſhip with Jehovah-Elohim, as to the ſoul. 2nd. The Bodies of Mankind, when generated and born, muſt, as well as the body of Adam, moſt certainly die in their reſpective ages and generations. Now the "Redemption which is in Jeſus" implies a Reunion of both ſoul and body to this firſt myſtical Head; of the ſouls of men by "Grace through faith in his blood," and of the bodies, by a Reſurrection in conſequence of his Reſurrection. By both being reunited to him, the ſoul will be made partaker of the divine nature, and the body be faſhioned like unto His Glorious Body, and will thus "bear the Image of the heavenly" Adam. All this was foreſeen and provided againſt by Him who worketh all things after the Counſel of his own Will, or according to his good Pleaſure which he had purpoſed in Himſelf, *Eph.* i. 9, 10.

Phil. And pray, what is that Work, the reſult of his Counſel and Purpoſe? *Didas.*

Didas. It is this, to Reunite, Rehead, or gather together *In Christ*, once more, at the least All Mankind, both Souls and Bodies; Christ being the same Person with *Jehovah-Elohim*, now incarnated; the Promised Seed of the Woman, and by her termed "The MAN, the JEHOVAH," *Gen.* iv. 1.

Phil. But will this *Anakephalaiosasthai*, or *Heading over again* of All Mankind, be entirely effected in this "Present Evil Age?" *Gal.* i. 4. Or in the "Ages to come?" *Eph.* ii. 7.

Didas. This Present Evil Age is, blessed be God, advancing fast towards its final Period. It was never God's Purpose to effect it in this present evil world, but in the "Œconomy or Dispensation of the Fulness of Times;" that is, "The Times of Restitution—the Times of Refreshing, or rather of Reanimation." These will be Christ's Own Times, but all included in the *Ages to come*. In these Ages, there will be Time enough to accomplish every Divine Purpose, Promise, and Prophecy, as is clearly, I hope, demonstrated below.

Phil. 1. If I then understand you right, that Divine Person in the Elohim was Constituted, at the Creation, the invisible Head of the soul of Adam and of his posterity in his loins. Sin cut off this head from this collective body of immortals; dissolved the Union; destroyed the divine Image in Adam; and thus put an end to his *Created* holiness and happiness together. 2. The divine Purpose was, to place Jehovah-Elohim once more as the Head of this Collective body; by Regeneration to Restore the Divine Image; and by increased degrees of holiness and happiness, communicated by the Holy Spirit out of His fulness, Raise from the Ruins of the Fall, this whole Collective Body, except the finally impenitent and unbelieving.

3. The

3. The ſame ſin of Adam that ſevered the inviſible Head from the body of theſe Immortals, brought temporal Death upon the bodies of the whole human Race, by depriving them of the fruit of the Tree of life as a natural means; which death was both haſtened and rendered much more dreadful by the influential Curſe upon the Ground, &c.
4. By an Act of Sovereign Pleaſure, both the Soul and Body of Adam, like a fountain, contained his whole Poſterity in himſelf. The *Guilt* of his ſin, by the ſame Sovereign Act, being *imputed* to his Poſterity, the judge doomed the whole race to Death Judicially; the Juſtice of which ſentence is to be the ſubject, I ſuppoſe, we are to examine.
5. As this one ſin of Adam introduced both ſin and death into the world, ſo to atone for the ſin, and deliver from Death, Emmanuel Himſelf, as Man, muſt Die; and, as the Head of the whole Race, raiſe Himſelf and all mankind from the Dead abſolutely; and in the *Diſpenſation of the fulneſs of Times*, advance the whole Body of mankind to Heaven, except the finally incorrigible and unbelieving.

Didas. This is the ſum of my meaning; after which introduction, let us haſten to our ſubject, as follows.

DIALOGUE

DIALOGUE VII.

Of our Justification from imputed Guilt, by an Imputation of Righteousness, Rom. v. 12.

Didascalos. LET us now attend to this infallible inspired Expositor, and to what has been already said, add a few short Paraphrastical notes and observations upon the very interesting subject.

Ver. 12. *By one Man Sin entered into the world*—The world of Mankind. This man is expressly called *Adam*, (*ver.* 14) who consisted of flesh and spirit, or spirit and matter, vitally united, by the inimitable Art of God! These mutually influence each other by inexplicable laws. Of his *One blood*, all nations of men that are, or that ever existed, were *Made*, as actually as Eve was, being seminally contained in that One Blood.

Phil. Methinks I here behold a double fountain, whose streams have spread the world over! a fountain of that blood that has circulated in every vein of Mankind, and conveyed in its crimson current the seeds of vice, that have deluged the world in every age and place, in which it has flowed!

Didas. Whoever reads this single proposition of the great Apostle with due attention, will not be at a loss to account for the origin of Moral Evil, the genuine spring of both spiritual and natural.

These bitter waters have naturally impregnated mankind with such bitter grape-juice, that only bitter or sower grapes have been produced from them all the world over. This is attested by histories of all ages and places.

Phil. From hence it appears, That sin is *natural* to man. "But if it be natural, is it not necessary? And

And if it be neceſſary, how can it poſſibly be *culpable?*" For who can be juſtly blamed for what they cannot poſſibly avoid?

Didas. Very true; the conſequence is good, where it cannot poſſibly be avoided. But how can ſin be *neceſſary*, ſeeing that, "Where ſin abounded, Grace did *much more abound?*" Is not that grace ſufficient, yea more than ſufficient to counteract it, which abounds more than ſin? let the Tide of the one flow ever ſo high, the Tide of the other overtops it. This will abundantly appear below. It is true, by the firſt offence, ſin found its way into the human heart, which has been its proper Throne ever ſince, *Matth.* xv. 18, 19. Here Satan erected an empire; and every unconverted man is his ſubject or vaſſal, and continues ſuch until converted.

AND DEATH BY SIN. Here another monſtrous Monarch is introduced into the creation! When Sin entered, and ſwayed his ſceptre in human hearts, having overturned that lovely moral Image ſet up in Adam by his Maker, in which his Maker, in a ſenſe, beheld Himſelf, which was not a dead, but a living Image, the divine ſpirit living in it; but no ſooner had Sin entered, than he ſevered the creating head from the created Body, as you have heard above; and thus produced the monſter Death: The ſoul firſt felt the deadly blow, by which the life divine was loſt. Man now being excluded the favourable intercourſe with his Maker, and diveſted of his royal robes, and the crown fallen from his Head, Naked he flew to a thicket, there by the foliage to cover his ſhame. Alas! what a poor ſubterfuge to hide in from an Omniſcient Eye!

Adam, having loſt his Dominion, both over himſelf and over the world, was ſucceeded by three Sovereign Powers, all of which obtained a degree of Empire. 1ſt. *Satan*, who now commenced the

Prince

Prince of this world, and at length was Deified, and became its God. The *Apotheosis* was performed by the profaneness of men, who almost all the world over worshipped him, and still he is worshipped every where. 2nd. *Sin:* The empire of Sin is confined to rational beings; and therefore not so extensive as his contemporary Monarch, being limitted to mankind. 3rd. *Death:* Death is a Twin-Sovereign with Sin. They both were born together, as the text says: But though sin brought death into the world with him, yet death will survive sin, for death is Christ's last Enemy; however, blessed be the Lord, he also, in due time, shall die. In the mean time, where is that human Hero, who, by stratagem, can elude his dart, or wield a shield sufficient to resist it?

AND SO DEATH PASSED UPON ALL MEN. Both the sentence passed, and the execution of it. Hence in Adam all die, infants not excepted. Such was the good pleasure of God! Which, however, is an appointment worthy of the divine wisdom, the effect of goodness and love, as the sequel will evidence, I hope, to your satisfaction.

Death is a daily monitor—its language to every survivor is, "*Prepare* to meet thy God!" It is a monument set up in every house, of God's universal hatred against sin, and displeasure against sinners. Like the voice of God, it daily cries, "Stand in awe, and sin not." Like an index, it points the gay and the ambitious to the house appointed for all living. It is a lesser evil sent to prevent a greater; yea, it is the asylum of the wretched; and puts an end to our woes, in order to conduct us through the cyprus shades and its dark chambers, to a Palace in the skies. Thus our glorious captain will vanquish the King of terrors; and, in the end, turn our last enemy into

 a friend,

a friend, by stripping us of these mortal habiliments, in order that we may put on immortality, and possess eternal life.

FOR THAT ALL HAVE SINNED, Or were constituted sinners, *ver.* 19. The Apostle gives this as the Reason why Death passed upon or into all men. Now death being the Wages of sin, and to condemn the innocent is against both the law of nature and revelation; this is therefore one great point in the divine plan, viz. to constitute innocent persons, as dying infants, guilty for a Time, in order to deal with them as if actually guilty; although in future, those very persons shall be acquitted of that imputed guilt, by the imputation of a righteousness, which is no more their own personally, than the guilt was; but shall at once deliver them from all the consequences of that guilt, and reinstate them in circumstances much better through that imputed righteousness, then otherwise they would have ever possessed if such imputation had never took place.

But this imputation of guilt, and of righteousness to acquit from it, is not the peculiar case of Infants, but of the whole world of mankind, so far as it respects death, and a resurrection from it.

Ver. 13. FOR UNTIL THE LAW, SIN WAS IN THE WORLD. And the old world, particularly, so abounded in vice and oppression, that every Imagination of the thoughts of their hearts were only evil, and that continually: And after the flood they were very little better; both of them together including a space of 2513 years, from the Fall to the giving of the Law by Moses, according to the Hebrew Chronology, which see.

BUT SIN IS NOT IMPUTED WHEN THERE IS NO LAW. This is certain; for where there is no Law, there is no Transgression. Had we no law in England that made murder hanging,

hanging, no murderer in England could legally be hanged for that Crime; notwithſtanding the crime is no leſs againſt God and civil ſociety. In like manner, notwithſtanding the multitude and magnitude of the crimes of the Antediluvians, Sodomites, &c. which fully demonſtrated, that "Sin was in the world;" yet, 1ſt. they did not and we do not die for perſonal ſins. Had not water drowned the old world, nor fire burnt the Sodomites to death, they would moſt certainly have died as well as other men. Their extra crimes brought extra puniſhment, ſhortened their lives, and made their deaths more terrible; notwithſtanding, if they had not been ſuch atrocious offenders, nor ſuffered ſuch exemplary puniſhment, in a courſe of nature they would ſtill have died, as we do, as the next verſe informs us. 2nd. After Adam had broken his law, there never was another law given that threatened death to the tranſgreſſor, ſo as that the tranſgreſſor would have eſcaped death, if he had not tranſgreſſed. Sin, or not ſin, ſince the days of Adam, every one muſt die, or eſcape by miracle. From all which, it is as clear as the day, that the people of the old world, &c. did not die for their own perſonal ſins, but for the ſin of Adam, which was the point to be proved.

Phil. The law given to Adam muſt have been as peculiar to himſelf as his own circumſtances were peculiar, being adapted unto thoſe circumſtances, I ſuppoſe.

Didas. Very right. Now Adam's Body was *conditionally* immortal, but ſo have none ever been ſince. The condition was, to abſtain from the forbidden fruit, by which he would maintain his natural Right to the fruit of the Tree of Life, and of courſe never die. Therefore he had a poſſibility for a happy immortality, without dying and riſing again. None in the world ever had this but himſelf, but by miracle. *Ver.* 14.

Ver. 14. NEVERTHELESS DEATH REIGNED FROM ADAM TO MOSES. All which time *ſin was in the world*, although not ſuch ſin as brought mortality into the world, for that was brought in before with Adam's ſin. Therefore Death reigned all that time over all, Enoch excepted:

EVEN OVER THEM THAT HAD NOT SINNED. Namely, againſt ſuch a law as had mortality for its Penalty. Sinned they had, and enormous ſins reigned in the world all the time. Now theſe that had not ſinned, were, 1ſt. Infants, who never had perſonally ſinned in any ſenſe. 2nd. Adults, who, though they had ſinned, yet not at all after the ſimilitude of Adam's ſin, viz. the tranſgreſſing a poſitive law in a ſtate of trial for immortality without dying—a law which had mortality for its penalty; a caſe peculiar to Adam, as the natural and federal head of Mankind.

Phil. All this ſeems plain, and infallibly proves the Apoſtle's doctrine, namely, That ſin entered into the world by Adam, and death by his ſin only. An affecting truth indeed! For one offence of one Man, a World of men muſt die! But if one ſin deſerved ſuch ſufferings, what ſufferings muſt the ſins of all mankind deſerve?

Didas. My dear Phil. muſt carefully obſerve, that as the loſs of the divine image, mortality, and death, were the direct conſequences of Adam's offence only; but grace here, and a Reſurrection hereafter, as infallibly ſecured to all men by Chriſt; ſo the ſecond death, from the beginning, muſt have been the certain penalty annexed to perſonal ſin in all finally impenitent and obſtinate unbelievers, whoever or wherever, when favoured with a ſufficiently clear Revelation. But of this, He only is able to judge, who is the Judge of all the earth.

Phil.

Phil. But if by one man's ſin, ſin entered into and deluged the world of mankind; and death, by the ſame ſin, gained an univerſal empire; and that all men Reputedly ſinned *in him*, as the Apoſtle aſſerted, (*ver.* 12) and proved, (*ver.* 13, 14) how is ſuch a procedure conſiſtent with that ſtrict juſtice, ſuch as the divine nature admits of no deviation from?

Didas. Beſide what has been already ſaid upon the ſubject, the Apoſtle, ſtill more clearly to account for it, and untie this gordian knot in divinity, lays open the divine Œconomy from its foundations; and exhibits, in the cleareſt terms, Adam and Chriſt as two Univerſal Heads of Mankind; and, in ſome reſpects, type and antitype. He ſhews wherein they agree, and wherein they differ, as we have noticed above.

In order to this, he terms Adam, expreſsly, The FIGURE (Type, Gr.) OF HIM THAT WAS TO COME: That is, that was to come "according to the Purpoſe of Him who worketh all things after the counſel of His own Will," *Eph.* i. 2. This was a purpoſe "which He purpoſed in Chriſt Jeſus our Lord." This divine Purpoſe was firſt diſcovered in a glorious Oracle, expreſſive of the ſum of both redemption and providence, *Gen.* iii. 15.

Now theſe two heads of Mankind in ſome things differ, with reſpect to their ſeveral connexions to the body; in others, they exactly agree as type and antitype. But obſerve, in both reſpects, the advantage is always in favour of mankind by the antitype. This demonſtrably proves, that the whole Plan is worthy of that GOD who formed it, the truth of which will appear below.

The Apoſtle begins to ſtate the ſuperexcellency of Chriſt's part of this aſtoniſhing plan, in

Ver. 15. BUT NOT AS THE OFFENCE,

SO ALSO IS THE FREE GIFT. For there is a wide difference between them in favour of Mankind. The clofer the fubject is ftudied, and the clearer it is underftood, this happy difference will appear the plainer, and afford the more fatisfaction to the pious enquirer after truth.

FOR IF THROUGH THE OFFENCE OF ONE MANY BE DEAD. *Many* muft here mean all mankind dead! becaufe cut off from that myftical head, from which alone it could have derived fpiritual life and nourifhment. Holinefs, derived by creation, was loft by the lofs of the image of God. This was myftical and fpiritual death. As to the body, naturally mortal, being debarred from eating of the tree of life, Adam communicated mortality to all his pofterity, which, for his offence, was confirmed by the divine decree, "Duft thou art, and unto duft thou fhalt return." Otherwife, had God fo pleafed, the pofterity of Adam, by eating of the tree of life, might have never died. But, then, it would have been at beft a mixed life of good and evil, and infinitely fhort of that holinefs and happinefs introduced by the Gofpel.

MUCH MORE THE GRACE OF GOD. Not only gracious favour, but the grace which was given us in Chrift Jefus *before the times of the ages*, 2 *Tim.* i. 9. Of which Grace Chrift is full, *Joh.* i. 14. becaufe it pleafed the Father, that in Him all fulnefs fhould dwell, on purpofe that out of his fulnefs, as from a fountain, we all might receive Grace for Grace, *Ib. ver.* 16.

Now this grace is the very effence of fpiritual and divine life, and is oppofed to fpiritual death: It is that which alone can quicken the foul, and reinftate us in the divine moral image of God. It is the Seed of God, (1 *Joh.* iii. 9.) which, if it abide and grow within us, will produce both gofpel

holinefs

holiness and happiness, almost infinitely superior to the Adamical state. The Apostle in this verse, beginning to treat of our Recovery by Christ the second Adam, mentions this grace in the first place, and before any other benefit; being, indeed, one of the greatest blessings, and that, which is most necessary for fallen man. The next, and the greatest of all, is the Crown of all, viz.

THE GIFT BY GRACE. "For eternal life is the Gift of God, by Jesus Christ our Lord," *Chap.* vi. 23. This Gift is twice termed the Free Gift, *ver.* 15, 16. Free indeed! free for all, and actually abounds unto all! But my dear Phil. will rejoice to observe, that both the Grace of God, and the Gift by Grace, flow unto us by that ONE MAN, JESUS CHRIST. Here the antitype that was to come, (*ver.* 14.) is expresly named. This was the person in the *Elohim*, in whose spiritual image and bodily likeness, proleptically considered, man was originally made: The Seed promised (*Gen.* iii. 15.) to come, and bruise the Head of the Serpent.

But it will exhilarate the spirits, and greatly rejoice the heart of my friend, to observe, that both the Grace of God, and the Gift by Grace, with a *MUCH MORE* HATH ABOUNDED UNTO MANY. That is, the same *many* who were *dead*, as is evident from the antithesis in the former part of the verse, namely, unto all.

Phil. From hence it is plain, that how *many* soever were dead, the grace of God, and the Gift by Grace, have *much more* abounded unto the very same *many*: So the *many dead* have no reason to complain!

Didas. Very true. On the contrary. They *have much* in their favour.

Phil. But my dear Didas. pray what does that *much more* refer to?

Didas.

Didas. Not to the number of perſons; for in both caſes, it is *many*. But this emphatical *much more* refers to the ground of the Apoſtle's compariſon to the ſubject. By the fall of the firſt Adam, he himſelf, and all his poſterity *in him*, loſt that Image of God in which he was created; and by this, he loſt all, both created holineſs, happineſs, and alſo the never-ending duration of them. Now here, to our unſpeakable comfort, the Apoſtle informs us, that the Grace of God, and the Gift of eternal Life, much more abound unto the many that be dead, ſo as to enhance greatly both the holineſs and happineſs of the ſame many, and to ſecure the duration of them: And that the Grace of God, and the gift of eternal Life, are *free*—*free to all*, without perſonal merit; and *free for the many* that were *dead*—Truths hereafter to be infallibly atteſted.

Phil. If I underſtand you right, in this compariſon between the offence and the effects of it, upon the many; and the grace of God, and the free gift by grace beſtowed upon the ſame many; it appears evident, that mankind, ſo far from having any reaſon to complain of that divine œconomy by which He ſo planted them in the firſt Adam as both in him to ſin and ſuffer, that, on the contrary, their ſituation in the ſecond Adam is vaſtly more eligible, not only with regard to the degree of both grace and happineſs, which by Chriſt have *much more* abounded, but alſo, as to the ſecurity of their continuance.

Didas. You take me right. But farther obſerve, both our created holineſs, happineſs, and the duration of them, were all embarked in Adam's veſſel; how he was ſhipwrecked, and our *all* ſunk with him, or daſhed to pieces, you very well know. The caſe is now quite different, as both our perſons and treaſures are put into the hands of

ſo

ſo glorious a ſecond Adam, being the Lord from heaven, our Head and Mediator, and all ſafe.

In him we have a fulneſs of grace—by him, a liberal out-pouring of the holy ſpirit for aſking for—a divine Interceſſor, poſſeſt of all authority both in heaven and earth—means of grace, or ordinances divinely inſtituted—In one word, though in a ſenſe like Adam, we are on our probation, according to the Terms of this new œconomy, yet we are candidates for future happineſs, ſuch as are ſure to ſucceed, if we do but give all diligence to make our calling and election ſure.

Ver. 16. AND NOT AS IT WAS BY ONE THAT SINNED, SO IS THE GIFT: In this verſe, we have a ſecond very material difference between the two divine Conſtitutions; (more eſpecially with regard to the number of offences) and their effects in both caſes.

FOR THE JUDGMENT WAS BY ONE (OFFENCE) UNTO CONDEMNATION. The ſentence paſſed upon Adam, (Gen. iii. 16, 19.) and all mankind in him, condemned the whole to a ſtate of ſuffering for his One ſin. But note well, That there is not the leaſt or moſt diſtant intimation of ſufferings *after Death* in that whole ſentence. There are two ſpecial reaſons for this; 1ſt. Adam had obtained pardon before, as to his ſoul: This was upon his believing the Goſpel when preached in his hearing, (*ver.* 15.) as we have obſerved above. 2nd. It was never intended, by the Father of the ſpirits of all fleſh, to conſign one ſoul to future ſufferings for the ſin of Adam. All the ſufferings mentioned in the whole ſentence, are principally ſalutary, and curatively intended. They all work together for good to them that love God, even death itſelf. And where it is otherwiſe, it is the fault of the ſufferer, not of the inſtitution.

Phil. Dreadful indeed, muſt thoſe diſeaſes be, that

that required ſo painful a regimen in their cure! If one offence introduced ſuch a world of woes, what ſhall we ſay to the innumerable offences of mankind collectively conſidered?

Didas. What ſhall we ſay? Let us hear what the Apoſtle ſays—THE FREE GIFT IS OF MANY OFFENCES UNTO JUSTIFICATION. For the free gift, is a gift of forgiveneſs, for the *many* offences of mankind. Hence nothing but final unbelief, and rejecting Chriſt and his ſalvation, can poſſibly prevent univerſal ſalvation to all mankind.

For the many offences, oppoſed to the One offence, muſt of neceſſity include all that the one offence affected; and the free gift extends to the juſtification of All thoſe who have been guilty of thoſe many offences; for unto all ſuch, the grace of God, and the gift by grace, abound.

Phil. From the above account, it ſeems fairly to follow, 1ſt. That not one will be finally condemned for Adam's ſin only. 2nd. Nor yet for their own many offences againſt the Law. 3rd. That unbelief is the only ſin that binds all other ſins upon the conſcience, as being the great damning ſin of the Goſpel; and that unbelief, the effect of wilful obſtinacy, againſt ſufficient evidence for conviction; as it rejects the only means of ſalvation by Jeſus Chriſt.

Didas. True. This will be more plain hereafter, by what follows.

Ver. 17. For if by ONE man's offence, *Death reigned* by ONE. If ſuch was the good pleaſure of God, that for *one offence* of *one man*, death ſhould obtain an univerſal Dominion—if, to evidence His hot diſpleaſure againſt ſin, and to deter ſinners from committing it, He permitted ſuch an afflicting Tyrant to dethrone the monarch and level him with the beggar—in a moment to raviſh

the

the infant from the weeping mother's breast—and the wife and husband from each others arms—to drown one world of people, and burn another, &c. &c.

Much more they which Receive Abundance of Grace, and of the Gift of Righteousness. Personally receive grace out of the fulness of Christ to sanctify them, and by holiness qualify them for heaven; and of the gift of righteousness freely imputed unto them, for their justification and title to future bliss: Without doubt, all such

Shall reign in life (eternal) by ONE, *Jesus Christ.* This is the proper end of Man's existence. An inferior life by Adam was forfeited; by One, Jesus Christ, an infinitely superior life shall be Restored! This life begins in grace, and will be consummated in glory. We may very naturally suppose, That as far as Emmanuel exceeded the earthly Adam in personal glory, so far the restored will exceed the forfeited life in glory also.

In the three last verses the Apostle shewed the difference, in the two next he shews the exact agreement between the type and antitype, respecting the offence of the one, and the obedience of the other; and their different effects upon all mankind. Let us parallel this beautiful antithesis, *ver.* 18.

Therefore, as by the offence of one judgment came upon all men to condemnation;	Even so by the righteousness of one the free gift came upon all men unto justification of life.

1. The *offence* is opposed to *righteousness*, as *one* is to *one*.

2. *Judgment* is opposed to the *free gift*, as *all men* are to *all men*.

3. *Condemnation* is opposed to *justification of life*. You may please to observe farther, that *condemnation*

demnation there means that sentence past upon Adam, in which his posterity were included, "Unto dust thou shalt return," as appears by justification *of life* being opposed unto it. The righteousness of One, must mean our Saviour being *obedient unto death*; without which, there could have been no resurrection.

Millions of infants die, but not for sins committed by themselves, no; but in virtue of this Judgment to condemnation. Now as dying infants are, too plain to be denied, included in the judgment upon all men; by a parity of reason, they are included in the free gift, or in the justification of life, and consequently will rise again. *Imputed* guilt condemns them—*Imputed* righteousness will justify them. *Imputed* guilt doomed the whole world to death—*Imputed* righteousness will raise the whole world to life again, both Infants and others.

Phil. And seeing that this is so undeniably the truth, upon what basis does this astonishing building stand?

Didas. Upon the important antithesis in the next verse. Let us again parallel them, *ver.* 19.

For as by one man's disobedience many were made sinners;	So by the obedience of one shall many be made righteous.

1. You may here see, that one man's *disobedience* is contrasted with the *obedience* of one, just as one is to one.

2. To be *made sinners* is opposed to be *made righteous*.

3. That *many* is opposed to *many*; and must, in every respect, mean the same persons, and the same number.

Please farther to observe, that to be *made* or constituted *sinners*, is to have sin *imputed* to them. This

This was done by the wise counsel of God, in order *justly* to treat them *as such*. For it is no injustice to condemn the guilty to suffer the penalty annexed to the law he has broken; the suffering being proportioned to the offence. The many, here you see, were all constituted sinners, or guilty, and the many must mean all mankind, because all mankind die. Again, to keep the opposition consistent, to be *made* or constituted *righteous*, is to have righteousness *imputed* unto them, in order to treat them as such. Now nothing can possibly make a person righteous, but an acceptable obedience to the law. Therefore the obedience of the *One*, must be *imputed* to the *many*, in order to *make them righteous* by *imputation*, which certainly is the case before us.

Phil. If I rightly apprehend you, in the very sense in which the Many were constituted, and so Reputed sinners by the disobedience of Adam, in the very self-same sense the *Many* are constituted and so Reputed righteous, by the obedience of Christ; that is, both by *imputation*. Thus Adam and Christ were type and antitype exactly. And that in both verses, viz. 18th. and 19th. both our personal Sins and Obedience are quite out of the question, i. e. both personal merit and demerit.

Didas. That is my meaning to a tittle, and I hope St. Paul's also. This two-fold imputation holds good universally with respect to a state of mortality, and a resurrection. But present personal holiness, and future happiness, are no more included here, than our own merit or demerit are. The former is the entire effect of the Adamic oeconomy; the latter as entirely belongs to the gospel Dispensation. The Apostle adds,

Moreover, *the Law entered*, both into the world, and into the grand Plan of our Redemption. "It was added (to the first Law of Adam) because of

N Transgression;"

Transgression;" for from Adam to Moses, Sin was in the world; but by the law only is the knowledge of sin; for when it is brought home to the conscience, sin will appear in its own proper colours, which are "exceeding sinful." God, therefore, in His wisdom, *added* the ten commandments by Moses on Mount Sinai, to the one commandment delivered in Paradise, *That the* OFFENCE *might* ABOUND. That is, that the first offence committed by Adam, might, as in a glass, be seen to abound in his sinful posterity, as branches from one root, or as streams from a fountain. For the offence here is taken collectively for the many offences, (*ver.* 16.) as the word Sin is below. This collective sense of the words *offence* and *Sin*, in this place, is very natural and proper. For in the 18th. and 19th. verses, and elsewhere in this passage, the Apostle had considered all mankind as one grand aggregate in no less than four different points of light, as is very easy to be observed. It is true, the law neither multiplied offenders nor offences, but it discovered and detected both. It shews the malignancy of Sin, and the danger of the Sinner; and therefore is an excellent Schoolmaster to document us, and bring us to Christ, where we may find all the treasures of divine wisdom and saving knowledge deposited: And among others, one of the greatest, and most glorious of all Revealed truths, viz.

WHERE SIN ABOUNDED, GRACE DID *MUCH MORE ABOUND*, Both over the One Offence of Adam, and the Many Offences of his posterity: But my dear Phil. must here very carefully Observe, that the One Offence is limitted to Adam's transgressing his One command—That the Many Offences are limitted to his posterity transgressing the Law that entered that the Offence might Abound; that is, the ten commandments of Moses.

Phil. Very well; to me it is quite plain ſo far. And what then?

Didas. Why, that alſo there is another *Law*, which is THE LAW OF FAITH, *Rom.* iii. 27. Now ſins againſt this law are not included in the Apoſtle's bleſſed declaration, that where ſin abounded, grace did much more abound, however boundleſs abounding grace may be over the One Offence, and the many offences of Adam and his guilty poſterity. This abounding grace falls ſhort, and in its utmoſt limits, ſo far as I yet can find, will never extend ſo far as to reach out a pardon to the final tranſgreſſor of the "Law of Faith." According to this law, "He that believeth not, is condemned already;" let his caſe or character in other reſpects, be whatever it may—the beſt or the worſt. Yea, farther, "He that believeth not the Son, ſhall not ſee life, but the wrath of God abideth on him." *See Joh.* iii. 18, 36. It has been obſerved above, that ſo ſoon as Adam had ſinned, for any thing that he knew to the contrary, his caſe was both helpleſs and hopeleſs; and this ſeems to me to be the caſe here with unbelievers.

But with reſpect to our former ſubject, ſuch was the exuberant goodneſs of God, That in Chriſt Jeſus, a moſt perfect and adequate remedy was provided for both the One offence of Adam, and the many offences of all his poſterity. This glorious abounding Grace, is more than ſufficient to remove all the ſin, guilt, and miſery, of mankind. On the one hand, it abſolutely takes away the guilt, and removes the miſerable conſequences of it, by the "Grace of God, and the gift of eternal life," after the reſurrection: And on the other hand, propoſes, for our acceptance, a full pardon for our own perſonal offences—a gracious acceptance with God, and an adoption into his family—together with ſuch a ſupply of the ſpirit of grace, as is

abundantly

abundantly sufficient to purify our hearts, and fill us with all those divine graces that will qualify us for the future Paradise of God. Here the broken heart may find a healing balm—the guilty conscience, pardon and peace—a rest for the soul, such as earth affords none—and all freely without money or price.

The last verse of the chapter sums up the subject relating to those two powerful Sovereigns, SIN and GRACE; let us contrast them and their effects together, *ver.* 21.

That as Sin hath reigned unto Death,	Even so might Grace reign thro' righteousness unto eternal life, by Jesus Christ our Lord.

1. The contrast is between SIN and GRACE.
2. Between Death and Eternal Life.
3. Grace, that sovereign Queen of Heaven, is obliged to employ two mediums, in order to gain her Conquest; 1st. Righteousness,—2nd. Jesus Christ. When sin is conquered, grace succeeds in the conquered domain; and not only gains the conquest by means of, but replenishes her whole empire with Righteousness. Jesus Christ our Lord is not only the sovereign of Grace, having enthroned her, and invested her with all her authority, being Himself the grand fountain of all authority; but he was here contrasted with Adam so long as the contest lasted, as appears through the whole passage; but now that Grace hath abolished the two empires of sin and death. Adam no longer appears in the field of action; but being himself subdued by grace, is become replenished with righteousness; while Jesus Christ our Lord will, in due time, for the ages of ages, possess that dominion which Adam lost so soon. Even so, *Amen,* LORD JESUS.

DIALOGUE

DIALOGUE VIII.

Philotheos. WILL my dear Didas. indulge me with an opportunity to make a few remarks, &c. upon the above very interesting subjects?

Didas. With the utmost freedom; and shall be glad of a little relaxation, as too constant and intense thought is apt to relax the animal fibres, and exhaust or depress the spirits.

Phil. 1st. Suppose Adam had never sinned, would not himself, and mankind in him, have been eternally happy, though, perhaps, in a very small degree? Seeing that we fell in him when he fell, should not we have stood with him had he stood? 2nd. When the promise was made, and he believed in the Seed promised, suppose he had immediately died, would his body have ever been raised? If it would, did not the bruising the head of the serpent imply the resurrection from the dead, as the bruising the heel of the Seed implied the death of the head or principal of that seed? If Christ had never risen, neither would Adam or mankind. 3rd. Had Adam stood and we in him, there would have been no abounding grace, or abounding offence, because no other law would have been added. In that case, would the primitive Earth and Paradise have continued the everlasting abode of mankind? If so, was not that primitive state far short of what the gospel promises, and that we now expect? And therefore, upon the whole, was not the permission of the fall a blessing to mankind; seeing that abounding grace will put an end to the empire of sin and death, and restore and advance us greatly in the scale of happy beings? But,

In the mean time, what an extensive empire did sin erect! By one offence of one man, it invaded the

the world of mankind! Quickly did it set up a splendid Throne, and establish an empire all over the inhabited earth. With a tyrannical sway, it maintained its dominion from Adam to Moses. The addition of his law greatly strengthened the power of the monster, and rendered him more formidable by arming him with as many instruments of vengeance as there were curses in that law. Under every dispensation, he has established a dominion as wide as the world, and, hitherto, as lasting. What multitudes are there of his wretched Vassals, who labour night and day to secure and extend his empire; at the hazard of their souls, and the ruin of others!

But, however long or secure he seems to sit upon his Throne, at best he is but an usurper, and the supreme Governor of the World is levying war against him. As the Judge of the world, he has already passed a sentence upon him, the execution of which he can neither avoid nor survive—*He has condemned Sin in the Flesh.* Let every christian rejoice, and daily pray for the time of its execution. But,

Behold! the King of terrors comes! Sin opened the Door, and another Monster found his way into all this lower Creation—"Death reigned from Adam to Moses;" and subdued the Antediluvian constitutions at length, though after a fight with some of near a thousand years together! He never met with his match till Christ engaged him. He even struck his sting into the heart of Emmanuel, which brought him into the grave a few hours! But as he descended, he fell, shouting, "O Death, I will be thy plague! O Grave, I will be thy destruction!" Ages will yet revolve, before the Saint, leaving his prison, will triumphant rise, and echo back Emmanuel's shout, "O Death, where is thy sting? O Grave, where is thy victory?"

He

He possesses a more extensive dominion than sin. He passes through the world in a thousand different and often most dreadful forms! He pervades every element; and lodges a while in every animal, vegetable, and mineral—Hides himself in our food and physic—Diffuses his poison throughout our constitutions in the shape of the high-seasoned delicious dainties we daily devour; and swims in the sparkling glass and wide-spread bowl, deceiving us with a fillip to our wasting spirits, which we interpret a fresh supply:—Thus the Sot drinks in death; and, without repentance, damnation, with it. He pervades nature, and almost has her at his control. He often rolls in the rattling thunder—Sits upon the pointed shafts of lightning—Flies in the whirlwind's furious blasts—Floats upon the tempestuous billow—Sinks the tossed vessel in shoals, or dashes its yielding bottom or sides against the unrelenting rock, and gathers his spoils out of the deep, or finds them hid among the rocks, or rolled upon the sands.

Dire diseases float in the air, wafted by every breeze from house to house, and kingdom to kingdom, which we imbibe with our breath, while death flies about on the wings of the wind! All these, and a thousand others, are the deadly artillery of this murdering monster! Time would fail to take an inventory of the stores deposited through the magazines of earth, air, and ocean, which this King of Terrors employs to enlarge the borders, and people his realms. But alas! Have not mankind put invention to the rack to supply him with weapons of cruelty, the faster to murder one another? How many sons of *Vulcan* dig in the mines, or scorch at the forge, to form the malleable metal into brandishing swords, glittering firelocks, or pointed bayonets—The cannon, mortar, &c. &c. fixed on the rampart, or floating in ships

of

of war, fire-ſhips, &c. like ſo many floating hells, laden frequently with theſe and ſuch-like weapons as theſe, calculated on purpoſe to ſhorten the lives of thoſe dying mortals who could not live long without them! Thus is the divine decree fulfilled, "Duſt thou art, and unto duſt ſhalt thou return."

But this is not all. The human ſpecies are not the only morſels daily devoured by this voracious monſter. His Empire, like Adam's, extends into earth, air, and ocean; from all which, he every moment collects his income, and yet forever cries, *give, give.*

The beaſts of the field, the fowls of the air, the fiſhes of the ſea, and the innumerable tribes of inſects, all fall a prey, in quick ſucceſſion! The vegetable world feels the fury of his attacks. The ſpiral graſs, the verdant foliage, the blooming flower, the luſcious fruit-bearing tree, &c. &c. fade, fall, and periſh, whether buried in living bodies, or the ſepulchre of mother earth. Not to mention the innumerable *animalculæ* that in countleſs millions feaſt on our herbage, foliage, fruits, and flowers—float in the air, or ſcud in the water, leſs than the mote in the ſun, yet all replete with animated life! Theſe, for a ſeaſon, ſport and feed themſelves at the expence of the lives of others; and, in their turn, many of them ſubmit to the ſame unnatural fate! We live by death, and die to give place to others, in ſwift ſucceſſion! O death! there is nothing ſo minute as to eſcape thy notice—nothing ſo hard or durable but muſt yield to thy power.

But ſhall he forever thus tyranniſe? Shall his reign have no end? Yes, bleſſed be God, yes; the Decree is gone forth, and *death itſelf* ſhall die. The enemy is already virtually aboliſhed—overcome—condemned.—The ſentence paſſed upon him, and the promiſe to the new *riſing* world is, "There

"There ſhall be no more death," *Rev.* xxi. 4. "Death ſhall be ſwallowed up in victory," 1 *Cor.* xv. 54. Loſe his dominion, and periſh for ever in the lake of Fire, *Rev.* xx. 14.

The mighty God—the Father of the future age—the Prince of peace—Emmanuel—the glorious Son of man—Son of God, unto whom the Kingdom and Dominion under the whole Heaven ſhall be given—He has ſet up a rival and competitor for an univerſal and never-ending Kingdom—GRACE ſhall REIGN over Sin—over Death—utterly aboliſh and deſtroy them—But of her kingdom there ſhall be no end! Grace ſhall reign through righteouſneſs unto eternal life, by Jeſus Chriſt our Lord; in whom it pleaſed the Father that all fulneſs ſhould dwell; in whom it was given to us before the times of the conſtituted ages began. This is the Grace of God that bringeth ſalvation unto all men, (*Tit.* iii. 12. *Gr.*). by which grace alone we are ſaved. Unerring Wiſdom drew the Plan of her Government—Divine Philanthropy and Goodneſs are the Pillars of her Throne, which is eſtabliſhed for perpetuity.

This divine Monarchy was ſet up on purpoſe to overthrow *effectually* every malignant effect of the One Offence—To dignify mankind, by exalting our nature into an *indiſſoluble* union with Emmanuel; by which Grace plants its principles, and extends its influences ſo powerfully in human nature, as to counteract our paſſions, mortify our corruptions, and purify our hearts, by ſo filling them with divine love and humility, as to render ourſelves and our ſervices an acceptable ſacrifice to God, through Jeſus Chriſt our Lord.

This Reſtored Life, unto all who receive and improve the abundance of Grace and the gift of Righteouſneſs, it may be rationally ſuppoſed, in my judgment, will be almoſt infinitely ſuperior, in every

every respect, to that life which we lost in Adam.

My dear Didas, after so long an interruption, please to inform me of your Judgment on this supposition.

Didas. My Judgment is, that it is neither irrational nor unscriptural. At the Times of the Restoration of all Things, the whole will be so far improved and changed for the better, as to bear a due proportion one thing with another. Both the state of mankind, and of the world itself, upon the Gospel-Plan, will be improved beyond all our present conceptions. The dignity of the Person of the second Adam, our great Restorer, above that of the first, sufficiently argues the superlative dignity and more exalted state of happiness in this lower world, in its Restored, above its primitive condition. Every member of Christ's mystical body, composing the bride, the Lamb's Wife, will possess a Glory suitable to the unparalleled dignity and honour of such a Head—such a Husband! This head, this husband, being Emmanuel, or God invested with human nature; flesh of our flesh, bone of our bone, all those glorious beatitudes which Deity will diffuse through human nature in his proper person, will, no doubt, be communicated to evey member in due degrees, and according to the rank or station such members will sustain in the body. Exalted bliss! "I in them, and Thou in Me." Experience in the ages of ages, &c. &c. can explain it! *Joh.* xvii. 23.

Phil. Will not the brute animals, at the Times of the Restitution, be partakers also in the glory then to be Revealed?

Didas. The *Times* of the Restitution seem to indicate more periods than one. And very probably, the Restitution itself will be gradual, at different times, progressively advancing from less to greater degrees of happiness, and to greater still, until

until we arrive at the ſummit of Perfection, if that be ever attained. But if the brute part of the creation were not to participate in it, how can it be ſaid to be the Reſtitution of *all things*, ſeeing that they poſſeſs ſo great a part in it?

Again. If a curſe took place upon the ground, and conſequently upon its produce, purely for the ſake of the ſin of Adam; may we not moſt certainly expect, that both that curſe, and all its baneful effects, will, in time, not only be totally removed, but that every ſubject affected by it, will be farther advanced in the ſcale of beings, and happineſs, than they were before that curſe took place? Is not the merit of Chriſt, reſulting from the dignity of his perſon, the perfection of his Obedience, and the greatneſs of his ſufferings, ſufficient to procure more and greater degrees of happineſs for the whole accurſed world, than the malignancy of Adam's ſin could deprive it of? If ſuch was the exuberancy of Creating love, as to make ſo glorious a world, and repleniſh it ſo richly, may we not juſtly expect, the divine nature being ſtill the ſame, that Redeeming love will go far beyond the bounds of the firſt creation, when He comes to make all things new? If God was pleaſed to plant ſuch a Paradiſe for a creature formed out of the duſt; and to repleniſh it, and the world without it, in ſuch a rich and reſplendent manner, eſpecially as He foreſaw the fall and the conſequent curſe upon it; what can be thought too glorious for His only beloved Son, the appointed Heir of all Things, in their Reſtored ſtate? It appears to me highly rational to think, that every animated Being, or that exiſts in the preſent evil age, will exiſt in a much greater degree of perfection in the ages to come, than ever they did at the firſt creation.

Were not all the creatures that inhabit the three

Elements,

Elements, the subjects of Adam's Kingdom? Shall the Heir of all things, by the fall, lose a great number of his domestic subjects, and break the beautiful scale of beings, by annihilating them? Is it not more consentaneous to the divine wisdom and goodness, to suppose, that he will rather exalt them? Were they not all, according to their respective kinds, capacities, powers, and uses, not only *good* by creation, but, no doubt, the intended instruments to be subservient to many holy purposes, if man had maintained is original standing? And though the fall, for a season, defeated those purposes, why may we not judge, that when all things are restored, these also will, both to a better situation, and to better ends and uses, in a better state of things?

These have long groaned in pain under the sufferings and curse of fallen nature; can we once seriously doubt, whether they will ever partake of the blessings of nature Restored? Why were they originally made *very good*, and endowed with the keenest appetites and sensations; and some of them with astonishing capacities, not much inferior to human; if they were all to be annihilated? If so, were these *very good* creatures, faultless and unblamable, to be plunged into all the miseries of the fall; involved in a curse they never deserved; and suffer its ills, though perfectly innocent? How often are they wantonly abused, and treated with unrelenting cruelty, by their tyrannic masters, and that without any pity or reward; but groan out a most wretched life, and that often from the badness of their treatment? Is there a God, whose tender mercies are over all his works? But are not these very creatures, so grand and curious in their forms and textures, the workmanship of God? But in what part of life do these tender mercies appear, unless it be by shortening them, and so re-

leasing

easing them out of their distress? If they will never rise to be recompensed, wherein shall we trace the foosteps of those tender mercies through the whole of their existence?

Phil. As the annihilation of beings, ever possest of vitality, was never an Article of my creed; so I leave it to Manichean principles to account for the cruel sufferings of such innocent creatures, without the least possibility of either recompense, or restitution to a better state. I may be mistaken, but I ingenuously confess, it appears to me, that the greatest advantages will result in the issue, not only to the far greatest part of mankind, but to the whole world in general, from the complete execution of the Gospel Plan.

Didas. Who that understands it, can once call that in question? He that runs may read in every prophecy, promise, and type, the transcendency of the New and Restored state of Things, under the conduct of the Son of God, above that of the Adamical, under which to this day the whole Creation groans, *Rom.* viii. 19, 26.

Phil. I begin to perceive, that it is not either to this present evil world, (*Gal.* i. 4.) or to the present conduct of a governing Providence, that we are to look for that light by which alone to form a right Judgment of things, in general.

Didas. That is most certainly true. Can any man of reason suppose, that the present state of Things are such as God created them? Or that the present Governing Providence is, for the most part, any other than the goverment of a world of Rebels under the displeasure of the Governor? Where are those Histories that prove the contrary in past ages? Where is the Kingdom existing, or what part of the Globe can furnish an instance to the contrary? Facts are stubborn things, and do not they plead in favour of the above remarks?

It is to futurity, that we are to look for a happy ſtate of the world, and of mankind in it. Now, *Satan*, the Prince of this world reigns—Sin, his own ſon, and of the ſame nature with himſelf, holds the ſceptre all the world over, and ever has done from Adam to this day. It is true, in every age God has employed a few fiſhers of men; but is it not equally true, that they have caught few, very few, compared with the innumerable ſhoals they left behind in the deep waters? Death, preceded with innumerable diſeaſes that give warning of his coming, in different ſhapes, knocks at every door—arreſts the giddy and unthinking—ſeizes him—and commits to the priſon of the grave—if terrene, worms devour him—if aqueous, he falls a prey to fiſhes—a few find a ſepulchre in the bowels of carnivorous fowls—others in the wild beaſts of the woods and foreſts. And thus he diſpoſes of his ſubjects at their exit out of time, and confines them in a priſon till a jail-delivery will ſet them at liberty.

Phil. Methinks you have, in theſe few remarks, ſufficiently demonſtrated, that it is not to this preſent ſtate of Things, but, as you ſaid, to prophecies, promiſes, and types, wherein, as in ſo many glaſſes, the world will appear in a dreſs comporting with the original deſign of its Maker, a world of happy beings and candidates for better ſtill.

Didas. Sin is the ſting of Death; of whoſe point, when it pierces the heart, every one feels the dying pain; its poiſon has infected the whole maſs of mankind: But the ſuperiority of grace over ſin, both antidotes its poiſon, and relieves its pain; and at length will gain a final conqueſt: For though Sin ſet Man in a ſtate of enmity with God, yet when we were "Enemies, we were reconciled unto God by the *death* of his Son," having actually made atonement for all ſin. Now,

being

being reconciled, how much more shall we be saved by his life?

Phil. When enemies, reconciled! Glorious news for guilty men! But, pray, how extensive was this reconciliation?

Didas. As extensive as the world of mankind. For Jesus Christ the righteous, is the Propitiation for the sins *Holou Tou Kosmou*, (1 *Joh.* ii. 2.) of the *whole of the world:* The reason is, that God was in Christ reconciling the world unto himself, not *imputing* their trespasses unto them, &c. 2 *Cor.* v. 19.

Phil. What! not *impute* them to those who had committed them? Unto whom then did he impute them?

Didas. Unto his own Son, "who Himself bare our sins in his own Body (prepared on purpose, *Heb.* x. 5.) upon the accursed tree. For, indeed, "God laid upon Him, or made *to meet in Him,* as in a centre, the Guilt of us all,"—all, who, like sheep, had gone astray, *Isa.* liii. 6.

Phil. One would be ready to think, from such infallible oracles as these, being delivered by divine Inspiration, that, "In the ages to come," by far the greatest part of mankind will be finally saved. Such sentiments as these, breathing nothing but Peace upon earth and good-will towards men, are sufficient to enflame every humane heart with the warmest gratitude unto God, and inspire the strongest and most fiducial confidence in the person and merit of our blessed redeemer.

Didas. True, they are so. But how far is this from being the case! Ignorance very often exposes us to very erroneous conclusions. And who knows not the fallibility of human Judgment? The greatest and best of men, and not seldom, even in the most solemn decisions, have often steered wide of the point of truth. In those very subjects,

ſubjects, in which the ſouls of men have been moſt concerned, how egregiouſly have whole Councils determined on the ſide of error! The right of private judgment is every perſon's birth-right; no authority upon earth ought to control it. Conſcience is ſacred to the Deity; It ought to be free as the breezes upon a plain, and as the ſolar beams at noon-day.

To the Law and to the Teſtimony we muſt make our appeal. Candor is ever ready to conſider and make due allowances for human infirmities. Notwithſtanding the preſent differences ſubſiſting among the fallible judgments of mortals, it appears to me, that when the laſt link of the golden chain of Providence will be exhibited to open view, thoſe will appear to have been neareſt the Truth, who have drawn out human Redemption upon the largeſt ſcale, that of *Origen's* perhaps excepted. When this appears, every embarraſſing difficulty will vaniſh—every ſpecious objection receive a true ſolution—and that contracted narrow bigoted ſpirit, which has ſo long rent the ſeamleſs coat of Chriſt into rags and tatters, will be no longer found among men.

At the preſent, it cannot be expected, that our fallible judgments and narrow conceptions of the conduct of Providence, the extent of Prophecy, and the height and depth of divine Purpoſes and Promiſes, ſhould be adequate to the almoſt infinite magnitude and variety of the ſubjects thereof. The prejudices of a bigoted education, the reluctance with which human pride admits of a change of ſentiments, &c. are reaſons ſufficient, with the generality of people, to keep them in the beaten track of their received ſyſtems, however eccentric it may lead them from the line of truth.

He who advances any thing new, expoſes himſelf to cenſure. But perſons who are ſo ready to

paſs

paſs them, ought firſt to conſider whether they are juſt. For inſtance; to limit our knowledge of the Scriptures of Truth within the bounds of our fathers and reformers, what is it but to aſcribe a degree of infallibility to their deciſions; and, contrary to the fundamental doctrine of Proteſtants, ſet up their Judgments, inſtead of the Scriptures, as the Standards of Truth? But this is not all: Do we not thereby ſhut up the avenues by which we might receive farther light and information, and of courſe bereave ourſelves of every acceſſion to increaſing knowledge, which, in all other Sciences, we ſee every where around us?

The progreſs that the liberal Arts, Trade and Commerce, &c. have made in the preſent century; the degree of perfection to which they are arrived within the memories of many living, is ſuch, that if an Angel from heaven had announced the fact a few centuries ago, it is a queſtion whether miracles themſelves would have gained him general credit.

Is ſuch an uncommon and almoſt miraculous increaſe in human literature, arts, &c. among us, ſolely owing to the ſuperior genius and induſtry of the preſent generation, above thoſe of our fathers? Human pride will ſuggeſt an affirmative anſwer. But will facts in any wiſe ſupport it? May we not both more piouſly and juſtly attribute it to a gracious ſuperintending Providence, who may be thus paving the way for the farther ſpreading of his goſpel, and diffuſing the ſaving Knowledge of Himſelf and of his Son Jeſus Chriſt our Lord?

This is certain, that an Angel informed Daniel of the fact, more than two thouſand years ago, "Many ſhall run to and fro, and knowledge ſhall be increaſed," *Dan.* xii. 4.

Many ſhall run to and fro. Has there ever been an age hitherto, that can put in a claim, equal to our own, for the accomplishment of this remarkable Prophecy? Do not our hardy Tars, sometimes attended with Gentlemen of rank and science, dare every danger of sea and climate, to explore the unknown regions of the earth, to acquire fame, accumulate riches, or satisfy curiosity? While every other science advances rapidly in its progress, shall religious, shall Bible-knowledge alone be at a stand? Can it be rationally supposed, that this divine knowledge is excluded a place in the angelic prophecy? Or have the formers of our creeds, confessions of faith, articles, &c. left no room for an increase of Bible-knowledge? Are the subjects of prophecy, and the full contents of the great and precious promises, so fully understood and explained, as to admit of on improvement?

Phil. Surely the book of sacred scripture, like the book of nature, is, comparatively, little understood. But do not both lie open to every one for inspection, examination, and farther improvement?

Didas. Most certainly. Prophecies and Promises, that respect the latter days, are far more in number, and abundantly fuller in their contents, I believe, than usually supposed to be. Narrow contracted sentiments are never friendly to that love and benevolence in which the very essence of religion consists. We have a glaring instance of this in the Jews, in the Times of our Saviour and his Apostles. The scope of the discourses of our Saviour and his Apostles being drawn upon a larger scale than the Jewish *peculium*, importing mercy for Gentile-sinners, militated so directly against their national pride and prejudices, that this very thing contributed not a little to the rejection of Christ and his Gospel.

The Prophecies contained in their own divine inspired oracles, did not afford evidence sufficient

to

to convince them of their folly, although fully believed and daily read among them.

Phil. Do not the ſame narrow principles at this day obtain too much among many profeſſed Chriſtians? How freely do Anathemas and damnatory Sentences fly about among thoſe who ſhould be the loving peacable followers of the Prince of Peace? A different ſentiment, perhaps about indifferent things—a mode of external worſhip, trivial in itſelf, will often ſteel the breaſt of one, and turn into ice the heart of another; and while they diſpute for a ſhadow, the heat of their temper, perhaps deſtroys the very ſubſtance itſelf, and renders the mind incapable of poſſeſſing it. Such are the effects of vain jangling!

Didas. Such contracted ſentiments, bleſſed be the Father or lights, had never a lodging in my breaſt. Senſible of the infirmities of humanity, with a conſcious ſenſe of integrity, the bible alone has long been my Rule of Judgment; and though I could not in every thing apprehend ſubjects as many do, and have done, yet I quarrel with none from whom I differ; but confeſs, that every contracted ſentiment in religion has always ſurprized me; being, to my apprehenſion, founded upon miſtake: And have often thought, that the miſtake itſelf principally originates from contracting the *duration of Time* much too ſhort, not affording opportunity for the accompliſhing the great things the Prophecies contain; and alſo, in conſequence of this, confining their views and forming their Judgments to the preſent ſtate of things; not knowing that this "Preſent evil *age*" (*Gal.* i. 4.) is but a very ſhort ſpace of that Time; which, in the deep counſels of heaven, is allotted for the fulfilling its myſterious purpoſes in.

Phil. As to myſelf, I freely own, whatever appears to me to limit the love of that God who is is love itſelf, and to contract within a narrow compaſs the extent of Chriſt's atonement, always give me pain; and the more ſo, becauſe I have uſually obſerved, that thoſe who do, are the very people who are the moſt jealous of the honour of Chriſt, and the moſt afraid of attributing that to human freedom and ability; which, as they ſuppoſe, belongs to Chriſt only. But, does not the Doctrine of general Redemption, as it is uſually underſtood, contract the love of God, and in the iſſue draw the atonement of Chriſt, and the effects of his merits, into almoſt as ſmall a compaſs as the Predeſtinarian ſyſtem?

Didas. With reſpect to the number of thoſe who will be finally ſaved or condemned, both ſyſtems nearly agree in the iſſue. Both ſuppoſe, that, comparatively ſpeaking, but few will get to heaven; and certain it is, that according to the ſyſtems in vogue among divines and caſuiſts, both are in the right. At the ſame time, both are agreed, that the moſt exquiſite torments imagination can point, fall infinitely farther ſhort of the anguiſh of the damned, than the pricking of a lance does to the amputation of a limb; but if we add perpetual duration, as both do, the horrid idea is too affecting to dwell upon.

This has induced ſome profeſſed believers of the Bible to ſuppoſe, "That there is no hell at all—That univerſal Redemption implies univerſal Salvation—That the only difference in this world, between a ſinner and a ſaint, is the improvement or non-improvement of abounding grace; and in the world to come, the only difference will conſiſt in their degrees of happineſs." Again, others admit of a long ſeries of ages, in which they will be puniſhed in proportion to their crimes; but that this puniſhment is only a very ſharp Diſcipline to correct them; and cordially believe, that it will have

have a happy iſſue, in which pain will for ever end in ſome degree of pleaſure: But ſome have doubted whether they will not then be annihilated. Others imagine, that the purifying flames of hell will purge them from ſin; after which, they will come forth, like Gold from the furnace, and be admitted to all the glories of heaven. To which may be added, that ſome think that this will be the caſe with devils alſo.

Phil. Such awful conceptions of the deity as *Reprobation* implies, have, I doubt, been often attended with the moſt pernicious conſequences to the intereſts of vital religion, and the truth of Revelation. It is eaſy to conceive, how perſons of bright and cultivated parts, and warm powerful paſſions and imaginations, may readily conclude, as it is to be feared thouſands have done, from the *Predeſtinarian* hypotheſis, either that there is no God at all; or, that the Bible, which is affirmed to be a Revelation of His Will, but, nevertheleſs contains Doctrines which afford ſuch awful concluſions, cannot be what it is ſuppoſed to be. For if there be a God, he muſt be infinitely good and merciful; and if the Bible be what it is pretended to be, it muſt diſcover Him to be ſuch; but as the contrary is concluded from that book, in his conduct towards ſuch a vaſt majority of mankind, that therefore, it cannot be a Revelation of His will.

With ſuch, therefore, it paſſes for nothing but a groſs impoſition upon the credulous part of mankind—an engine of ſtate-policy—or an invention of Prieſt-craft. What a fruitful womb muſt this be of Atheiſts, Deiſts, Arians, Socinians, &c. eſpecially the two former—as well as of diſtreſſing doubts, jangling diſputes, and a thouſand perplexities among the more ſober thinking part of mankind!!

Didas.

Didas. Whatever ambiguity may be ſuppoſed in ſcripture Terms, expreſſive of future puniſhment, the reality of its exiſtence can never be denied by a ſober judgment, nor the terribleneſs of it deſcribed by the pens of mortals.

Eternity has been frequently deſcribed as a *nunc ſtans*, or a *ſtanding Now*. However this may be reſpecting God, or in heaven properly ſo called, when God will be All in All, 'tis moſt certain that Time is a ſeries in perpetual ſucceſſion. St. Paul informs us, as has been already noticed, that God has appointed his Son the "Heir of all Things." Though foreſeen by divine preſcience, yet, this appointment, in fact, could only take place when Adam, the firſt Heir, by rebellion had forfeited his Title. By Him *then* it was that He "Conſtituted the Ages," *Heb.* i. 2.

Phil. What Ages, do yo ſuppoſe, are intended?

Didas. Eternity, and He who inhabits Eternity, can never be meaſured in their duration by Ages. The Ages of Angels we now nothing of. Beſides, can there be any propriety in uſing the Term age or ages, to any thing of endleſs duration? Muſt not both age and ages have beginning and ending, a terminus *a quo* et *ad quem?* Is not to make an age of eternity, and eternity an age or ages, to erect a new Babel in Language and Philoſophy? He who inhabits Eternity is no older *now* than when time firſt commenced; nor is He any younger *now* than He will be when Time is no more. Neither God nor Eternity have any relation to Time or Ages. Obſerve, for inſtance, St. Paul informs us, that God is Able to do exceeding abundantly above all that we aſk or think; and then adds, "Unto him be glory in the Church by Chriſt Jeſus throughout all ages, world without end," *Eph.* iii. 20, 21. Conſult the Greek, and it is very different; inſtead of *all ages*, it is

all

all the Generations; and for *world without end*, it is *of the age of ages*. Now I ask,

1. For God to receive Glory *by Christ Jesus*, is it not to receive it through him, as through a medium, i. e. as he is Mediator? But will Christ be a Mediator when God is *all in all*? 1 *Cor*. xv. 28. Most certainly not.

2. This Glory is to be *in the Church*, or by the Church: Now where will that Church exist? Doubtless it means the Church upon earth; for

3. It is to exist throughout *all the generations*, &c. But I ask what generations there can be in heaven, when Christ hath delivered up the Kingdom to the Father? Will procreation, birth, and death, there exist?

4. These Generations are to proceed in succession, as it appears plain, throughout *the age of ages*. Can this mean an endless duration? Rather, is not the age, or ages of ages, an Hebraism, put for the greatest or longest of all ages, exactly corresponding with our Saviour's magnificent Titles that He will then sustain, and justly, when His own proper Times commence, namely, "The blessed and only Potentate, King of kings, and Lord of lords?" 1 *Tim*. vi. 15. Are not these those happy halcyon Times so long foreseen, and foretold by the sweet Singer of Israel? Then will the mountains bring Peace to the people—then will He judge the poor of the people—save the needy—and break in pieces the Oppressor, (*Rev*. xix. 11, 20.) Then shall the People fear Him *as long as the Sun and Moon endure, throughout all Generations*—in His Days, (or his own Times) shall the Righteous flourish; and abundance of Peace so long as the *moon endureth*—He shall have Dominion from sea to sea, to the ends of the earth—yea, all Kings shall fall down before Him; all Nations shall serve Him—His name (Jesus) shall endure

endure for ever; that is, His Name ſhall be continued as long as the Sun—all Nations ſhall call Him Bleſſed—and let the whole Earth be filled with His Glory; Amen, and Amen. *See Pſa.* lxxii. *tot.* being the laſt, probably, that David ever wrote.

Permit me here to aſk every ingenuous and intelligent reader,

1ſt. In what paſt age, and where are thoſe Hiſtories of that age, wherein this laſt Pſalm of David's have had an accompliſhment?

2nd. Are not through "All the generations of the age of ages," and "As long as the Sun and Moon endure," Terms expreſſive of the ſame duration?

3rd. Do not the Sun and Moon meaſure Day and Night? And is not the *Age of Ages* meaſured by day and night? *Rev.* xx. 10.

4th. If ſo, will not the age of ages *end*, when the Sun and the Moon ſhall endure no longer, or ceaſe to meaſure day and night?

Phil. But if the age of ages *end* with the duration of the Sun and Moon, (and moſt certainly they will end when heaven and earth ſo flies away, that no place will be found for them) will not the ſmoke of the torment of the Beaſt's Worſhippers then vaniſh, and riſe no more? for certainly the ages of ages is the limitted time for that ſmoke to aſcend. *Rev.* xiv. 11.

Didas. Moſt certainly. But my dear Phil. is not ſo inadvertant as not to obſerve, That this awful ſcene will be, beyond contradiction, exhibited "in the *Preſence* of the holy Angels, and in the *Preſence* of the Lamb;" nor yet ſo ignorant as not to know, that the holy Angels, in whoſe preſence this tormenting fire and brimſtone is, nor yet the Lamb, as a Lamb, that is, as a Mediator, will, for an endleſs ſeries of duration, continue where that

that ſmoke of torment is, nor yet where the fire and brimſtone are from which the ſmoke aſcends.

Phil. I hope I am not ſo ignorant, for that would be to confound hell and heaven together; in the latter of which, the lamb, when he has thrown off that enſign of his Mediatorſhip, together with his holy angels, no doubt, will paſs this endleſs duration, where and when God will be All and in All.

Didas. But obſerve, the ſmoke of their torments aſcendeth up for the very ſame term of duration, that the Kingdoms *of Koſmos* will be the Kingdoms of our Lord and of his Chriſt, (*Rev.* xi. 15.) for the very ſame words are uſed in both places. Now if Koſmos will continue for an endleſs Duration; and if the Kingdoms of Koſmos, (or of this World) will be the Kingdoms of our Lord and his Chriſt, for an endleſs Duration; then, ſo will the ſmoke of their torments aſcend for an endleſs Duration. But, 1ſt. Koſmos, yea, the Earth itſelf, and Heaven, will both ſo fly away, as that there will be found no place for them. 2nd. When this event will take place, then ſhall the Son deliver up the Kingdom to the Father. But this will not be, ſo long as the ſun and moon endure, as you have juſt now ſeen.

Phil. But my dear Didas. when do you ſuppoſe that theſe worſhippers of the Beaſt, &c. will enter upon this awful ſcene of ſufferings?

Didas. St. John expreſsly tells you, that it will be at our Saviour's next coming. Then will be the ſolemn ſeaſon, when the Beaſt will be taken, and with him the falſe Prophet, and their followers, and be caſt *alive* into the lake that burneth with fire and brimſtone, *Rev.* xix. 20. And as our Saviour informs us, that this Puniſhment is Prepared for the devil and his Angels, (*Matt.* xxv. 41.) ſo, agreeable thereto, you read, "That the

Devil was caſt into the lake of fire and brimſtone, where the Beaſt and the falſe Prophet are," and had long been, *Rev.* xx. 10.

Phil. I ſuppoſe they had been from the time of our Saviour's coming, all the time of the Millennium, and of Satan's little ſeaſon. But ſay, my dear Didas. if the ages of ages, being the time of the puniſhing both the Beaſt, falſe Prophet, and the Devil, will have an end; that is, if the lake of fire and brimſtone, ſituated during the age of ages, in the preſence of the holy angels, and in the preſence of the Lamb, will only burn until Chriſt delivers up the Kingdom to the Father, as you ſaid above; then, is it not plain to demonſtration, that the puniſhment of wicked men and devils will have a final end?

Didas. Not ſo plain as my dear Phil. may ſuppoſe. By all probability, that ſentence that finally fixes the never-ending ſtate of the wicked, whether men or devils, will be the laſt act, or nearly ſo, of the great Judge, before he ſurrenders up his Mediatorial Office to his Father, and at the concluſion of the ages of ages: *See Rev.* xxii. 5. *comp.* 11. "He that is unjuſt, let him be unjuſt ſtill: And he which is filthy, let him be filthy ſtill: And he that is righteous, let him be righteous ſtill: And he that is holy, let him be holy ſtill." As I look upon it, that the Mediator's Kingdom will continue ſo long, and no longer, as there are any of the human kind within the *reach of mercy*; ſo I look upon it, that innumerable multitudes will be deemed ſuch, by their merciful Judge, of which none but Himſelf is capable of judging, who are and who are not within that reach.

In this preſent age, ſhort-ſighted mortals are very apt to draw erroneous concluſions when they judge by appearances. It has been before obſerved, that prophecies, promiſes, and types, alone hold a

Torch

Torch into the dark Place of futurity; nor can human penetration see the least object there, farther than they shine upon it. The vulgar supposition, that when the present state of things ends, which most people think will not continue long; and that human generation will then entirely cease; that the day of judgment will immediately follow, and a burning world close the scenes of Time: Such people must certainly have very narrow and imperfect conceptions of the works of God, and his Providence, not to mention their ignorance and inattention of what sacred writ records.

Is it not evident that this present earth, in the space of less than six thousand years, is in its third state; and has suffered changes in its qualities, sufficient to denominate it, in a sense, a new earth, in each change it has undergone? No doubt it was very different when it first came out of its Maker's hands, and while all things were *very good*, from what it afterwards was, when the Curse for Adam's crime had taken place upon it. And it is certain, that St. Peter distinguishes the heavens and the earth which *now are*, from those that perished at the flood, 2 *Pet.* iii. 5, 7. By which it appears, that this is its third state from the creation. How many more it will pass through, before it finally will pass away, I know not. But this I know, that it will advance from worse to better; it will be *changed* like a garment; but how often, the "Ages to come" will discover. Garments are frequently changed, in the course of human life, as life itself is changed, from infancy to old age; and so it both has and will be with it.

We may here remark, that at the creation, when all things were *very good*, man was then in a state of probation, not of perfection; and is it not reasonable to suppose, that the fruits of Paradise, and the creatures, in general, possessed qualities adapted

to

to his then present condition? And has not divine Providence pursued the same rule ever since? This affords reason to suppose, that in future the rule will be followed, so as to adapt the changes in the natural world, at the different *Times* of Restoration, to the state of the world of mankind. The case of Gog and Magog, and the Holy City subsisting together in Time, and this time being in a future age, demonstrates that both Saints and Sinners will inhabit our earth in that age. Are not Gog and Magog *Nations* of Mankind? *See Rev.* xx. 8.

Hitherto Satan has deceived the whole world, *Rev.* xii. 9. But the mentioning the Holy City, and the Camp of the Saints, but not one word about the Jews expresly, but only the Gentiles, seems plainly enough to inform us, that Satan's deceptions will be confined to gentile nations only. Must not these Nations be in a state of probation, similar in substance to that of our own? But is it reasonable to suppose, that they will have no means of information about Satan's design against them? Yea, is not that *Aionion* Gospel, (*Rev.* xiv. 6.) or Gospel of the Age, to be preached unto them, as now it is to us?

The Gospel will be continued down from our Times for many thousands of years yet to come. This I have demonstrated elsewhere. Ever since the Adoption of Abraham, from whose loins the Messiah was to proceed, a preference, in point of Time, the Jews have always experienced. The labours of our Saviour, of his Apostles, and seventy Disciples, all the time of his Ministry, were expresly limitted within the bounds of the Jewish Peculium. The lost sheep of the house of Israel were the proper Pastoral care of that good Shepherd. The advantage they had over the Gentiles, from the time of Moses, was *much every way*.

The

The Stock they ſprang from, growing upon the Root of David, made naturally a Good Olive Tree. The Root being holy, the Branches were holy alſo. By Unbelief, many of theſe branches, by the great Huſband-man, were cut off: The inciſions made, by the ſame hand that made them, were healed, by His ingraffing the Gentiles in their room. Theſe new branches, naturally wild, only grow by being ingraffed, and by Faith only maintain and retain their Places in the Good Olive. But if ever a general Apoſtaſy from Chriſt ſhould happen, the Gentiles will, in their turn, be cut off by the ſame hand that ingraffed them.

Phil. As what you have juſt obſerved is evidently St. Paul's Doctrine, (*Rom.* xi.) it almoſt makes me tremble! Look around through all the nations of Chriſtendom, what do we ſee but ſuch a growing Apoſtaſy? Whole Nations and whole Communities denying the Lord that bought them—Original ſin—the Divinity of Chriſt—and his Atonement made for ſin. Alas! I fear, leſt we ſhould ſuffer the ſame exciſion that the Jews did, and that by the ſame hand, for a ſimilar Cauſe, *Unbelief*, which deluges Chriſtendom!

Didas. The proſpect is truly alarming, and greatly affecting to all who love the Lord Jeſus in Sincerity, and the Truth as it is in Jeſus. Foreſeeing this Apoſtaſy, juſt before he left the world, among other things, he ſaid, "Ye believe in God, believe alſo *in Me*." But ſo little is this duty attended to in our day, that, among the profeſſors of Chriſtianity, there are few that *poſſeſs* that faith that works by love—purifies the heart—and overcomes the world; that is, the luſt of the fleſh, the luſt of the eye, and the pride of life.—This is no cenſure, as the tree is known by its fruits. Yet, bad as the caſe is at preſent, before Chriſt comes it is ſure to be worſe. With regard to morals, christendom will be as it was in the days of Noah and Lot: But with respect to orthodox faith, He himself asked, "When the Son of Man cometh, shall he find Faith on the Earth?" Importing that it would be at a very low ebb, at the best.

When, therefore, He will come, though the Gentiles will be cut off for unbelief, and the kingdom will be Restored to Israel, and from that time will never be given to any other people, then will the Deliverer come out of Zion, turn away ungodliness from Jacob, and so all Israel shall be saved. Their own Olive Tree, good by nature, will receive them, by a new inoculation, "as alive from the dead."

Phil. What, think you, will then happen to the Jews extraordinary?

Didas. The *Sabbatismos*, or the Keeping of a Sabbath, will be gloriously celebrated all the world over. The people of God; consisting, first, of all converted Jews in every preceding age; secondly, of all converted Gentiles in preceding ages; all which compose the Saints of the first resurrection—called, by our Saviour, the Resurrection of the just: These are the persons, together with the few living righteous who will then be changed, "Who will, from the East, and West, and North, and South," assemble together, in the holy city, and the camp of the Saints, and with "Abraham, Isaac, and Jacob, sit down in the Kingdom of God. Our Saviour will be personally present, in all the *Regalia* of divine Majesty upon Earth, and will then, with his followers, as Emmanuel, drink new wine in this Kingdom of his Father, which was *prepared* in Paradise, but forfeited by Adam, from the foundation of the world, *Luk.* xxii. 16, 18, 29, 30.

Tertullian flourished in less than an hundred years after the death of St. John: He informs us, that

that it was customary for Christians, in his Time, so near that of the Apostles, to pray, "*Ut partem haberent in prima Resurrectione,*" that they might have a part in the first Resurrection. This Father, in his Book against *Marcian*, says, "We confess that a kingdom is promised us *on earth, before the heavenly one*, but in another state, (i. e. of the world) *after* the Resurrection, for a thousand years, in a City of divine Workmanship, the new Jerusalem coming down from Heaven, &c. This, we say, is provided of God for the Saints, to be there refreshed with all spiritual good things, in recompense of those things which in this world we have either despised or lost: For it is a righteous thing and worthy of God, that his servants should exult and rejoice where they have been afflicted for his Name's sake." *Hanmer.*

"A settled religious faith in this holy and glorious state of the Church, as prefigured, foretold, and promised, in the scriptures throughout, pours amazing light on the sacred volume—is a Key to many wonderful secrets in the system of this world—and opens Paradise lost, in Paradise Restored: Whilst man rises in a gradual ascent on the scale of Perfection, and is changed from Glory to Glory." *Hartley.*

"It justifies the ways of God towards man, by providing a gratuitous retribution to the Saints in Time, for the greater injuries they have suffered in Time for Righteousness sake. It gives full display to the wonders of God's wisdom and power in the beauties and riches of creation, and opens a free communication between heaven and earth." *Ibid.*

A divine Theocracy will be restored, and all wicked oppressive governments will govern no more; for the Wild Beast will then be taken, who so long had trodden mankind underfoot—The false

Prophet

Prophet will never more impose upon the ignorance and credulity of Mankind—Henceforth there shall be no more Tyranny exercised over the consciences, persons, or properties, of Mankind. Every promise, and every type, respecting the Millennium, will have a most certain accomplishment. One of the greatest blessings of that happy time will be, that Satan will be bound. All the time that he is confined in the abyss, the will of God will be done on Earth as it is in Heaven. Happy time! Swords will be beat into ploughshares, and spears into pruning hooks—Wars shall cease to the ends of the earth, and they shall learn its murdering arts no more; but they shall sit every man under his Vine, and under his Fig-tree, and none shall make them afraid, *Mich*. iv. 3. 4.

Phil. In that glorious time of Refreshing from the personal presence of the Lord, do you suppose that Mankind will multiply?

Didas. The Jews, the lineal descendants from Abraham, will multiply, in a manner, like fishes. Confining the words to the Jewish nation, *Lactantius*, in part, speaks my meaning. The Jews "shall abundantly multiply, and beget a holy generation dear to God; but as to the *Resurrection Saints*, these shall lead a more heavenly life, Preside over the others, and neither marry nor be given in marriage, but be as the holy Angels." In Israel, iniquity shall be sought for and not be found. At the beginning of this happy season, "A nation shall be born in a day." And in that nation, a man shall have no need to say to his neighbour, or brother, "Know the Lord," that is, preach and call and invite them to him; for they (the Jews) shall all know the Lord, from the least, unto the greatest; for their sins and iniquities I will remember no more, *Jer*. xxxi. 31, 35.

Phil. And how will it fare with the Gentiles, properly

properly fo called, in that happy *Sabbatifmos?* I mean, fuch as are not derived from Jacob in a direct line by the male fide.

Didas. 'Tis only He who made all nations of One blood, who can poffibly tell where that blood flows. In the Primitive ages, thoufands of Jewifh families intermarried with Gentile Chriftians; which formed fuch a coalition of Seeds, as it is not poffible for any to know, but He who knows all things. But to me, it does not appear improbable, that their number is almoft numberlefs. And whether the defcendants of thefe, fcattered among the nations, will be collected, converted, and incorporated among their brethren of the unmixed blood of Abraham, it is not poffible to determine; but I incline to believe the affirmative.

As to the gentile nations, whether Heathen, Mahometan, or profeffed Chriftians, they will in a great degree be cut off, and ceafe to exift as a Governing people, as will be demonftrated below.

The weekly Sabbath typified our Saviour's Reft in the Grave; and accordingly on that day He refted there. The *Shemittah*, or Seventh-year Sabbath, typified the *Sabbatifmos* of St. Paul, and will be glorioufly celebrated in the Millennium. The former was bleffed and fanctified at the Creation, and confequently all Mankind were obliged to keep it, becaufe all mankind were interefted in that day's Reft of Chrift, which *fuppofed* the labour of his life and painful death; and *implied* his Refurrection the following day, as man returns to his labour the day after his keeping the fabbath. But the feventh-year Sabbath typified the feventh millenary of the world, and was peculiar to the Jews; for no people but them ever enjoyed fo great a bleffing, or were ever enjoined fo peculiar a Duty. But as the Jewifh fervants, bought of ftrangers or bred in the houfe; and alfo profelytes from

from heathen countries, enjoyed or partook of the blessing of that year-rest; so all the saints of the first Resurrection will be happily united with the natural Jews, although not lineally descended from the Jewish Patriarchs.

The Saints of the first Resurrection will occupy the Holy City and Camp around it; in the midst of which, Christ, during the Millennium, will dwell, but at the end of it will ascend to heaven, and leave the twenty-four Elders to reign in his room over those Jews not raised again who will dwell in other parts of the world.

All this time of Christ's personal stay upon earth, Satan will be a Prisoner in the abyss, or probably in that vast collection of subterraneous waters, the fountains of which being broken open, helped to drown the old world. Of this the Devil seems not to be unapprized, which made him exclaim, "Art thou come to torment us before the Time?" Our Saviour permitting him, in the swine, to descend into the deep, was a type of this binding in the Abyss.

It is probable, that when our all-conquering Redeemer shall return to heaven, that countless numbers of the Saints of the first Resurrection will ascend with him to grace his triumph, and rise to greater advancements in bliss and glory. These, as I take it, were typified by those *many* who rose when our glorious Head arose, by which he opened the Gates of Death, and set *many* prisoners at liberty; and, doubtless, carried them in victorious triumph with him at his ascension, although invisibly to mortal eyes.

Phil. But will he never return to earth again after this second ascension?

Didas. Most certainly he will. But not till he comes to judge the wicked, Create all things new, and take up his abode for the ages of ages in the

the new Jerusalem that descendeth from heaven from God. At this last advent, he will cast the Devil into the Lake of fire and brimstone, (where we hear no more of him in holy writ) which will be his proper Hell.

The whole process with the Devil, respecting mankind, seems in short to be this—1st. He deceived man in Paradise, and thereby laid the foundation of a mighty Empire over mankind, and over the world. 2nd. Being an enemy and an usurper, at the *first* Judgment he was degraded in Paradise, in the body of the Serpent, the assumed vehicle of his imposture. 3rd. When the Judge appeared in human nature, a campaign of forty days was fought in the Wilderness, in which the Devil was worsted; but quitting the field, he retired to prepare for a more bloody engagement. Here his Antagonist got such a blow and a bruise upon his heel, that it kicked him into the grave; however, not before a sentence was passed upon Satan, by which the "Prince of this world was Judged," *Joh.* xvi. 11. But, though judged, the execution of his sentence was postponed. The sentence was, 4th. To be imprisoned for a thousand years. Afterwards to be liberated for *a little season*, for the same purpose that he was first permitted to practice his arts of Deception upon Adam. Being but too successful in his hellish attempts, 5th. He will finally be apprehended, and executed in the lake of fire; which, to human kind, is the *second death*; and here we will for ever leave him to suffer, agreeable to his Judge's Pleasure, throughout the ages of ages; and afterwards, for any thing I know to the contrary, unto endless Duration. Secret things belong unto the Lord, but they that are Revealed unto us.

DIALOGUE

DIALOGUE IX.

Philotheos. ST. John mentions a Firſt Reſurrection, *Chap.* xx. 6. As firſt is a relative term, and implies a ſecond, &c. ſo how many Reſurrections do you ſuppoſe will take place in future?

Didas. Three, at leaſt, of a general kind.

I. Firſt at the commencement of the Millennium, termed by our Saviour, "The Reſurrection of the juſt." This will be the time, when they who in this world, avoiding luxurious feaſting of thoſe who need none, ſhall lay out themſelves to feed the Poor, &c. who not being themſelves able to make any returns in kind, the Judge himſelf will make the recompenſe, *Luk.* xiv. 12, 14. *See alſo Rev.* xi. 18. This will be the time of general Remuneration to the Righteous. For the Son of Man having taken poſſeſſion of his Kingdom, and being in all the ſolemn ſplendor of Heavenly Majeſty, ſeated upon his ſuperb Throne of glory, He will then give a reward to his Servants the Prophets, to the Saints, and unto thoſe who in all former ages have ſerved Him, and ſuffered for his ſake. Thoſe whoſe narrow circumſtances in this world enabled them to give only a cup of *cold* water, out of love to one of the leaſt brothers of the Judge, ſhall not be forgotten, *Matt.* xxv. 31. This will be the firſt Reſurrection, when the Dead in Chriſt will riſe, among whom the Angel promiſed Daniel that he ſhould ſtand in his Lot, *Dan.* xii. 13.

II. The ſecond Reſurrection will take place at the end of the *Sabbatiſmos*, or the Millennium. Now alſo will a new Revolution in Time take place, attended with ſuch a change of circumſtances in the world, in ſome reſpects ſimilar to thoſe

before

before the fall, insomuch that in some sense it may be said, that the world is beginning anew.

Phil. Pray, how do you evidence the certainty of a Resurrection at the end of the Millennium?

Didas. Very plainly. But the better to understand it, observe, that the three last Chapters of the Revelations abound with Transpositions. This is as clear as the light to the least attentive reader. To save time, one instance at present shall suffice. Consider *ver.* 11, 12, 13, in *Chap.* xx. Thus in *ver.* 11. you read, that from the Face of the Judge the earth and the heavens fled away, and that there was no place found for them: This must certainly be posterior to the following Judgment—How could the sea give up the dead which were in it, (*ver.* 13.) after the earth and heaven had fled away so as to have no place found for them? *ver.* 11. Which, nevertheless is thus proleptically set down, or transposed. Now, carry down the former part of the fifth verse, and insert the words in their proper place between the sixth and seventh verses, and the whole will read thus—"And they lived and reigned with Christ a thousand years," namely, those mentioned in the former part of this fourth verse—"This is the first Resurrection."

Ver. 6. "Blessed and holy is he that hath part in the first Resurrection, on such the second death hath no power; but they shall be Priests of God, and of Christ, and shall reign with Him a thousand years."

"But the rest of the dead lived not again until the thousand years were finished," *ver.* 7. And when the thousand years are finished, Satan shall be loosed out of his prison. Hence it is evident,

1. That a thousand years intervene between the first and second Resurrection.

2. That this thousand years, in which these Priests of God and of Christ reign with Christ,

 are

are ſynchronical or contemporary with the thouſand years of Satan's impriſonment.

3. That the *reſt of the dead lived again*, at the expiration of the ſynchronical thouſand years, in which both God's Prieſts reigned, and Satan was bound.

4. Therefore Satan's impriſonment is bounded by two Reſurrections; that of the ſaints, and the reſt of the Dead, excluſive of the finally impenitent.

5. Conſequently, there will be a third Reſurrection but of the wicked only, *after* the deſtruction of Gog and Magog, at the expiration of Satan's *mikron chronon*, or little ſeaſon, *Comp. ver.* 9, 10, with the 11, *ad fin.* *

6. This

* *The following was lately given to me by a Friend; but who Mr. Johnſon is, I know not, but am glad to find two or three Perſons think like myſelf upon this important Subject.*

Mr. JOHNSON ſuppoſes, that "As a great part of the world never heard of Chriſt, and yet the Goſpel of the Kingdom was to be preached in all the world for a witneſs to all nations; ſo ſuch of them as have died in ignorance of the chriſtian diſpenſation, will be raiſed from the dead to have a time of probation allowed them in the uttermoſt parts of the earth, in a condition ſuited to their ſtate; and ſhall have the goſpel preached to them by Emiſſaries from the kingdom: That many of them will be converted and eſtabliſhed in grace, and have their portion with the Elect; but that a great number of them will be ſeduced by Satan, on his enlargement at the end of the thouſand years; will invade the kingdom, and be deſtroyed by fire, as mentioned in the Revelations." Such a ſuppoſed diſpenſation of grace and trial as this, vouchſafed to the poor heathens, does certainly, in the eye of human judgment, ſet the divine proceedings towards the human race upon a foot of nearer equality in mercy; enlarges our conceptions of God's goodneſs; aſſigns greater extent of efficacy to the Chriſtian ſacrifice, the Redeemer's blood; and removes that rock of offence, and abomination of a ſyſtem, which excludes the far greater part of Adam's fallen offspring from all benefit in the covenant of grace eſtabliſhed by God in Chriſt, the ſecond Adam,

6. This third and last Resurrection will be a long time after the second. This is plain. 1st. Satan's *mikron chronon* allowed him to deceive the nations in, has no limitted or specific time fixed. But as Scripture is the best interpreter of itself, so it is very probable, That this *little season* is here left indefinite in order to be collected by a diligent examination of the same Phrase elsewhere. This we find in *Chap*. vi. 11. Now

(1.) Upon opening the fifth Seal, The Souls of all the Primitive Martyrs, from John the Baptist and St. Stephen, down to the end of the heathen Persecutions by the conversion of Constantine, are introduced crying, "How long dost thou not judge and avenge our Blood, &c.?" The answer was, "That they should Rest yet for *A Little Season*, &c." Now

(2.) This Little Season will not end until the last Martyrs are slain, Rome destroyed, "And the Time of the Dead that they should be Judged," at the first Resurrection. For that is the Time when God will Reward, in the Time of the Millennium, the Prophets, Saints, Martyrs, &c. as you may infallibly learn by *comp. Chap*. xi. 17, 18. with *Chap*. xx. 4.

(3.) But

Adam, who tasted death for every man, without excepting one single individual. Mr. Johnson allows, that such a purpose of mercy in God towards the heathen world, is not expresly or particularly revealed in the Scriptures; and he quotes the two following probable reasons assigned for it from STAYNOE's Treatise of Salvation: "First, because this Resurrection and Probation of the Gentiles does not concern those who have the Scriptures, as by these they may come to the knowledge of the Saviour, which is as much as concerns them. And secondly, Had this Resurrection and Probation been put into the Scriptures, yet those who had them not, could have known nothing of the matter in this life; and so as to them it had been put into the Scriptures in vain."

HARTLEY.

(3.) But this *chronon mikron* connot be lefs than about two thoufand years. From whence I conclude that fo long will Satan's little feafon continue. And by all probability, abfolutely confidered, it will be no lefs, though when compared with the fix thoufand years before his imprifonment, it may be termed *a little feafon*. 2nd. The Beaft and falfe Prophet, (*Chap*, xix. 20.) according to St. John's laconic way of relating it, appear to have been *Taken and caft alive* into the burning lake without the leaft formal procefs, or trial in Judgment. But our Saviour himfelf had given a particular account of the fame event, *Matt*. xxv. 31. *ad fin*. And St. John's conftant Rule was, to be fhort whenever the fame event had been related at large. In like manner here, he feems in *ver*. 10. to reprefent the Devil as caft into the lake of Fire to the Beaft, &c. as if there would be no more to do about it; whereas, in fact, the cafe will be far otherwife.

Phil. How fo, I pray my dear Didas?

Didas. Muft I have my dear Phil. to afk as St. Paul had the Corinthians? "Know ye not that WE fhall Judge ANGELS?" 1 *Cor*. vi. 3. Surely not thofe good Miniftering Spirits, (*Heb*. i. 14.) who are fent forth to Minifter for thofe who fhall be heirs of falvation! No my dear Phil. no. The Evil Angels are to be Judged by a *Confiftory* of Saints. Nor would it in the leaft furprife me, if Adam himfelf prefided in it. How would He detect and lay open the fubtility and fraud of that old Deceiver, who fo grofsly impofed upon his innocent and beautiful Bride!!

But rightly to underftand this, my dear friend muft obferve,

1ft. This devouring of Gog and Magog, and judging of Evil Angels, fall out in the interval between the conclufion of the Millennium, and the laft laſt Judgment. This is evident in the face of the text, as half an Eye may ſee.

2nd. It has been before obſerved, that at the end of the thouſand years, Chriſt returned again to heaven himſelf, as is ſufficiently implied in this, that the "Prieſts of God and of Chriſt Reigned *with* Him a thouſand years;" which, though it imports that they reigned *with Him* no longer, he then returning to heaven; yet it does not intend that they themſelves reigned no longer; No. Theſe Elders expreſsly inform us, that they ſhall "Reign upon the Earth," (*Chap.* v. 10.) without the leaſt intimation, that it will be a joint Perſonal reign *with Chriſt*. The fact, as it ſeems to me, will be this—So long as Chriſt vouchſafes his perſonal preſence, they will reign with Him *as Prieſts* only; every branch of Sovereign Prerogative being exerciſed by Himſelf Perſonally. But upon his return to heaven, the whole time of Satan's little ſeaſon, and for ſome time after, the Elders are left to exerciſe Sovereign Authority, as ſo many Viceroys or rather Kings in Chriſt's perſonal abſence, *See Ibid.*

3rd. This Judging of Angels, or Devils, will be left to theſe Delegates of Chriſt; who, after the little ſeaſon of Satan's liberation is over, will try and paſs ſentence upon him, as the great Accuſer and enemy of Mankind.

Phil. But Devils are ſpirits, and is it not incongruous to ſuppoſe that Men ſhould judge ſpirits?

Didas. As to the fact, we have Apoſtolical Authority for it. And as to the manner, we muſt leave it, 'till time ſhall explain it. But, does not Satan uſually appear, and often act in a tangible vehicle? Did he not firſt clothe himſelf with the body of the Serpent? Beſides, this heavenly Conſiſtory, being raiſed again, will be clothed with their ſpiritual bodies; which, no doubt, being tangible or not, at pleasure, will equally capacitate them to judge Devils as to converse with holy Angels, now their familiar companions.

Phil. As it appears to me, that you have made it sufficiently plain, that there will be no less than three Resurrections, at three very different and distant periods; pray who do you understand will rise again at the second Resurrection, at the End of the Millennium, or Beginning of Satan's Little Season?

Didas. This is a very difficult question. St. John terms them the *Rest of the Dead.* I suppose that no person, of any age or place, who died under absolutely unpardonable guilt, will ever rise again, until the sea, &c. gives up her dead, at the time of the third Resurrection. But at that solemn day, all finally unbelieving wretches will then be raised, condemned, and tormented, in torments proportioned to their different degrees of guilt, in the lake of fire, prepared long before for the Devil and his Angels. And such will all those be, whose names will not be found registered in the "Lamb's book of life," which is very different from the book of life simply considered. *Comp. Chap.* xx. 15. with xxi. 27.

The "Lamb's Book of Life" is a Register containing the names of all those who, in every age, lived and died in the Faith of Christ, as the promised Seed, and only Saviour. The "Book of Life" contains the names of Unbelievers also, which will be blotted out of this Book when they die the Second Death.

The œconomy of grace and providence is truly wonderful, and such as comports with the wisdom of Him who works all things after the Counsel of his own will, who can do what he will, with his own; against whom none can say, why doest thou thus? Poor short-sighted mortals, can we comprehend

hend the thoughts of Omniſcience, or ſet bounds to that divine Philanthropy, which, in its own nature, is boundleſs?

Plans of grace and providence, founded upon every amicable attribute in deity—conſiſtent with the moſt rigid juſtice, accompanied with the richeſt diſplays of mercy and goodneſs.—Plans formed by the wiſdom of the ſacred Trinity, having omnipotence and omniſcience to direct them—and every poſſible exertion of all created beings, inſtruments in the hands of the great Supreme, ready to uſe every effort to accompliſh them—can they, or is it poſſible for ſuch finally to miſcarry?

Phil. Certainly not. However highly improbable from preſent appearances, or contrary to commonly-received ſyſtems--Every plan, formed by ſuch wiſdom, directed by ſuch unerring guides, and executed by ſuch inſtruments and exertions, while they act in concert with human liberty, muſt certainly promote every deſirable end of human happineſs, and ultimately accompliſh all the grand purpoſes of heaven.

Didas. Such is the plan I am about to exhibit before you; and which, I am perſuaded, however the novelty of it may at firſt ſurpriſe your imagination, the due underſtanding of it will be homogeneous to your humane feelings; and if I can but convince your judgment of its more than probable Truth, there will be no fear of your giving it your hearty approbation. However let us proceed to obſerve, that, as you have already heard, the Juſt, the dead in Chriſt, were the ſubjects of the firſt Reſurrection. That the wicked—the unpardonable guilty, will not riſe until the third Reſurrection—That the Gentile nations will be cut off at the next coming of Chriſt to ſet up his kingdom, as is evident in every Parable of our Saviour himſelf—That all the Time of the *Sabbatiſmos*, or all the time

time that our Saviour perſonally Governs upon the earth, the inhabitants will all be Righteous; and, having paſſed the time of their probation, they are out of the danger of Apoſtaſy.

The grand queſtion is, From whence do Gog and Magog proceed? I anſwer, at the preſent till I can find a better, but which I utterly deſpair ever to do; that Gog and Magog will ſpring from thoſe perſons who will Riſe again from the dead at the *ſecond* Reſurrection, or at the end of the thouſand years; perhaps not all at once, but in ſucceſſion.

Phil. And who, my dear Didas. do you ſuppoſe thoſe perſons to be?

Didas. *All thoſe in this preſent evil world, who never either did or poſſibly could enjoy the benefit of divine Revelation*, or hear that Goſpel that aſſures us, that "Chriſt Jeſus came into the world to ſave Sinners."

Phil. That is an uncommon ſuppoſition indeed.

Didas. It is ſo; and with many will be looked upon and treated very probably as a fooliſh vagary, or with ſome as a madman's dream. Be it ſo. And ſhall for ever be willing that it ſhould paſs for ſuch, when what will be ſaid in ſupport of it is fairly confuted by ſcripture and reaſon, and a better hypotheſis ſubſtituted in the room of it. My dear Phil. I doubt not, will attend with candor while I proceed to remark, that the very reaſon why Satan was bound ſo long as the grand *Sabbatiſmos* was celebrated, appears to be, becauſe not any but ſuch as had on the wedding garment were admitted to that holy feſtival. The company were ſuch as bid defiance to all the ſtratagems of Hell to ſeduce; and ſuch an unclean ſpirit was very unfit to go to and fro in the earth, and to walk up and down in it, (*Job* i. 7.) as uſual, while the ſons of God were banqueting on the bounty of their elder Brother.

It

it was reasonable that the false God of this world, the Ruling power of darkness, who had engaged earth and hell against the poor righteous few to persecute and make them as miserable as he could, should be degraded, imprisoned, and punished, while the objects of his hatred were keeping Holy-Day with their beloved Saviour, and banqueting upon the bounty of Him, for whose sake many in life had cheerfully suffered the loss of all things otherwise dear to them, and even loved not their lives unto death, but freely sacrificed them at his sacred shrine, but are now receiving a just compensation.

Phil. I do not desire to indulge an idle curiosity, or dive into the secrets of Providence: But if you think the enquiry is not too bold, it would afford both pleasure and satisfaction to hear, Why Satan should be liberated from Prison, in order to try to deceive the nations again?

Didas. The hypothesis above will supply, what appears to me, both a rational and scriptural answer. It ultimately resolves itself into those reasons that induced Providence to permit him at first to deceive Eve. But of this, enough above and below.

Phil. But if your supposition be true, why has it not been more explicitly Revealed in scripture?

Didas. I answer, *cui bono?* If it had been ever so explicitly revealed, where Revelation never comes, they would have been no better for the discovery. But as to the truth of my supposition, I ask, Where can we find any other to Rise again but them at that second Resurrection? All the Righteous were risen a thousand years before: All the Wicked not till long after. Whom but them can Satan possibly deceive? Not the righteous; they had passed the time of their probation, and probably almost all taken to Heaven to return again in in the New Jerusalem with their glorious Redeemer—the rest were in the Holy City and the Camp of the Saints: Not the wicked; they were in their graves, there to remain till the last Judgment.

The people tempted by Satan must be in a state of probation either as Adam was or as we are. If they had passed through it, they would either have been conquerors, or conquered; but in either case Satan's attempt must have proved abortive, which, alas! was not the case. Nor can they be another generation of men springing from some other stock than Adam. Concerning the Heathen, the great Apostle told the Athenians, (*Acts* xvii. 30.) that at "The Times of this ignorance God *winked at.*" But why? Because "In Times past (He) *suffered* all nations to walk in their own ways," *Ib.* xiv. 16. Now let any rational man consider whether infinite wisdom and goodness would ever have permitted all nations, the Jews excepted, to walk in their own ways, *and wink at them* for so many Ages, if it had not been some part of a great Plan—some remarkable scene of a grand Drama?

Phil. Certainly no; it cannot be: For with God there is no respect of persons. "Is He the God of the Jews only? is He not also of the Gentiles? yes, of the Gentiles also," *Rom.* iii. 29. How then can we acquit him of partiality, or respect of Persons, without supposing, That God must have mercy some time upon those very identical people, whose *ignorance He winked at*; which ignorance proceeded, no doubt, from no other Reason than the want of a divine Revelation. But, my dear Didas. do the Scriptures give us no intimation of such a gracious design in God to exhibit his love towards these nations, who, in appearance, in Times past hitherto have been left in such ignorance?

Didas.

Didas. Such intimation we certainly have. *But the dispensation of the Grace of God* towards the Gentiles was a profound mystery; *a mystery which from the beginning of the Ages* (apo ton aionon) *hath been hid in God*—the mystery, *which by Revelation*, was first made known to St. Paul; and *which in other Ages had not been made known unto the sons of men*, but by St. Paul was preached *among the Gentiles*.

Phil. And, pray my dear Didas. what important mystery was it?

Didas. It was, in short, THE UNSEARCHABLE RICHES OF CHRIST. And farther, "That the Gentiles should be fellow-heirs, and of the *same body* (with the Jews) *and partakers of his promise in Christ, by the Gospel.* This divine plan is termed the *manifold wisdom of God*—a plan which is intended, by the medium of the Church of Jew and Gentile coalesced, to make known to other heavenly worlds this manifold wisdom of God, *Eph.* iii. 1, 10. The magnitude of this subject is such, that volumes might be wrote upon it. However, at present, a few remarks and enquiries must suffice. And

1st. The subject is, "That the Gentiles," indifinitely or without limitation, "should be fellow-heirs, and of the same body, and partakers of his promise in Christ, by the Gospel," *ver.* 6. The substance of the Promise is, "The unsearchable Riches of Christ," *ver.* 8. Now I beg leave to appeal to unbiassed Reason, enlightened by Church-history ever since the Apostle's days, whether these unsearchable riches of Christ have so much as been Preached among all the Gentiles the world over, and that in every successive Generation? the Apostle informs us, that God has made the Gentiles *fellow-heirs* with the Jews; that is, heirs of the promise, and of the same body, incorporated into One;

One; and partakers of the Promiſe. But where is the body to be ſeen? Or to what degree have either Jew or Gentile to this day experienced the promite? Let hiſtorical facts anſwer.

2nd. This grand Plan in all its parts, is "According to the Eternal (*or Aionion*) purpoſe, which He purpoſed in Chriſt Jeſus our Lord," *ver.* 11. But are not the greateſt and moſt eſſential parts of this purpoſe to be yet accompliſhed? It is true, Chriſt is come, &c. But has He yet done any more than lay the foundation of his immenſe Kingdom? Or will he, ſo long as this "Preſent evil Age," (*Gal.* i. 4.) continues? So long as the united Kingdom of the Dragon, the Beaſt, and the falſe Prophet governs? *Rev.* xvi. 10, 13. Certainly no.

3rd. This whole divine Plan "In other ages was not made know to the Sons of Men," *ver.* 5. And are we aſſured that the *whole of it* was revealed to St. Paul, &c.?" Or if it was, that he has fully Revealed it? Or only rather hinted at it, as in the caſe of the man of Sin? Or that we moſt rightly underſtand the intimations given?

Phil. The purpoſes which the Father purpoſed in Chriſt Jeſus our Lord, are firmer than the foundations of the earth, and ſhall ſtand until the whole be realized by every circumſtantial accompliſhment. But ſeeing that there is not the ſmalleſt probability, or even poſſibility of ſuch accompliſhment in this preſent evil age or ſtate of things; has the Apoſtle hinted at any future age or time for the execution of theſe grand and important purpoſes?

Didas. Very plainly, and in this very epiſtle. You muſt here remark, that the out-pouring of the ſpirit of God at Pentecoſt, and in the Apoſtolical times, was only conſidered as the firſt-fruits (*Rom.* viii. 23.) of the ſpirit, the whole harveſt

being

being to be reaped afterwards. But when or where, I pray, ſince thoſe days, has ſuch a vaſt harveſt grown, or is now to be ſeen? In perfect harmony with ſuch a view of the out-pouring of the ſpirit in the Apoſtolical times, they looked upon the extraordinary converſion of the heathen, which in a ſmall degree then took place, as a pattern or ſample of ſtill much greater converſions that would in future take place; and that juſt as the firſt-fruits were a ſample of the corn, &c. in the following Harveſt. For inſtance,

In the ſecond Chapter of this Epiſtle, all the vaſt ſupernatural gracious work which the Epheſians ſo happily experienced, the Apoſtle conſiders as a ſample, "That in the Ages to come He might ſhew the exceeding riches of his Grace, in his kindneſs towards us, through Chriſt Jeſus," *ver. 7.* Now here I aſk, are not the *Ages to come* indefinitely put for all future ages? Will not thoſe Ages extend far beyond the limits of the preſent ſtate of things? Do not they include the Age of Gog and Magog? If they do, I aſk farther, will not God have the ſame kindneſs for the people of that Age, that he had for the Epheſians? Will not "The exceeding riches of his Grace," extend unto, and be as ſufficient to ſave, through faith, the people then as now? Or will the Riches of that grace be ſpent and exhauſted before that Age commences? If ſo, the Apoſtle muſt certainly have been miſinformed, and conſequently miſinform us. But who, that believes the bible, can or ever will believe, or ſo much as doubt it?

If then the Grace that ſaved the Epheſians through faith, will be extended unto thoſe as well as to other future ages, muſt they not have the goſpel preached unto them as well as the Epheſians, in order to be ſaved through faith in that goſpel? Again, was not the quickening the Epheſians when dead in trespasses and sins, as great a miracle, as great a mystery, as little expected by both Jews and Christians, and as much surprising to them, as the Raising the Heathen from the dead and sending the gospel among them, possibly can be to us? Or can we urge sufficient reasons to prove this hard negative, that such an hypothesis as the above, is no part of the divine Purpose, nor included in the aforesaid Mystery?

Phil. I confess, from what is already advanced, that I begin to suspect Gog and Magog will spring, probably, from their Ancestors, who, in sacred scripture, long have borne that name; and that such as never heard the Gospel here, will rise again to hear it hereafter. Nor is it to me improbable, but that they will have the advantage of us, as there will be neither Beast nor false Prophet in Being, no more than in Adam's days; and because hitherto every divine Dispensation has been on the advance, and probably will from less to greater degrees of divine favour. Indeed, since I have got the hint, abundance of scriptures occur to me, which seem to countenance the supposition, and which, without it, I am at a loss, and long have been, fully to account for their extensive contents. Pray, my dear Didas, let me beg a few of your thoughts upon a few of them, as they affect me in a very striking manner.

What think you of our blessed Redeemer's extensive commission to his Apostles, "to go and Preach the gospel to every creature?" *Mar.* xvi. 15.

Didas. Certainly that Commission can import no less, than that every rational creature has a divine and indefeasible right to hear that Gospel, and upon believing it, to enjoy its immense privileges. And as Christ, who gave the commission, is the real Trustee or Preserver of that right, will he, he, can he, consistent with that Trust or Office, for ever suffer his rational creatures to be deprived of that privilege? Since then to hear the Gospel is every rational creature's right, and Christ himself is the Preserver of that right, who will be hardy enough to say that he will so far fail in the discharge of that Trust, as for ever to suffer by many degrees the far greatest part of mankind in every age and nation to be defrauded of that Right? If he does, it must certainly be because he either cannot or will not prevent it. But who can reconcile the former with his universal sovereign Authority both in heaven and earth; and the latter with his fidelity, universal love, essential goodness, and benevolence to mankind? ..

Again, "Behold my servant whom I uphold!—I have put my spirit upon him. He shall bring forth Judgment to the Gentiles—I the Lord have called Thee in righteousness, and will hold thine hand, and will keep Thee, and give Thee for a Covenant of the People for a light of the Gentiles. To open the blind eyes, to bring out the Prisoners from the Prison, and them that sit in darkness, out of the Prison-house." To which permit me to add, what ascertains the whole, "*He shall not fail, nor be discouraged,*" whatever obstructions he may meet with; but how long will he persist? till he hath *set Judgment in the earth.* *See Isa.* xlii. 1, 8. Here, my dear Phil. observe,

1. Christ is his Father's Servant, and upheld by him; that is, by Deity; otherwise his humanity would have failed in the arduous discharge of his offices.

2. For whatever office he was called unto, he was duly qualified; "I have put my spirit upon him." *Comp. Luk.* iv. 18, 21. *Joh.* iii. 34, 35.

3. The Gentiles are the subjects of this Prophecy, and the Heirs of these Promises.

4. He

4. He is *a Light*, a Sun to the Gentiles; but when did a twentieth part, taking in all ages, ever see him? or were ever either enlightened or enlivened by him?

5. When did he ever bring forth judgment, or real religion unto 'em?

6. May not the *Prison-House* mean the Grave? Is not the Grave a Prison? Who can prove the contrary? May it not be both literally and spiritually true?

7. Observe the extent of the undertaking, which is, to "Set Judgment in the earth: And the isles, &c."

8. Observe the certainty of his fulfilling the *whole* of his Mediatorial Office, "*He shall not fail*, nor be discouraged."

9. Lastly observe, the Father's veracity is here pledged by promise for the performance of the *whole* of this grand undertaking for the Gentiles.

Phil. I give it as my humble opinion, that he that *Runs* may read promises here made to the Gentiles, which, if he was to *sit* and read all the histories in the world, he would never read their accomplishment. And if he was to *rise* and travel all the world over, he could not meet with a single place to take a prospect from, that there is the least probability of their accomplishment in this present evil world. But please to consider *Matt.* xxiv. 14. in the next place.

Didas. "This Gospel of the Kingdom shall be preached in all the World, for a witness unto all nations, and then shall the End come." The Greek word for world here is *Oicoumene*, and always means properly the habitable world, and is used in *Heb.* ii. 5. for *the world to come*. It is evident from this text, that the end of the world is suspended upon the Preaching of the Gospel throughout this habitable world. But this is what

never

never yet has been, but most certainly will be before the end comes, and that to the very end of it. But where is there the least likelihood that this should be, so long as the Dragon reigns? But the end of *Oicoumene* will not arrive until Gog and Magog be devoured, *Heb.* ii. 5. Therefore the Gospel of the Kingdom will be preached to those Nations, amongst whom the liberated Devil will go out to deceive all he can, i. e. Gog and Magog, &c. *Rev.* xx. 3, 8.

Phil. How reasonable is this! While every diabolical art is exercised to deceive them, He who made them has such mercy upon them, that he sends his Heralds to proclaim his everlasting gospel, to counteract the deceiver, apprize them of their danger, and invite them to be citizens of the Saints, and enjoy those privileges which the Devil is enlisting them to march against and overthrow.

Didas. True; but this is not all: The Gospel is to be preached for a "Witness unto all Nations." But what is it to witness? Is it not that worthy, faithful, and invaluable apostolical Proverb, "That Christ Jesus came into the world to save sinners?" To destroy the works of the Devil—to effect which, that he gave himself a Ransome for all—tasting Death for every man—and rose again to abolish death—and justify us from that sentence dooming us to those dreary regions! Conferring upon us a title to honour, immortality, and eternal life?

Phil. What other Testimony does the Gospel give but these, and such doctrines as have the closest connexion with them? But does not St. Paul refer this Testimony to be given both to this very subject, and the very Time also, in 1 *Tim.* ii. 6.? You will very much oblige me to open that passage a little, which, if I mistake not, appears very much in point.

Didas. *A little,* my dear friend, it must be;

 for

for a volume may be wrote upon it. The words are, "Who gave Himself a ransome (or a price of redemption) for *all*, to be testified in *due Time*," or in his own proper Seasons. *See the Greek, and comp. Chap.* vi. 14. The better to understand which, we must observe,

1st. That the great Apostle introduces the subject very properly, by exhorting, that, first of all, supplications, prayers, &c. be made *for all men*, *ver.* 1. But if by far the greatest part of men, by a secret decree, are either doomed to an inevitable damnation, or passed by in the means of Redemption, and so left to perish under the ruins of the fall, why did the Holy Ghost exhort us to pray for them? What! Has *Elohim* decreed one thing, and commanded us to pray against the thing decreed? Who would attribute such inconsistency to infinite wisdom and goodness? Not even Devils.

2nd. The more forcibly to urge his exhortation, he assures us, that "This is good and acceptable in the sight of God our Saviour," *ver.* 3. Upon what possible ground of truth can this assertion stand? Is it good to pray against God's secret will and purpose? Or is it good to pray for that which God before had determined not to grant, although he even exhorts us to do it? Is it possible to acquit an earthly Sovereign of duplicity in such a case, or any thing like it? Again, the Apostle adds, that it is *acceptable* as well as good. If God has enjoined it, 'tis most certainly our duty to obey. And if, in humble obedience to that injunction, we properly address our Maker in prayer and supplication for the *salvation of all men*, (for that is to be the subject of our prayers, *ver.* 4) such obedience and service, no doubt, are both Good and Acceptable, suppose that we can pray in Faith; that is, believing that God both can and will

will grant what we pray for. But if we believe, that an irreversible Decree is passed in Heaven, by which *any part*, and much more by far the *greatest part*, be consigned to eternal sufferings, how is it possible for a Believer to pray in faith? And if, when he pray, he believes that it is for what God will never grant, how can such prayers be either good or acceptable in the sight of God our Saviour?

3rd. The solid foundation upon which our duty stands, when we make prayer and supplication for the Salvation of all men, and that which renders them both good in themselves and acceptable in the sight of God our Saviour, is this, that God our Saviour "Will have all men to be Saved," *ver.* 4. How can such prayers be otherwise than both good and acceptable in God's sight, when they tally so exactly with His own Will? But is this true, that God *will* have *all men* to be saved?

Phil. No doubt. For the Apostle roundly asserts it without either *if* or *and*—without any restrictive condition.

Didas. If so, it is impossible that the *contrary* can be true. It can never be his positive will that any one should be damned. If, then, God will have all men to be saved, why should any short-sighted mortal imagine, and that in direct opposition to the positive will of God, our own prayers, and our own feelings, that very few will finally be saved? Before we draw such a horrid conclusion, which militates so directly against both the letter of scripture, our natural notions of a Deity, and the common feelings of humanity; had we not better wait for the event, than dogmatize upon such precarious grounds as that whole hypothesis stands upon? For my own Part, so far as I know myself, nothing but such an event can reconcile it to my judgment and feelings.

God's Thoughts and Ways as far surpass ours,

as Himſelf is above us. Such are the narrow limits of our underſtandings, and ignorance both of the works and word of God, that we often egregiouſly err contrary to our deſign. *Neſcire and errare humanum eſt.* This ſhould make us cautious and modeſt in our deciſions of matters of the greateſt moment. But is any thing too hard for God ?

The Apoſtle having informed us of the reaſon why our prayers, &c. for the ſalvation of *all men* are good and acceptable, &c. viz. becauſe God *will have all men* to be ſaved, now hints at the means which the divine Plan has appointed to compaſs ſo great an end. And they are,

4th. Firſt, He wills all men "To come to the Knowledge of the Truth." Whatever God does immediately Himſelf, one word is ſufficient. But when He employs ſubordinate cauſes, the means are always calculated by infinite wiſdom ſufficient to effect the end. Now one appointed means to bring about this divine will is, the *Knowledge of the Truth*, or of the Goſpel. But how ſhall all men come to the knowledge of this, except they either hear it, or read it ? Under the Jewiſh diſpenſation, how ſmall was the country, and how few its inhabitants, who were bleſſed with the ſacred Oracles, when compared with the reſt of the world ! Under the preſent Chriſtian diſpenſation, who will plead for its univerſality, except the Pope and Papal votaries ? Not a word need to be ſaid in proof of what none will deny, namely, that from the beginning of Chriſtianity to this very day, a very great majority has gone out of the world with little or no knowledge of it at all. If, then, God wills all men to be ſaved ; and, in order to that great end, to come to the knowledge of the Truth, to give them an opportunity to believe it ; and if the far greateſt part of men go out of the world

without

without a possibility of ever acquiring that knowledge here; I conclude, that God will most certainly find means to communicate that knowledge hereafter. And I ask, by what more probable method than this hypothesis suggests? To hear it in *Hades*, is not surely so probable.

6th. Second, The grand medium by which the Salvation of Man is to be effected, is contained in the two following propositions, 1. "There is One God." And do not the unity of his nature and attributes imply an unity of design with respect to creatures of the same kind? Will his nature, which is uniform, admit of partiality? Suppose it possible for his will to incline to it, would his essential love, justice, and goodness, admit of it? Are not all equally related to Him? 2. "And One Mediator between God and Men, the Man Christ Jesus."

As this man was made of the seed of Abraham and David, he must be of the same nature identically. From this nature, then, is there any thing to induce him to regard one man above another? Are not all equally related to him? Again, Sin set God and Man at variance—without Reconciliation, Man must suffer—a Mediator must be equally related to both Parties, or he could not negotiate for both. According to the natures of the parties at variance, he must have the interests of both equally at heart—He must be authorized, and in every thing perfectly qualified, for the important office—Such, in every respect, is the man Christ Jesus. Again, the Apostle says in General, between God and Man—here the Nature is regarded, and personality in one sense is excluded. God consists of three Persons; and Man of so many as there are individuals of the kind. With regard to Personality, both sides are considered collectively. If an *indefinite* be equal to an *universal*, 'tis plain, that

that He officially mediates for every individual person. What shall we say?

Can any man in his senses suppose, that this mediation will, in its issue, prove so far abortive, as that it will fail in its effects on the greatest part of Mankind? To say that he mediates only for the elect, is to say what the Apostle neither said nor thought of. Where do we read it? That the Great Mediator acted officially for all mankind, the Resurrection of all fully demonstrates. Is it then rational to suppose, that but very few, out of the whole, will ever have the possibility of benefiting by this mediation? It cannot be. Sooner or later, most certainly, every one will have such opportunity.

Phil. Humanity can have no objection. Notwithstanding the appearances of Providence at the present are far from being favourable, I doubt not, but that every future scene of the grand Drama will exhibit upon the stage of Time such astonishing subjects, though some of them very Tragical, as will gradually open and display the design of the great and astonishing performance, as directed by the Principal Undertaker.

Didas. That will undoubtedly be the case sometime, and the very next verse tells us when. And therefore the Apostle informs us,

6th. That the great Mediator, in the discharge of his Office, "Gave Himself a Ransome *for all*," *ver.* 6. In which words, we have the Pillar that props up the fabric of the Apostle's building in the passage before us. Who will say that this *price of redemption* was not *sufficient*, in the estimation of the Father, for *every man*? Who hath so far been admitted into the Privy Counsel above, as to be able to demonstrate, that it was never *intended for all*? Or in which of the Archives of God's Court is it written, that it was not *accepted for all*? If

the

the negative of these queries can never be proved from scripture, and that in explicit terms, we may venture safely to depend upon the affirmative, which is so often explicitly affirmed. And let me tell you, my dear Phil. that if the closing scene, when this Mediation is at an end, should evidence the negative side of the question to be true, I will then cordially believe it; but till then, hope to be excused if I believe the exact contrary.

But I am inclined to think, that long before then, such a Testimony will be publicly produced, as will silence all objections, answer all arguments, and turn all opposition into full acquiescence; for so the Apostle tells me, and with me his Authority is sufficient. "Christ Jesus gave Himself a Ransome for all, to be testified in due time," or a Testimony, &c.

Setting prejudice (that Jaundice-eyed Judge,) aside, with every preconceived opinion, let rational criticism speak—I am mistaken if it will not candidly allow, that this verse clearly informs us, that Christ's *own proper times or seasons* will produce a *Testimony*, that He gave Himself a Ransome for all mankind.

1. Our business is to enquire, When these Times commence. And as they have not yet commenced, or are not now current, we need not be surprised if there be different sentiments upon this weighty subject; more especially when we consider, that the Times we live in are those of the Dragon, Beast, and false Prophet.

2. The words rendered in our Translation *In due Time*, in the greek are found exactly the same in the last Chapter of this Epistle, and are there translated very differently, and much nearer the greek, *In His Times. See Chap.* vi. 15. But may be more closely still, *In His own*, or *proper Times*; *Times*, note, in the Plural. These times are, 1st, The

The *Sabbatismos*, or the Millennium. 2nd. Satan's *Little Season.* 3rd. The Age of Ages, or the New-Jerusalem state. These are the *Times* of the Restitution of all Things—The *Times* of Refreshing, or Revivification, because in them all the dead will rise again, in the Presence of the Lord, *Acts* iii. 19, 21. The commencement of these Times will be at Christ's next coming, as is quite plain in the passages referred to.

Phil. Here is time enough indeed to testify any thing in! But, pray my dear friend, what Testimony will it be that will be then attested?

Didas. Our Saviour tells us, that it is the Gospel that is to be Preached in all the world to come, (*Heb.* ii. 6.) for a Testimony unto them. For as the Testimony is to be given in his own Times, so that world to come is his own world, as is plain enough at first sight. Now the sum of the Gospel we have just heard from this passage; and according to the Apostle, it is in substance the very same with that which will then be attested, or as our Saviour adds preached also. *Matt.* xxiv. 14.

1. God will have all men to be saved.

2. To come to the knowledge of the Truth, viz. By hearing it Preached in all that world.

3. That Jesus Christ is the One Mediator, and consequently the only Saviour. That in discharging that important office,

4 He gave Himself a Price of Redemption for all, being the very same for whom he was a Mediator.

Phil. Glorious Truths indeed! But who do you suppose will give this decisive Testimony?

Didas. Without doubt every person whom the king of kings shall think proper to employ, as his Embassadors and Heralds. But in the Time of the Millennium, and in the New Jerusalem, Christ himself will be personally present, and as an infallible sible Judge of all Controversies, will decide them all infallibly right.

Phil. Happy Time! Blessed Sabbath! Then will God's will be done on earth, as it is in heaven. "The spirit of God, which animates the Saints, will then unite them together under Christ their Head, in the same knowledge of divine Truth; in the same love and obedience to God; in the same affection one towards another; and in the same endeavours to promote the good of the whole. The Being of God, his Perfections, and Authority, will be fully acknowledged; his laws obeyed with cheerfulness; his mysteries understood, or received with humility; his justice revered; his goodness admired; and Himself worshipped in Spirit and in Truth. The œconomy of the Word in a body of flesh, and the dignity of his nature, will no longer be matter of contradiction and strife, but confessed in a manner becoming those who enjoy the Redemption obtained by his blood; and Himself be joined with the Father and Holy Spirit, in the worship and praises of Angels and Men. Religion will be pure, without hypocrisy; virtue without presumption, love without dissimulation, honour without pride, power without oppression, and knowledge without conceit. No one's abundance will create envy, where every one is full, and selfishness will be lost in the spirit of Love." *Dr. Knight.*

Didas. After this agreeable relaxation, for which I thank you, we must now return to our subject. Well, as I hope it appears sufficiently evident, that our Saviour gave himself a ransome for all, it follows that all are ransomed—all bought with a Price—yea, the same Price, and that Price of inestimable value: Consequently all men are Christ's Property by Purchase. Will reason, then, ever admit, that he will part with his Purchase, or

 any

any part of it, on any account whatever, without the greatest reluctance? Do not justice and mercy both unite to plead the cause of all the ransomed World? Let reason and revelation both be heard in this common cause of humanity. Their verdict is unanimous—Here or hereafter, they all avouch, every individual of the human race ought to hear the gospel of the Grace of God, to afford an opportunity to believe and be saved. But it must be allowed on all hands, that here it has not all the world over. Yea, are we assured that all the inhabited parts of the earth are known at this day? And how lately have one half of it been discovered?

As Christ gave himself a Ransome for all, and of course all are his purchased property, so He enjoys a prior right to all. For "all things were made by Him, *and for him*:" Yea, and he has his Father's Promise, that, in future, "The Heathen, (indefinitely) shall be his inheritance, and the uttermost parts of the earth His Possession." Will he *inherit* them only to destroy them? though, at his next coming he will the *then* living Generation, as you have already heard. But if he does not raise them up again, how can the ends of the earth be His Possession? This will be in a future state, as is too plain to be denied, *Rev.* ii. 26, 27. What subtility can defraud, or opposition violently extort this Possession from him? Does not He Possess in order to dwell *in* or *among*, and so make them happy? If reason dictates to Man to secure and make the most of his property, surely the fountain of reason will much more; unless, in this case, the streams rise higher than the fountain!

If all were made for Him, can we reasonably imagine, that the devil will have by far the greatest part, for ever? At present they are the Dragon's Possession—Christ and Christianity are not heard of among

among them—and so they will continue till the Dragon is bound. But after that period, will they always remain so? The whole tenor of scripture-prophecy announces the contrary. Christ's own Times will then commence, and henceforth the Heathen will be his peculiar People and Property.

Phil. Seeing, then, that God will have all men to be saved—that Christ gave himself a ransome for all—with how great propriety does the Apostle term the living God the Saviour of *all men*, (1 *Tim.* iv. 10.) but especially of those that believe?

Didas. Very true: And upon those two Pillars, General Redemption will for ever stand. And as this was a principal doctrine enjoined Timothy to teach, why should any refuse to preach it now?

Phil. But if God be the Saviour of all men, why does the *Apostle* add, "Especially of those that believe?"

Didas. For this substantial reason—Because, in the issue, only they who believe will be saved, under every dispensation. But how can those believe the Gospel who never heard it? And how few either have or possibly can hear it in this life? Therefore they will rise to hear it, in order to prove God to be the Saviour of all men by Grace through Faith, except a comparative few, incurably obstinate, whose obstinate cry is, "We will not have this Man to reign over us."

One principal design of Preaching is, To proclaim, as the Heralds of Heaven, Peace upon earth, or Reconciliation on God's part, and to announce his good-will towards men. Is it possible that this good-will should shine more brilliantly than upon the cross? See, my dear Phil. see! The only-begotten of the Father, divested of his heavenly glory, clothed in human flesh, and crowned with Thorns! exchanging his Father's Bosom for an accursed tree for his humanity to expire upon

upon—the object of man's indignant fury—the object of angelical adoration, and his Father's love! And why all these unexampled sufferings, but because "He is the Propitiation for the sins of the *whole of the World*?" 1 *Joh*. ii. 3.

After all, may we not reasonably ask, If this was the way in which the Father of the spirits of all flesh discovered his benevolence towards his disobedient children, when every act of disobedience was in full prospect before him; and for which his beloved Son expired in unequalled agonies; can any thing change this good-will into such implacable wrath, as nothing but endless and inexpressible sufferings inflicted upon most of these very children can ever satisfy?

Phil. Reason recoils at the thought!

Didas. One Thing only can do it. An absolute rejection of that Propitiation, from an absolute refusal of accepting the Son of God to be their only Saviour. But how can this possibly be the case of those to whom this propitiation was never tendered, and who therefore die totally ignorant of it? And as this indisputably is the case of the most of mankind—as the propitiation is made for all—and all must believe in it to receive the saving benefit of it—I conclude, that it must certainly will be Preached unto them after they rise again.

It was in consequence of this good-will, that God was in Christ reconciling the world unto Himself, *not imputing* their Trespasses unto them, 2 *Cor*. v. 19. This non-imputation follows upon reconciliation, as that does upon Christ being made a sin-offering for us, who knew no sin. Now, the Apostles were sent as Embassadors for Christ, in this peculiar point of light, "As though God did *beseech you* by us," saith the Apostle. How abundantly must He be Reconciled, when he condescends to entreat the guilty to accept of Reconciliation!

liation! But this is not all: For the Embassy was, "We beseech you, *in Christ's stead*, BE YE RECONCILED UNTO GOD."

1. God *imputed* sin or guilt unto Christ, who was personally free from it.

2. In consequence of this imputation of it to Christ, it is not imputed to the World. And now, sin is not imputed, God is reconciled unto the World.

3. And in virtue of this Reconciliation, God himself *Beseeches*, and Christ, by his Embassadors, *Prays* the World to be Reconciled to God. Astonishing proceeding towards a whole guilty World!

Let my dear Phil. here observe, that God is essentially loving and merciful to every rational creature. This love sent Christ from Heaven, *Joh.* iii. 16. By a transfer of guilt from the guilty World to Christ, Christ suffered. God, who always willed that all should be saved, by this expedient took away every impediment that stood in his own way against it, in a course of Justice. Hence, nothing hinders the salvation of the world, or stands in the way of it, but want of reconciliation unto God, and faith in our Lord Jesus Christ. As to the former, both God and the Mediator evidence their most earnest desire for it, in that they beseech and pray the World to be reconciled unto God. And as touching faith in our Lord Jesus Christ, certain it is, "That Faith comes by Hearing." And if so, must not all the whole world, and every individual Person that has been, is, or ever will be born into it, Hear the Gospel somewhere, sooner or later? Can they be saved any other way than by Grace through Faith? Can any ever be Justified from personal Guilt, otherwise than "Freely by (God's) Grace, through the Redemption that is in Jesus Christ, whom God hath set up a Propitiation through Faith in his blood?"

blood?" Or where in Scripture do we read, that God can "Be just, and the Justifier of him that believeth in Jesus," upon any other Plan? From the whole, I conclude, that they who never heard the Gospel in this life, will rise to hear it in another; or the Gospel Plan of Salvation be either varied, or in the issue fail very much in its vast design. But when Christ's own Times arrive, who can disprove the Preaching of the Gospel then? And, Gog and Magog excepted, upon what reason, founded upon Revelation, can we ever suppose that many will then disbelieve it to their final condemnation?

Again, our Saviour by Oath was established a High-Priest in things pertaining to God. His office was to make Atonement for the sins of the People. Now let any one point out that Scripture, which informs us of any People, or any sins, (except the sin against the Holy Ghost) that he has not made Reconciliation for? The People mean His Brethren in a natural way, all that are Partakers of flesh and blood, *Heb.* ii. 14, 17. Atonement is made for all who are made of human flesh and blood. Is it then probable that very few will Receive that atonement? Did not God foresee this, if it be true? But is it just in Deity to receive satisfaction for an offence, and to punish the offender also? It cannot be, except on certain conditions, and I know none except final unbelief. If Christ actually suffered adequate punishment for sin, the more sin, the more severe the punishment. Now the guilt of all who went astray God caused *to meet in him* as a common centre, (*Isa.* liii. 6.) and he bare the whole in his own body upon the Tree. Hence the Guilt of us all was transferred virtually from the guilty to the innocent. But as perhaps eight out of ten will suffer themselves, why should the innocent suffer for them also?

If,

If, then, the High-Priest made atonement for all, I conclude, upon the principles of justice and equity, that all have a Right to the benefit of that atonement. And why may not the benefit be accepted in general by those who will hear it attested in Christ's own Times?

Again, "Christ was delivered for Our Offences, and raised again for Our Justification," *Rom.* iv. *ult.* *For ours*; he speaks not here of Adam's. Sin is a debt, the world of sinners debtors, God the creditor, and the Man Christ Jesus the responsible surety. The Creditor justly demanded payment from the Surety, because the principal debtors "Had nothing to pay," no not one farthing per Pound. Himself therefore, Paid the uttermost farthing of penal future sufferings. If this be denied, why did He suffer the just for the unjust, not only to bring us out of the grave, but to bring us to God? But if so, must far the greatest part of the unjust suffer also? When the Surety has paid the uttermost farthing, shall the original and proper debtor pay it over again? What Law of God or man requires this? And will God himself exact it? Again,

The Lord is *Good*, saith the Prophet. God is *Love*, saith the Apostle. But goodness and love are essential to his Nature, infinite in themselves; and have, among others, Mankind for their object. This goodness and love *intentionally* created us to make us happy. It could not possibly comport with this love and goodness to make one immortal spirit designedly to be miserable. Can we then in reason suppose, that God's design will easily be defeated? Can it be reconciled to those amiable attributes in deity, to give an existence to mankind, and then place the far greatest part in such circumstances, that their eternal misery should be inevitable? Is it not more agreeable to reason,

and

and our natural notions of a deity, to suppose, that either he would never have Created them, or his wisdom and power would have prevented the possibility of such a dreadful event?

If God's original design was to communicate from himself such a degree of his communicable Perfections to mankind, as to make us the bright images of Himself, according to our nature and capacities; are not his wisdom and omnipotent power sufficient to effect that design in spite of any opposition it can meet with? Or what hinderance could possibly occur, which Omniscience could not foresee, or his power and goodness prevent?

Men, deceived by the Devil, may militate against their own interests; and some, no doubt, prove finally incorrigible; but when the deception is discovered, the principles of self-preservation, connatural to mankind, in such a situation, must greatly alarm them. Is it not highly rational to suppose, that he who made them will have mercy upon them, and Rise to their Rescue from eternal torments? Or who can reconcile the idea of the infinitely amiable attributes of Deity with the endless torments of the greatest part of mankind, thus deceived? If justice be satisfied—if God be reconciled to the world—what attribute in Deity, or policy of Hell, can hinder the final salvation of all men, who have not committed the unpardonable sin?

What is the Gospel but glad tidings of great Joy? Ought not those Tidings to reach every Ear, seeing they were intended for all People? Or did the Angels mistake the extent of their message?

But, in what sense can the birth of a Saviour, Christ the Lord, be matter of great joy to all People; if, alas! in the issue, he will prove the eternal Condemner of the far greatest part?

Adam,

Adam, it is true, Rebelled; and, by that rebellion, involved all his Posterity, without their knowledge or consent, in his guilt and forfeiture, and, consequently in partial and temporary misery, and no more. For could you descend into the infernal shades, among all the horrid exclamations, not one would be heard to lay his damnation at Adam's door. But the Second *Adam*, instead of effectually removing all the sad consequences of the fall, 'tis commonly supposed by many, that He will add Eternity to the torments; and, instead of a Grave only, kindle a hell of fire and brimstone, never to be quenched. And, this it is supposed, by the Orthodox in General, whether *Arminians*, or *Calvinists*, will be the most certain Portion of the greatest part of mankind, in every age and part of the world! A horrid supposition indeed!

But upon this supposition, reason and candor are ready to enquire, in what sense can the birth of Christ the Lord be justly accounted matter of great Joy to all People? It must be confessed, that the coming of Christ is the sole cause of a Resurrection, as the *second* Death is the consequence of that resurrection. And if the far greater number of mankind in all ages and places will die that death, as usually supposed; what shall we say? I shudder to think of it, yet who can deny it? That instead of being the Saviour of the World, He must certainly have Come into the world "To condemn the world," notwithstanding his own express declaration to the contrary, *Joh.* iii, 17. Must it not then have been better for those devoted Immortals, had He never come at all? I ask, what sort of glad Tidings must those be, that justly infer a conclusion, like this? Surely not those of great Joy to all People!

As these glad tidings must be heard by all People, before they can minister great Joy; I beg to

know

know when or where they are to hear them, as I suppose it must be with their own Ears, if they do not come out of their graves to hear them; as it is confessed that only a comparative few ever heard them before they were consigned thither? Must they hear them in *Hades*, or in some Popish Purgatory?

Since both the knowledge of Gospel-truth, contained in these glad tidings, and faith must come by hearing them: Since God wills that All should come to the knowledge of them, and few do in this world in the least degree; what is their either unreasonable, antiscriptural, impossible, or absurd, in the supposition, that they will hear them hereafter? If, instead of militating against, it harmonizes with the soundest reason, most impartial justice, the divine attributes, and the necessity of the subject, why should it be discountenanced for its novelty? How then can knowledge *increase*?

However strange the above supposition may appear; can we do justice to some of our Saviour's Parables without it? For instance; the Leaven that was hid in three measures of meal, until the whole was leavened. Providence has distributed mankind into Jews, Heathens, Christians; does not the word *Lump* intend mankind in a collective sense? And what does the Leaven intend but Grace communicated from the fulness of Christ? The circumstance of its being *Hid*, very clearly intimates the slowness and mysteriousness of its operation, gradually fermenting, until it has incorporated itself with the whole mass of Mankind, as our Saviour seems to intend.

The Parable of the Mustard-seed—Can any thing be more to the point? Here we have the least of all seeds shooting out into a Tree sufficient to find habitation for the fowls of Heaven. The time of its growth, and the difference of soil or climate,

mate, are not here noticed. The absence of these restrictive circumstances are intended to point out the universality of its progress, until it arrives at the utmost limits of its Perfection. From the smallness of the grain, the swelling idea must expand to the utmost size of the Tree, imperceptible in its growth, yet astonishing in its size, from so small a seed! The purport of which is, to shew from what small beginnings the kingdom of Grace takes its rise, and the progress it makes, until it arrives at its perfection. Now if the whole lump be leavened, there can but be a very small *residuum*—And the expanding mustard-seed, surprises Reason itself, in its growth!

Nebuchadnezzar's dream is very worthy of notice. The image is standing, but the Sovereign Authority has long resided in the ten toes. These, as the remains of the four Monarchies preceding, are only to be destroyed by the Stone cut out of the mountain. The Dominions of the Beast and false Prophet are within the limits of these ancient Empires, and will fall when they fall. The size of the stone is three-fold. When first cut out of the mountain, it is very small—it gradually increases, like a rolling snow ball, till it swells into a mountain—then the mountain spreads till it covers the whole earth. The first small size corresponds with Christianity in its current state. It reaches from Pentecost unto our Saviour's next coming: At this time it will break the whole Image to pieces, and then commence a mountain gradually, when the kingdoms of the world become the kingdoms of our God and of his Christ. This growing stone will arrive at its mountain-size in the Times of the Millennium and of Satan's little season. But the New-Jerusalem state is reserved for its last size, when, in the Age of Ages, it will cover the whole earth; but this it never had done before, witness

Gog

Gog and Magog. This last period includes the dignity of Christ's Kingdom both temporally and spiritually, and will continue to the end of Time, when his Mediatorial Office ceases.

It will appear below, that the Gospel of the Kingdom will be Preached throughout all those long periods, and "Then will the End come." It will be then, and not till then, that the fermenting leaven will temper the whole Lump of Mankind, to the great Joy of angelical beings!

Phil. My dear Didas. whence can originate those tremendously awful, if not horrid ideas, that have found entertainment in many human heads, of the Governor of the Universe; as if implacable wrath was his darling attribute, and vindictive vengeance his principal delight; or as if to hurl hundreds of millions into hell was a trifling thing with Him, and the most of them for no other reason than His own good pleasure, or at most, for a Crime which they never committed? To attribute a sentiment to the Deity, at which humanity shudders and reason recoils, is certainly to suppose our Maker worse than ourselves; nor is it less contrary to the very spirit and genius of Christianity, whose origin and essence is Love itself.

Didas. As it is impossible to reconcile such sentiments with reason, our natural feelings, or the genuine doctrines of the Bible; so it is vain and absurd to resolve them into some supposed secret occult Decrees of Heaven, as such supposed decrees directly contradict what is confessedly the Revealed will of God: Such sentiments therefore can have no existence but in the mistaken judgments of fallible mortals.

How many thousands have been involved in the inextricable Labyrinths of vain reasoning—overwhelmed and plunged into the deepest distress, and that without the least glimmering beam of hope,

or

or certain clue to lead them out of thofe gloomy Principles of Defpair!

But the Doctrine here advanced, how fweetly is it calculated to difperfe the gloom—adminifter comfort to fuch difconfolate minds, being pregnant with rational grounds of hope for every individual of the human race, whofe inveterate obftinacy, and malignant contempt of Chrift and his Crofs, have not tranfported them beyond the almoft boundlefs limits of redeeming love and mercy, which far tranfcend our moft exalted conceptions, as Scripture afferts, and Reafon confeffes.

When "Ages to come" have difcovered thofe limits; exhibited them to public infpection; and realized them by an univerfal Salvation of Adam's Race, except as above excepted; how many erroneous conclufions, derogatory to divine Philanthropy—depreciating the merits of our glorious Redeemer by a contraction of their limits, and reducing his Redemption into fo narrow a compafs, as to exclude from its benefits the moft of Mankind—furely fuch conclufions, and the Principles from which they were drawn, will vanifh like Dreams, and the Perfons who drew them, now broad awake, ftand aftonifhed to fee their miftakes difcovered!

Such a glorious difplay of the vaft dimenfions of Redemption, realized according to the letter of Scripture, will teach men and angels how it originated from univerfal Love and Benevolence—was concerted by Omnifcience—conducted by unerring Wifdom and Omnipotence—and at the fame time, the whole of it adminiftered upon Principles of the ftricteft Juftice, and moft inviolable Truth. Here every attribute of Deity fhines in its divine luftre; join in concert in the fweeteft harmony to the glory of God; fecuring and advancing the honour of the world's Redeemer; dignifying, with a divine nature, countless millions of happy Immortals, henceforth possest of every possible degree of glory which that nature is capable of. Thus is discovered a boundless and endless theme of gratitude and praise for Men and Angels!

You recollect, my dear friend, this is one of those Foundation-Truths we intended the Pile of our Essay to stand upon, viz. that there is no other Name given under heaven among men whereby we can be saved, but the Name of Jesus. But here permit me to ask, is it Scriptural to suppose, that those many hundreds of millions of Adult Heathens, being by far the bigger half of mankind, *may* be saved without ever hearing of the Name of Jesus? If so, they are saved without believing in his name! Can they believe in Him of whom they have not heard? and how shall they hear without a Preacher? These countless myriads have left the world without ever hearing a syllable of the joyful sound: Are we not here reduced to this dilemma, That those already dead must either never hear it, or rise to hear it in ages yet to come? If this be denied, I ask, must they all for ever perish—be annihilated? If not, how or by what means must they be saved? But if by far the greatest part of Mankind may be saved without ever either hearing of Christ or believing in Him, why not all? And upon this supposition, where is the absolute necessity of either preaching or believing? If there be any cogency in this mode of reasoning, is it not much more likely, that the Ages to come will give to those Heathen an opportunity both to hear and believe, in order to their salvation, rather than conclude that there never was any intended for them, or that Christ will save them without either? both of which suppositions are absurd in the extreme.

Phil.

Phil. But as final ſalvation or damnation in the Balances of the Sanctuary are ſuſpended upon the believing or not believing, the neceſſity of both preaching and hearing are the neceſſary conſequences. Had not this been the caſe, why did our Saviour commiſſion his Diſciples to Preach it to every creature, but that every creature might believe and be ſaved; ſeeing the world through him *might be ſaved?*

Didas. True. That certainly was his deſign. For either He intended it for every creature, or he did not. If he did, who ſhall *finally* fruſtrate this intention? If he did not, what did he mean? If the meſſage was not *deſigned* for every Creature, how ſhall we vindicate Him who gave the commiſſion from inſincerity?

If it be allowed, that the Merit and conſequent Satisfaction of our Saviour were adequate to the guilt of Mankind, it follows, upon the meritorious ſatisfaction being accepted, that the World of mankind *are* virtually forgiven; does any thing but unbelief hinder the actual application of that pardon? Can Juſtice inflict farther or future puniſhment, having received compenſation; or hinder Mercy and Benevolence from effecting the Salvation of all, in ages and by means beſt calculated to diſplay the manifold wiſdom of God, except as above excepted; that is, final Unbelievers?

Phil. But can Unbelief be a damning ſin unleſs it is obſtinate and wilful? Or will abounding grace abſolutely ſave one ſoul who never heard of it, whether Infant or Heathen?

Didas. Invincible ignorance merits excuſe, but none can ever, upon Goſpel Terms, get to heaven in that ignorance. He who will have all men to be ſaved, wills, in order thereto, that all ſhould come to "The knowledge of the Truth." Abound-

ing

ing grace will ſave none but thoſe *who receive it.* To me it ſeems evident, that the everlaſting goſpel muſt be preached to the heathen hereafter, as unto us now; and that they will be ſaved as we are now, viz. By Grace, through Faith, or periſh in unbelief, as it is to be feared too many now do. If this be denied, they muſt either be ſaved by a way not diſcovered in the Goſpel, or, periſh. Which is the moſt rational way to ſolve this difficulty? Shall we cut the Gordian knot, and either damn or annihilate them all at a ſtroke? Some writers do the one, and ſome the other. Others land them all in heaven by the Tide of abounding grace. Others ſuppoſe, that a few, and but a few, will find their way to heaven, by living up to the ſtar-light of their dark diſpenſation. Vain ſurmiſes!

May I here be permitted to make an appeal to enlightened reaſon? Which of thoſe very different hypotheſes is moſt eligible, moſt rational, and moſt ſcriptural? Who can allow leſs limits than I have done, reſpecting both Perſons, Time, and Place, and do no violence to the very letter of the Scriptures? Objections and cavils, wit and learning may make; and what Truth is it, againſt which they cannot eaſily levy an army? But one ſingle ſubſtantial proof will ſtand out a ſiege againſt them all.

It may, at firſt thought, be ſuppoſed incongruous for perſons raiſed from the dead to hear the goſpel, believe it, and be ſaved. But wherein does that incongruity lie? Is not death analogous to ſleep, and in the Scripture language, is it not ſo denominated? Is it unreaſonable to ſuppoſe, that the Holy Ghoſt foreſeeing this vaſt event, accommodated the term to that daily neceſſary reſt, in order to familiarize it to our ideas, as well as to leſſen the horror of dying? We are not to ſuppoſe that the heathen will riſe with ſuch glorious bodies

dies as the Saints will have, ſuch as St. Paul deſcribes in 1 *Cor.* xv. Where is the difference between making Adam's body, and raiſing the duſt of the dead? May not the one be as eaſily reanimated, as the firſt of the kind was originally animated? The body of Adam was qualified to perform every animal function intended for it in his then condition; and why may not theirs? What quality will they riſe with incompatible with hearing the goſpel? If there will be a *Reſtitution* of all Things, then ſurely of human bodies out of the duſt, ſuch as Adam's may be ſuppoſed to have been. Does not a Reſurrection properly mean, that the very ſame identical or numerical body will riſe again? Can the different circumſtances of bodies raiſed from the dead, or quickened from the duſt, make ſuch an eſſential difference, ſo that the minds of the one ſhall be qualified to hear the Goſpel, and the other incapacitated? What metaphyſical abſurdity is there in ſuppoſing, that a body raiſed from the duſt may hear the Goſpel, believe, and be ſaved, as well as a corrupting Lazarus called forth from the grave could? Adam was made out of the duſt: Where will be the difference in the *Stamina* of the duſt of the riſing dead, being originally *derived* from his, and the duſt of mother earth that gave being to his? In reaſon, the reanimated duſt, if any difference at all will ſubſiſt, may put in a plea in its own favour, as being a ſecond edition of the ſame building, the former being pulled down with a view to improvement. With God nothing is impoſſible. To make Adam's body out of the duſt, or compoſe Eve's out of his, are equally eaſy to Omnipotence.

The body of Eve had a prior exiſtence in the body of Adam to her own perſonal exiſtence. But was not the operation performed upon his body, in order to extract the materials for the compoſition of of hers, much more ſolemn than is uſually conceived to have been? This operation is thus related by Moſes: "And Jehovah Elohim, or Jehovah one of the Elohim (*Chap.* iii. 22.) cauſed *a deep ſleep* to fall upon Adam, and he *Slept*: And He took one of his ribs, and cloſed up the fleſh inſtead thereof," *Chap.* ii. 21. The Jews have three words for ſleep, expreſſive of its different degrees; but Lexicographers tell us, that the word *Thardemah* here uſed by Moſes, is the deepeſt ſleep of all. But I aſk, is not this language of the Holy Ghoſt identical in its meaning, as uſed here, and in the New Teſtament? In this laſt, ſleep means Death. Can it mean any leſs here? We muſt confeſs that the ſkill of the operator here was far above human, but that does not hinder from ſuppoſing that Adam actually died under the divine operation. If ſo, we here have the reaſon why the New Teſtament calls Death ſleep. And without a miracle, could ſuch an Operation be performed and the perſon ſurvive it? To ſuppoſe that this was a temporary death, is more agreeable to experience and matter of fact, to the uſe of the term by our Lord and his Apoſtles; and the miracle of reſtoring him to life again, is much more inſtructive than to ſuppoſe otherwiſe. In this point of light, how can it be viewed otherwiſe than as a myſtical, proleptical, and inſtructive leſſon? Does it not plainly teach us, as in other things, ſo in this alſo, that Adam was *Typos* or a Figure of Him that was to come?

Phil. Wherein, my dear Didas?

Didas. Among other things, in this eſpecially, that the Bride, the Lamb's Wife, would coſt him his life by the opening of his ſide; and that, 1ſt. He muſt Himſelf riſe again from the dead; and 2nd. Form her anew, by a new nature communicated from Himſelf unto her, as Eve derived hers

from

from Adam, before he could enjoy her in such a relation. "This," Apostolical authority warrants us to call a great Mystery! But this only by the bye.

Now if Adam himself was raised from this deadly sleep, with the seminal "Blood of all nations that dwell upon the face of the earth" then within him, with the greatest degree of evidence we may most truly infer, that virtually and in a sense all the bodies of his posterity both died and rose again in him. And may not the language of the Apostle be understood as analogous to this, when he represents Christians both as dead and quickened *together* with Christ? Once more! Can the Restitution of all Things imply any less, than that the bodies of all Adam's Posterity shall rise again from the dead, as certainly as Adam did from the Type of it, namely, his deadly sleep, in which, in a sense, they themselves had both died and risen again? And hence their mystical Resurrection in Adam may be looked upon, not only as an Earnest of their own, but also of their rising in circumstances similar, in various respects, to those of Adam after the formation of Eve. From which it will follow, that the circumstances in which the dead will rise again, will be no more incompatible with hearing the Gospel, and believing unto Salvation, than Adam was incapacitated from hearing the Seed promised, and believing that promise. The bodies of Saints, as described in the Epistle to the Corinthians, we may be sure will be very different in quality from those of sinners. For instance, the bodies of Saints will be "Raised in Glory;" nor will they be capable of the second death, &c. neither of which will be the case with sinners. Again, as to ancient Types I shall notice, 1st. That Noah, by living the *same man* in both worlds, is a very clear one, as is obvious at the first sight. See the introduction in the first Dialogue.

and.

2nd. Abraham was the Patriarch of the Jewish Nation. The Promise that his Seed should vie with the Stars for multitude, was limitted to Isaac. But before Isaac had begotten any issue, his Maker demanded him for a Burnt-offering, who was the destined Father of them all.

Now how was it possible for him to be the Father of many nations, whose body was burnt to ashes? In this, consisted the very strength and supernatural excellency of Abraham's Faith, that after the body of Isaac had been burnt, he proceeded stedfastly to believe the divine Promise with little less than a miraculous Faith. Such was the plethory or full assurance of the Faith of Abraham; So unwaveringly did he confide in the veracity of his almighty and all-sufficient God, that he proceeded without the least hesitation to comply, according to the sacred Oracle to make the bloody and burning Sacrifice!

Phil. But, how was it possible for him to have an issue to vie in number with the Stars, when his body, from which they were to proceed, was by fire reduced to ashes?

Didas. How indeed! Faith not only silenced every paternal complaint, for we hear none, but triumphed over nature, and death itself. "Accounting that God was able to raise him up, even from the dead!" And as what the Patriarch performed, was, even in the Judgment of God himself, tantamount to the actual burning of him as a sacrifice, so when he unbound and took him from the Altar, of course he must receive him "As alive from the dead," *Comp. Gen.* xxii. and *Heb.* xi. 17, 19.

Here we have a typical Resurrection, equal in the eye of Abraham, and equally accepted by Abraham's God, as if it had been realized by an actual sacrifice and consequent Resurrection. He

I 2 did

did it require from Abraham one grain less faith. Hence it is evident, from the whole Transaction, that Abraham believed that the ashes of his darling son would again be reanimated, beget an issue, and perform every animal function, as much and as well as if he had never died. Here let me ask, what difference can there be between the ashes of Isaac recently burnt, and the ashes of others dead thousands of years? Suppose we were possest of the faith of Abraham, could not we more easily believe in the numerical Resurrection of the heathen, in order to give an accomplishment to divine promises, than he did, in sacrificing his own son for the same purpose? Abraham believed that an innumerable offspring would issue from Isaac's loins, and that therefore the Oracle would be fulfilled; "In Isaac shall thy Seed be called," though burnt to ashes before he had any. We have not the difficulty to grapple with that Abraham had; we have no Parental feelings to divest ourselves of: Abraham believed in the Resurrection of his Son, type of the World's Redeemer, type and earnest of his own; and why may we not tread in the steps of his faith, and believe, that God may raise the Heathen, in similar circumstances, that Abraham expected his son to have been in, after the Reanimation of his ashes? The faith of Abraham argues the possibility of the fact.

Phil. Astonishing and triumphant faith indeed! This heroic act was worthy of the Father of the faithful! To believe that his darling Isaac's Ashes would be reanimated—the very same particles collected by Him who numbers our hairs; and like the body of Adam formed out of the dust into a second edition of that Fabric in whose seminal cells the World's Redeemer lodged! Which shall we most admire? His faith, or obedient love springing from it? To make a Burnt-offering of the

the ſon of his old age—the ſon of his faith—the hope of his family—the centre of all the promiſes, and the Heir of the World, (*Rom.* iv. 13.), embarked in the loins of which earthen veſſel, all the hopes of Man's Salvation were depoſited! This Action, expreſſive of the moſt complete obedience, perfect love, and paſſive reſignation, all which were confirmed by the ſanction of Heaven, was a Mirror in which might be clearly ſeen that love of the Father of the ſpirits of all fleſh, by which he ſent his only-begotten ſon to die for our ſins—riſe again for our Juſtification—the conqueſt of death, and conſequent Reſurrection of all mankind, and that in the ſame identical bodies which dropt into the duſt, and with the ſame degree of certainty that Iſaac was releaſed from the ſacred Altar to beget a numerous iſſue, and perform all human functions.

Didas. All this is true. And by this you may ſee, that the Jews had no farther to look than to their own great Anceſtor for the original ground of a future Reſurrection, and faith in it—A Reſurrection of the ſame numerical body that dies and moulders into duſt.

Joſephus ſeemed to think, that the wicked are not to riſe again, and many of the Rabbins affirm the ſame thing. But this is not the doctrine of the Jewiſh Church. The *Chaldee Paraphraſe* upon *Iſa.* lxv. 6. ſpeaking of the wicked Hypocrites of that day, ſays, "Their vengeance ſhall be in hell, where the Fire continually burns." Then he adds, the Almighty denouncing, "I will be revenged on them for their ſins, and deliver their bodies to the *ſecond death.*" This plainly ſuppoſes a preceding Reſurrection. The famous Jewiſh Rabbi *Maimonides* defines the Reſurrection to be "The Return of the ſoul into the *ſame body* from which it had been ſeparated." "The Catholic faith throughout the whole chriſtian world is this, that the SAME body

body which dies, consisting of the *same Particles*, shall rise again out of its grave, and be reunited to the soul." *Dr. Hody*.

Some few have thought, that the doctrine of the Resurrection, as asserted in the New Testament, was known to the Antediluvians, and by Noah transmitted down to his Posterity; though the Author of the *Clementine Recognitions* makes Abraham the first who taught it. See the Introduction to this volume.

That the ancient *Magi* were acquainted with it, seems to be certain. *Plutarch* informs us, that the Books of *Zoroastres*, or *Zoroaster*, assert, "That there will be a Time when the earth will be made plain and level, and that all mankind will live happily together in one Community, and speak but one language." And according to *Theopompus*, "That this shall happen after a term of six thousand years."

Æneas Gazeus affirms, out of *Theopompus*, that *Zoroaster* foretold, that there will come a "Time when there will be a Resurrection of all the dead." It is said, that the remains of the ancient *Magi* in *Persia*, called *Guchars*, still maintain this doctrine, "That there shall be an Universal Resurrection. At that time, all the souls, either in Paradise or Hell, shall return to take possession of their bodies."

Lactantius also informs us, that the *Magi* taught *Anabiosesthai tous anthropous, &c.* that men shall live over again, and be then immortal. Again, *Lactantius* cites *Chrysippus*, that prop of the Stoicks Porch, as *Cicero* termed him, saying, "It is manifest that it is not at all impossible, that after a certain Revolution of Time, even we may be restored from death *to what we now are*." *Lact. de Vita Beata*, L. 7. C. 23.

How

How clearly this doctrine was understood in the Time of the Maccabees, and how it animated the Mother and her seven Sons to suffer Martyrdom, may be seen at large in the 2 *Maccab. Ch.* vii. The second Martyr told his Murderer, "Thou, like a fury, takest us out of the present life, but the King of the World shall *raise us up*, who have died for his Laws, unto everlasting Life," *ver.* 9. The third Martyr putting out his tongue, and holding forth his hands, manfully said, "These I had from Heaven; and for His Laws I despise them, and *from Him I hope to receive them again*," *ver.* 10, 11. The fourth Brother, when he was ready to die, said thus, "It is good, being put to death by men, to look for hope from God *to be raised up again*," *ver.* 14. The courageous Mother cried, "Doubtless the Creator of the world, who formed the Generation of man, will also of his own mercy *give you life again*," *ver.* 23. Christian Martyrs could have said no more.

Our Saviour informs us, that "All that are in the graves shall come forth." If *all*, then all Infants, and all Heathens; and what will become of the former who never sinned, or the latter at whose sins God winked?

Some say the greatest part will be annihilated; and others say, for ever damned. But what says reason, humanity, and christian charity? "What have these Sheep done," that they must thus be doomed, and for who knows what? You have already had a few gleanings from Heathen and Jewish Authors, all which are unanimous, that the very identical body that dies, "shall come forth," composed of all its former parts and particles; and I may add, as the Foundation of the whole, that the very same body of flesh and bones that was buried, our Saviour brought forth out of the grave again, and carried up to heaven with him, making the clouds his chariot, riding upon the wings of the wind; and doubtless took those along with him who rose when he rose, as the ensigns of his victory over *Death* and *Hades*, which he carried as Trophies of honour into the invisible world!

Phil. As Jew and Gentile have given in their united suffrages to the momentous subject before us, please to call for the votes of the Christian Fathers of the Church, to discover whether the same unanimity, in general, subsists amongst them; which if it does, we may venture to term it, The voice of Nature—the voice of Reason uniting in unison; and where does the voice of Revelation bring in a discord?

Didas. Permit me first to introduce a few single voices, and then a few in certain Concerts when assembled in Council. Shall only name a few.

1. The venerable *Polycarp*, a Disciple of St. John, when he was bound to a stake to be burned, he "thanked God that he drank of the Cup of Christ in order to the Resurrection of both *soul* and *body* to everlasting life."

2. *Papias*, Bishop of Hieropolis, believed, "That *after* the Resurrection we shall eat and drink as *before* we died." Did not Christ *eat* after his Resurrection? Was not his the sample of ours? Did not he promise his Disciples that they should eat and drink new wine, the *Fruit of the vine*, with him in his Kingdom? And why not, as well as Adam in innocence?

3. *Justin Martin* would not allow those to be Christians who denied the Resurrection of the Flesh. He wrote a Book entitled, "Concerning the Resurrection of the Flesh," as being less ambiguous than the word *body*.

4. *Origen* was, in some part of his life, for an Ætherial Body; yet owns, "That the Resurrection of the Flesh was the Doctrine preached in the

Churches. What is that which died? Is it not the Body? The Resurrection therefore will be of the body. The bodies that fell are said to rise again; for nothing but that which fell, can properly be said to rise again, and so of all others. For it is not equitable that the soul which sinned in one body should be punished in another; neither does it become a just Judge to reward a body when it was not *that*, but another which suffered for Christ. That the Promise of a Resurrection of the dead, is concerning this body that died, appears from many proofs of the holy scriptures. Christ is called the First-born from the dead. It is certain that our Saviour arose in that very body which He received from many." Thus *Origen* asserted the Resurrection of the same numerical substance. And, according to *Photrius*, he plainly affirms, that the body, when it rises, will be true and real flesh, and retain its old form and shape.

5. According to *St. Irenæus*, the primitive universal Church believed, "*Et in carne in cœlos assumptionem*," that Christ in the flesh was taken up into Heaven.

6. *St. Athanasius* says, "He carried up into heaven the very same flesh which He had when living." The primitive Fathers maintained, "that he sits at the right hand of the Father in the Flesh, which he had when living; and that he will come in the same to judge the quick and the dead." Yea, some were excommunicated who believed to the contrary.

Both Creeds and Councils speak the same language. For instance, in the Apostles Creed, what is in English, "The Resurrection of the *Body*," was originally, according to *Ruffinus*, *St. Austin*, and *Jerome*, "*Carnis Resurrectio*," The Resurrection of the Flesh. One ancient Creed, says *Dr. Hody*,

Hody, expressed it emphatically, "The Resurrection of *this Flesh*."

In the Creed of the ancient Mother Church at Jerusalem we read it, "*Sarcos Anastaris*," the Resurrection of the Flesh.

The Creed of *P. Damasus* expresses it thus; "We believe that we shall be raised up *in hac carne qua nunc vivimus*," in the same flesh in which we now live.

The Creed of the first Council held in *Toledo*, A. D. 400, is this, "*Resurrectionem vero futuram humanæ credimus Carnis*," We believe there will be a future Resurrection of the Flesh of Mankind. In the fourth Council held there in 633, it is said, "We are to be raised up in the same Flesh in which we now live, and in *ea qua resurrexit idem dominus forma*, the same form in which the Lord rose.

In a Council held in the same place in A. D. 675, we are told that, according to the example of our Head, we confess that there will be a true Resurrection "*Carnis omnium Mortuorum*," of the Flesh of all the Dead.

What need of adding any more human Testimonies to prove that which must be granted by every one whose ignorance or prejudice has not biassed their Judgments? For, from the whole, we may safely conclude, and that is enough for my purpose, that the Dead, whether reduced to ashes or not, will rise clothed with the same numerical body, composed of every particle which it put off when it went to rest in the bosom of Mother Earth. For which, besides what has been already said, we evidently have the suffrage of one when living, and example when dead, that must be decisive with all Christians.

When Herod had heard of the Fame of Jesus, he said unto his Servants, "This is John the Baptist:

Baptist: He is risen from the dead, and therefore mighty works do shew forth themselves in him." *Matth*. xiv. 1, 2.

Phil. But John the Baptist had been lately beheaded by Herod, and might not his guilty fears have suggested such a fancy? Besides, John's body, though corrupt, could not be reduced to ashes.

Didas. Whatever might be in Herod's fears or fancy, it certainly was the received Doctrine at that day, that the Dust of the Dead, yea of the ancient Dead, might be reanimated, and in their former human form appear, and transact any business as formerly, and that without any apparent symptom to indicate their death and resurrection.

All this is evident from the opinion of many who said, "That one of the old Prophets had risen again," *Luk*. ix. 8. such as Moses, Elias, Jeremiah, &c. To this sentiment, the silence of our Saviour, in a measure, gave a sanction: For tho' it was not true that he was one of the old Prophets risen again, yet it was true that the people thought so; which thought, had the thing been either in itself impossible or absurd, would not have passed unnoticed by Him, seeing that it directly led them to form a very wrong Judgment of his Person and Character. Once more;

Our Saviour expressly forbids us to fear those who can kill the body only; but commands us emphatically to fear HIM who can kill both body and soul in hell. It is this body that men can kill; it is the Resurrection-body that may be cast into hell; and wherein does he mark any difference? Do not both his language and argument suppose no difference? Or what difference does he intimate in either the nature or qualities between the maimed bodies here, being without eye or hand, and those which he will cast whole into Hell, wanting neither?

Phil. It appears to me, that the two facts, viz. Abraham receiving Isaac from the Altar, "As alive from the dead;" and the Resurrection of Christ in the same body that was buried; lay a sufficient foundation for the doctrine of an Universal Resurrection of all Mankind, by a reanimation of the dust of the body that died.—A superstructure sufficient to withstand the shocks of infidelity, and support the faith and hope of the genuine Christian in his dying moments.

Didas. Yes, friend Phil. a foundation, upon which "Ages to come" will erect millions of living monuments among Heathens, Jews, and Christians, with this inscription upon every one of them, "I was Dead, but am Alive again." And from what we have heard upon the subject of the Resurrection, we have met with nothing to confute, but with much to confirm our general hypothesis, in a great degree of probability.

DIALOGUE X.

Philotheos. MY dear Didafcalos, it appears to me that your hypothefis would gain an univerfal confent, were it poffible to found the depth, foar to the height, comprehend the breadth, or meafure the length of the love of God in Chrift Jefus. Such an intuitive view would afford a profpect aftonifhing to our contracted minds—banifh infidelity from the human breaft—foften the hardeft heart—and, like a live coal from the heavenly altar, thaw the moft icy one; and enkindle fuch a facred fire of heavenly love, as would burn up a whole army of cavils levied by our ignorance and narrow conceptions. Were the unfearchable riches of Chrift exhibited to view, they would command and obtain the warmeft applaufe from enlightened reafon—appear infinitely fuperior to every thing human—and approve themfelves, in every thing, abundantly worthy of a general acceptation.

Thofe intricacies in the divine Prefcience, and predetermining will of God, with refpect to ages, nations, and individuals among mankind, would be eafily and rationally accounted for, to general fatisfaction. Thefe, could the plan of Providence be exhibited in a picture, like well-drawn fhades, would heighten and brighten every line, and illuftrate every part of the plan in greater perfection. How would the World be aftonifhed to find, that ineffable love is the fountain and root of every difpenfation flowing from the Deity unto mankind, from the beginning to the end of time! "Ages to come" will difcover the whole.

Didas. Thofe Ages will realize the Fact, that the "Grace of God bringeth Salvation to All Men,"

Men," *Tit.* ii. 11. In the Apoſtolical Times, that Grace *appeared*, but it was only like the ſun-beams gilding the mountain-tops in the morning. It was only the firſt-fruits of the ſpirit: A beam of this grace firſt darted from the Sun of Righteouſneſs in the Promiſe made in Paradiſe. From thence, at "Sundry times, and by divers Tropes or Figures," (*Heb.* i. 1.) God, by the Jewiſh Prophets, explained that Promiſe, and illuſtrated it by more explicit Promiſes, Prophecies, and Types. When God ſent his Son, the promiſed Seed, it was only, in his perſonal Miniſtry, to the "Loſt Sheep of the Houſe of Iſrael," being a ſingle family among all the families of the earth. However the Apoſtolical Commiſſion extended unto *all nations*, and to *every creature*; but the preſent and paſt hiſtories of all nations that have any, are mournful Monuments, on which are inſcribed, "Lamentation, Miſery, and Woe." Hitherto, inſtead of his Head being completely bruiſed, he "Deceives the whole world," and will, ſerpent-like, until he is impriſoned, *Rev.* xii. 9.

As St. Paul ſeems to have conſidered the mode of his own miraculous converſion, by Chriſt's perſonal Appearance to him, as a *Pattern* to his own Nation, whoſe converſion will only be accompliſhed by his next appearance in the Clouds; ſo, as we have touched above, he evidently conſidered the Converſion of the Epheſians, and, doubtleſs, of other Gentiles, as *Patterns* of the Converſion of the Heathen "in Ages to come."

To the Epheſians God ſhewed the exceeding Riches of his Grace in Chriſt Jeſus; and to the *Heathen* he will the ſame in Ages yet future; for to this day he has not. The great love wherewith God loved the Epheſians *before* their Converſion, and the exceeding Riches of his Grace in his kindneſs towards them at the time of their converſion, he he confiders as a *Sample* which God will follow in the Converfion of thofe who, like them, were dead in trefpaffes and fins—children of wrath—without hope—and without God, or *Atheifts*, in the World, &c. Now as God quickened, pardoned, adopted, and faved, by Grace through Faith, the Ephefians; fo in Ages to come he will fhew the fame; and they who hereafter *believe*, which they cannot do without hearing, Grace will equally fave them.

Now do not the Ages to come include all future ages, until Chrift fhall deliver up the Kingdom to the Father? Does not the current language of Prophecy point at thefe Ages, or *latter*, or *laft days*? Are not thefe the Seafons of Grace—the Times of Refrefhing or Revivification—the Times of the Reftitution of All Things—the Times peculiarly Chrift's—the Times, of which God hath fpoken by the mouth of all his holy Prophets fince the world began—the Times when the "Myftery of God" will be fulfilled—when Promifes, Prophecies, and Types, will have their full accomplifhment; and the Holy Spirit poured out in a degree as fuperior to the Apoftolical Ages, as the whole harveft exceeded the firft-fruits? Former Ages have never, but future Ages moft certainly will experience all the great and precious Promifes in the Bible. In thefe days, the whole Plan of human Redemption will be difplayed, and the manifold Wifdom of God will fhine in every part of it, to the confufion of his enemies and gratification of his friends, in worlds vifible and invifible!

Phil. What a glorious Theatre will the world then be! The manifold wifdom of God will exhibit fcenes of divine Grace and Philanthropy in every glorious form before men and angels! Then Juftice and Mercy will each act their aftonifhing parts, and kifs each other! The eternal falvation of countlefs numbers, by our ignorance and narrow principles

principles doomed to annihilation or damnation, will then add a brilliancy to each divine Attribute —discover dimensions on the scale of Redemption, little suspected—confound the devil, and add to the society of heaven glorious subjects of the Sovereign, objects of the love and sharers in the glory and dignity of the great Emmanuel!

Didas. When the bright Morning Star appears, harbinger of that happy day when the glorious Sun of Righteousness shall expand and stretch forth his healing wings the world around, then shall the Ends of the Earth look unto Him, as the bitten Israelites to the brazen Serpent, and be saved. Then will that Grace of God which teaches us now, teach all nations the delightful Lessons of Redeeming Love and Evangelical Obedience. But certain it is, that the far greatest part of those nations have been swept off this into the invisible world untaught, by Gospel-preaching, any part of the Plan of Salvation.

Christ is the great Prophet, the true Shepherd and Bishop of Souls, the Proprietor of the Sheep. Had it comported with the plan of his Providence, He, doubtless, would have sent faithful labourers into every part of his dominions; endowed them with Wisdom to win Souls, and convert a world. As He is possest of all Authority in heaven and earth, want of Power can be no reason why the far greatest part of Mankind have left the world altogether uninstructed in the lessons of Grace. The pious and prudent will resolve this into the "Mystery of God;" a mystery spoken of by the Prophets, (*Rev.* x. 7.) scarcely at all understood, nor will it, but by a few that are Wise, (*Dan.* xii. 10.) till the blasts of the Seventh Trumpet sound its commencement to the ends of the Earth. Then will a nation be born in a day; in which, the light of the moon will be as the light of the sun, and the light

of

of the ſun will be ſeven-fold brighter than ever, while Jehovah ſhall Reign in Zion, and amongſt His Ancients glorioufly, throughout the *Sabbatiſmos* of St. Paul, *Heb.* iv. 9.

The Sound of that Trumpet will aſtoniſh the world, by publiſhing the contents of divine Purpoſes, Promiſes, and Prophecies, which, at the preſent, few either underſtand or believe. Among others, will be the Gentile-Diſpenſation, or the Myſtery of Chriſt, which from the Beginning had been hid in God. The more myſterious in itſelf, the more marvellous will it appear, not only unto Mankind, but unto Principalities and Powers in heavenly Places, or to the Inhabitants of different and diſtant worlds. Take the whole of this Gentile-Diſpenſation together, and I am greatly miſtaken if the unfolding of this Myſtery will not diſplay "the manifold Wiſdom of God," in a way ſuperior to any other Diſpenſation, to the aſtoniſhment of Men and Angels—prove a principal part in the grand Drama of Providence—the whole of which will be entirely tranſacted in a vaſt variety of ſcenes in the Times of the Reſtitution, or of Chriſt's own Seaſons.

Phil. If Adam had never ſinned, there would never have been ſin in the world, I ſuppoſe; or if the Law had not intervened, would perſonal ſins have been either imputed or puniſhed? Whether of the two Adams, may we juſtly ſuppoſe, influenced Mankind moſt powerfully?

Didas. This may be anſwered by aſking, whether of the two were more dignified in their Perſons and Offices? Was the Sin of the firſt more malignant to deſtroy, than the Grace of the ſecond to ſave? Will not the *tenders* of Grace and Mercy, through the redemption which is in Jeſus, be as univerſal as the imputation and propagation of ſin? If there be a ſufficient plenteouſneſs of the Re-

demption

demption which is in Jesus for all Mankind, wherein does the deficiency lie, that so few will receive its saving benefits, as is commonly supposed?

Phil. Is it not solely in Unbelief?

Didas. Certainly. But can unbelief damn those who never either did, or possibly could hear of that Redemption? That he who hears, but obstinately refuses to believe and obey the Gospel, is condemned already, and the final unbeliever will be finally condemned, are Truths which the Judge himself has informed us of; but where has he said that they either are, or ever will be condemned who never enjoyed the benefit of Revelation?

The Apostle, speaking of both Jews and Heathens, says, When we were without strength—ungodly—sinners—enemies—we were Reconciled unto God by the *Death* of his Son; and if so, much more being reconciled, we shall be saved by his *life*. Here, then, the Reconciliation of all mankind is certain. Can any thing, except unbelief, render the Salvation of any child of Adam uncertain? Shall the greatest part of these reconciled enemies be lost, notwithstanding the *much more* certainty of Salvation resulting from Christ's living an Intercessor for them?

The grand design of this Reconciliation of enemies, ungodly, &c. was the more amiably to recommend and illustrate God's love and favour towards these ungodly enemies. The greater enemies, and the more ungodly, the more the love and grace that reconciles them is displayed, and must appear to better advantage. The more extraordinary effects flow from the death, resurrection, and intercession of Christ; that Love, both of the Father and Son, that induced them to the whole process, must stand recommended as more eminent and extraordinary. But it was not to mankind only

only that this Love was intended to be ſet off with every poſſible ſtriking circumſtance of advantage, but alſo to inhabitants of other worlds. But in order to this extraordinary recommendation of this Love, is not an explicit knowledge of it abſolutely neceſſary, eſpecially to mankind? But it muſt be granted, that only a very ſmall part of mankind either have, or ever can be bleſt with an explicit knowledge of it in this life. Unleſs, then, a future life in "Ages to come" afford them ſuch an explicit knowledge, the far greateſt part of mankind muſt for ever remain in ignorance, as to the true cauſes of either their ſalvation or damnation, which conſequences it is impoſſible to avoid. Which, whether my hypotheſis, or ſuch abſurdities, afford the ſweeteſt harmony in judicious ears, I leave others to judge.

Many ſuppoſe that Goſpel-bleſſings will be transferred to ſome without any explicit knowledge of them. But ſuch a ſuppoſition deviates very far from the divine œconomy of our Salvation—evidently prevents the grand and previous recommendation of love and grace from which they ſpring—and is by no means conſentaneous to the conduct of Providence, and the divinely inſtituted means of Grace. Is man a machine? Is he altogether a paſſive ſubject in Goſpel-ſalvation? But this laſt ſuppoſition infers ſuch conſequences. If five parts out of ſix of mankind, infants, idiots, heathen, &c. in all ages and places may be ſaved without an explicit knowledge of the Goſpel, then they may be ſaved without Repentance, Faith, Love, or Evangelical Obedience. But if ſo, theſe are not abſolutely neceſſary to ſalvation. If an explicit knowledge of theſe things, and a practice flowing from faith and love, be the ordinary and eſtabliſhed methods of Salvation, either this knowledge muſt be obtained in "Ages to come," or by far the greateſt

part

part of mankind muſt be ſaved without it, or damned for want of it; either of which Propoſitions let him believe who can!

As the Goſpel in itſelf is ſo great a bleſſing, what can unbiaſſed reaſon object to the whole world enjoying it? Inſtead of militating againſt, do not the harmony of divine attributes, and the impartial conſiſtency of the ways of Providence, ſtrongly plead for it? Surely we ought not to meaſure the mind of our Maker by our own imperfect and contracted conceptions! Univerſal Love and equal Juſtice are the two Pillars of Impartiality. The contrary appeared to be the foundation of the Jewiſh *Peculium*. Partial favours ſeemed to be diſtributed among them with ſo liberal a hand, that he that runs may read them in almoſt every page of their early hiſtory. Yet, after ſo many Ages had elapſed, and inſtances of apparent partiality in their favour, the myſtery at length unfolded, and the out-pouring of the ſpirit upon a few Gentile-converts convinced even Peter himſelf, "That God is no Reſpecter of Perſons."

That this is a truth, none but ſuch bigots as Peter was can call in queſtion. But who can demonſtrate it from that part of the plan of Providence hitherto purſued? Could we comprehend the whole of this Plan, all the ways of the Lord would appear equal and juſt in the eyes of every one. This, at the preſent, is far enough from being the caſe; but it is becauſe we ſee not the whole of it. When this appears, the rectitude of the divine nature, and his equal diſtribution of Juſtice and Mercy, will appear in the execution of every part of that important Plan. There will be no jarring diſcords in the whole piece: Thoſe parts which ſeemed to be moſt exceptionable, will all accord in the harmony, heighten the muſic, and accent the Praiſes of the grand Performer.

Before we draw conclusions derogatory to the Deity—conclusions that mutilate his mercy—arraign his justice—contract and concentre his love to a few objects—shade the bright beams of universal benevolence and essential goodness—even case with steel the heart of our common Parent against the far greatest part of his offspring—and deny him to possess that paternal compassion and sympathetic tenderness which his hand planted in our nature; before we thus judge the Judge of all the earth, and pass sentence upon Him who will sentence us all, we ought to be very certain that we have infallible Authority from Himself for so doing; lest, while we think that we are doing God service, our ignorance should occasion us to fight against Him; and, under the colour of vindicating His absolute Sovereignty, we act vindictively against those amiable attributes that are the glory of his nature, the dignity of his throne, the reasons and motives of our creation, and the very basis of His natural and moral Government of the world.

If an Angel from heaven taught doctrines whose visible tendency gravitated towards such a centre, the principles of reason and natural religion forbid us to wish him success. Reason in a moment subscribes to this divine axiom, *God is Love*. This is the fountain from which all creation flowed. This is the foundation of every rational creature's hope—the ground and basis of moral Government. Justice itself owes its existence to Love. What is the very essence of Justice but that inviolable love of giving every thing its due? Every divine attribute that Reason discovers, or Revelation reveals, most perfectly harmonizes with Love. He that loveth is born of God—knoweth God—dwelleth in God, and God in him. This is the epitome of all religion—the pinnacle of holiness—the sum of happiness—and a degree of heaven upon earth.

How

How far ſome of our commonly-received ſyſtems of religion are reconcilable with this eſſential principle, let others judge. When the laſt link of the golden chain of grace and providence appears, it will diſcover that Love united every link together—runs through the whole Piece from the beginning to the end, as the woof through the warp. This will unriddle the greateſt Ænigmas—untie every Gordian knot—unfold every myſtery in the manifold Wiſdom of God—level what now appears inſurmountable difficulties with human capacities—

" Aſſert eternal Providence,
" And juſtify the ways of God to men."

Phil. I incline to think, that the ſurveying the immenſe works of Creation—Redemption—and Providence—diving into the depths—ſoaring up to the heights—and endeavouring to find the bounds, tracing, as we paſs, the footſteps of infinite wiſdom, love, and goodneſs, will conſtitute no inconſiderable part of our heavenly employment.

Didas. That ſeems to admit of no doubt. As the profoundeſt myſteries in Revelation will be then unfolded, and the divine conduct in every age vindicated, ſo love will be read in every line, and found to breathe in every page of divine inſpiration. Matters of the greateſt moment, God uſually opens up at ſundry times and in divers manners. But every ſcene, even where ſeverity at the firſt ſight appears in the grand Drama, diſplays new diſcoveries of parental Kindneſs and divine Philanthropy. Did the complicated wickedneſs of a whole world at once unſheath and whet the ſword of divine Juſtice? Muſt her ſcales, ſuſpended in the hands of heaven, weigh at once a world of wickedneſs? Does the Judge of all the earth, when the laws of divine œconomy require, ſolemnly folemnly proceed to denounce a fentence of death, to drown a world of Animals at once? Whether fhall we moft admire, the parental tendernefs of the Judge, or the Juftice of the Sentence?

While the heavy hand of Juftice waits to execute the juft decree, the heart of the Judge relents: Hearken, my dear Phil. to what the pen of infpiration has recorded—"It repented the Lord that he had made man, and *it grieved him to the heart.*" And as the determined mode of Punifhment neceffarily involved Fowls, Cattle, and Creeping Things in the common ruin, the tender mercies of their Maker moft fenfibly felt for his devoted creatures; and, as if he had done wrong in creating them, movingly cried, "It Repenteth me that I have made them," *Gen.* vi. 6, 7. How was it poffible for Juftice to pronounce the world's doom attended with more tendernefs or more divine compaffion?

Phil. Has it not been fuppofed by many, that our Saviour, in the interval between his death and refurrection, went and preached unto thofe fpirits, who had lived in the antediluvian world, in *Hades?*

Didas. "It is plain, that the moft ancient chriftians, whofe books are left, do generally, if not without exception, expound this Text, (1 *Pet.* iii. 18, 20.) and that in *Chap.* iv. 6. of Chrift, during the Time that his body lay in the grave, going into the ftate (or place) of the dead, and preaching there to the fpirits of the men of the old world; *Hermas*, *Irenæus*, *Clem. Alexandrinus*, *&c.* and *Ocumenius* in his Prologue to this Epiftle, &c." As the earlieft and pureft antiquity immediately following the Apoftle's days unanimoufly thus underftood it, and as other expofitions appear unfatisfactory, Proteftants might admit it without the leaft fear of inferring a Popifh Purgatory. There is no fimilarity between them. If, according to our Creed,

Creed, our Saviour descended into Hell, upon what better Errand could he go, than to spoil Principalities and Powers—Preach deliverance to the Captives, having first raised them from the dead, as he did those many Saints St. Matthew mentions. If he actually visited these repositories of departed spirits, it could not be to finish his penal sufferings, for they most certainly expired with him upon the cross.

Phil. This supposition seems rather to be countenanced than condemned, by the melting tenderness of the Judge that punished them.

Didas. Most certainly it does. But did not the same compassionate heart reside in the breast of the blessed Jesus—transpire in the sighs and tears of Emmanuel, when he gave up his once highly-favoured people to hardness of heart and a judicial blindness, to continue for ages, and only to be cured by a sight of Himself coming in clouds! *Luk.* xix. 41, 45. Here the inspired Penman has pourtrayed the Picture of his heart, and, in lines taken from the life, exhibited those tender mercies which are over all his works. Where does an implacable vindictive spirit breathe in his language, or appear in his attitude? Who that reads it can possibly believe, that such a heart can have any "Pleasure in the (second) death of him that dieth?"

Though, therefore, the Wisdom and Justice of divine Providence required such coercive measures and penal sufferings to be inflicted upon the old world, to warn the present to beware of its wickedness—and the awful destruction of the body of that nation from whom himself derived his humanity, for unbelief to be cut off, as a warning to others not to deny the Lord who bought them; yet, in the former case, we have already heard of the probable tenders of mercy made to those very

 sinners

finners by a triumphant Saviour in a future ftate, after a reunion of body and foul; and with regard to the latter, though it is indeed a very myfterious conduct of Providence, yet it is fuch as St. Paul would by no means have us to be ignorant of. While the Jewifh *Peculium* continued, and the partition-wall, erected by the hand of heaven, ftood firm, the Gentiles were as great ftrangers to the God of Ifrael, as Ifrael has fince been to the Meffiah. But foon after the times of the Gentiles expire, the Deliverer will come out of Zion, and turn away ungodlinefs from Jacob. At that glorious period, all Ifrael will be faved.

This œconomy of Providence will be fo furprifing when exhibited upon the ftage of Time, that, could we comprehend that Myftery as clearly as St. Paul, we fhould equally acknowledge both the wifdom and knowledge of God, as therein moft richly difplayed; and, in aftonifhment with him, cry out, "O the depth!" When the apologue of the whole drama is heard, "Of him, and through him, and to him," will be the univerfal Plaudit of every rational creature; nor is it poffible, when fully known, that it fhould be otherwife.

The fum of this myftery is the caufe and the cafe of the prefent partial blindnefs of Ifrael—the time of its continuance—and its final iffue in their future Salvation. This iffue, befides the promifes made unto them, the Apoftle concludes from the following grounds: 1ft. If the firft-fruit be holy, the lump or whole crop is holy. But the firft-fruits were holy, Ergo. 2nd. If the root be holy, fo are the branches: But the root was holy, Ergo. 3rd. As touching the Elect, fuch as were then converted, were beloved for the Father's fake: And will not the reft, except the final obftinate unbeliever, be beloved for Chrift's fake? Such an an entail of Love was exactly agreeable to *Exod.* xx. 6. And it ſtands upon this foundation—That the Gifts and Calling of God are without Repentance. For God to give and confer national favours, and then retract them, would evidence a mutability in his diſpenſations by no means comporting with the immutability of his nature, and certainly reflect upon his infinite wiſdom.

If, then, the Apoſtle infers the future call, converſion, and ſalvation of that part of Iſrael that was blinded—cut off—and that to make way for the engraffing of the Gentiles into their ſtock, upon the preceding grounds, will not the like grounds afford ſimilar concluſions in favour of the Gentiles in future? Under the Moſaical Diſpenſation, the Jew had *much* advantage every way over the Gentile; ſince the Apoſtles' days, ſome Gentiles have had as much over the Jews. In future, the Jews will again gain the advantage, and the Kingdom of a divine Theocracy will be reſtored to Iſrael, as before the days of Saul, until the whole œconomy of Government ſhall iſſue in One Shepherd, One Flock, and One Fold! The Lord alone will be exalted in that day!

Phil. But my dear Didas, are not the Gentile-nations as much beloved for Chriſt's ſake, as the Jews for the ſake of their Fathers? If the Gifts and Calling of God be without Repentance towards one People, why not equally towards another? In both caſes, they equally ſpring from free Grace. What is there in God, or what in one man or nation of men above another, to induce the common Father of all always to diſtribute his favours with a partial hand?

Didas. What indeed! 'Tis true he has an unalienable right to do what he will with his own. But, as his own univerſal benevolence diſcovered, and flowing through the univerſal Mediation of Chriſt

Chrift in behalf of all men, are the fole fountains of every bleffing, when, where, or upon whom, or by whatever channels conveyed, fo we have reafon to believe, that among mankind the objects will be univerfal alfo. Every circumftance of time, place, manner of beftowing, &c. muft and ought to be left to his fovereign will, which is always influenced by infinite goodnefs, and fuperior wifdom which can never err.

The world was upwards of two thoufand years old when it pleafed the Almighty, in purfuance of his wife defigns, to call Abram alone and blefs him. To him was the original Promife renewed, but limited to his iffue by Sarah. *Judah*, the fon of Jacob, was the Patriarch in whofe Tribe the World's Redeemer defcended. In lefs than other two thoufand years, the Defire of all nations appeared in the likenefs of finful flefh, and by the Sacrifice of Himfelf in that nature, for ever abolifhed every other fin-offering. It was at that important period when the election of one people in preference to another firft began, which for wife reafons has continued ever fince.

This long promifed Seed, the Saviour of the world, had a two-fold Character to fuftain, which implied a two-fold coming. This double Advent, in very different forms, caft a vail of confiderable thicknefs about his Perfon. With this, his real glory was fo fhaded, that when he came to his own, they knew him not—they received him not. A man of forrows and acquainted with grief, by no means comported with their received fentiments of a Son of David, a King of Ifrael. His latter appearing, as yet in future, being by the Prophets defcribed in very pompous and poetic language, and their moft conquering and exalted Princes being well known types of their Meffiah, their carnal eyes dazzled with thefe fplendid defcriptions,

their

their fancies alſo dreaming about the perpetuity of the moſaic rites and ſacrifices, they utterly rejected him when he firſt came as a devoted ſin-offering. His gracious tenders of a ſpiritual Salvation they utterly refuſed: And by procuring the crucifixion of their long-expected Meſſiah—reſiſting the external evidences and internal impulſes of the Holy Spirit—and adding Perſecution of his goſpel, both its Preachers and Profeſſors every where—they brought upon themſelves the guilt of that very blood which was ſhed for the remiſſion of their ſins, and the ſins of the whole world.

In conſequence of theſe things, a very great and ſudden change in the diſpenſations of Heaven took place in the world. The Myſtery, that from the beginning had been hid in God, began to unfold. The Jews, as a body, were cut off from their own Olive Tree for obſtinate unbelief; and the Gentiles, merely by free Grace, were adopted or engraffed in their room. Thus were the ſcales fairly turned. And the Jews, as a nation, became as utter ſtrangers to their own Meſſiah, as the Gentiles had formerly been to the God of Iſrael. From that time to this, the currents of divine favours have, for the moſt part, flowed through Gentile-nations, while Iſrael has been left like the barren heath in the deſert.

The ſuddenneſs of theſe great events, and the effects that followed, were, I doubt not, as much unlooked for, and as ſurpriſing both to Jew and Gentile of that age, as the Preaching of the everlaſting Goſpel to the raiſed Gentiles, &c. probably will be. To me it appears plain, that, were all the Bible-Prophecies rightly and fully underſtood, they would be found fuller and more in point, with reſpect to the future, than the preceding event.

Why ſhould our ignorant contracted conceptions ſet bounds to the immenſity of divine benevolence?

Why

Why draw, within our narrow compaſs, the extenſive deſigns towards the Children of our common Parent? What either reaſon or religion can there poſſibly be, in not allowing to the Father of Mercies to poſſeſs as much and as tender compaſſion for all his offspring as we do for ours? Pauſe, my dear Phil. pauſe for a moment: Conſider; will the divine Philanthropy, and the eſſential love and goodneſs of God, refuſe their voluntary ſuffrage in favour of this benevolent ſuppoſition? According to revealed diſcoveries of the Deity, can you conceive infinite wiſdom refuſing to contrive—infinite goodneſs to admit of—or infinite power to execute ſuch a laudable Plan? Do not the dignity and honour of the Deity, and the infinite Merit of the Redeemer, render it neceſſary, in order to ſhine conſiſtently in all their glorious ſplendors? What can Juſtice, however ſtern or rigid, fairly alledge againſt it, if it be true, That God laid upon him the iniquity of us all—that he himſelf bare our ſins in his own body upon the Tree—and is, in conſequence, the Lamb of God that *beareth* away the SIN OF THE WORLD?

If, by his ſufferings, Juſtice has received ſatisfactory recompenſe for all the repeated affronts and indignant injuries that ſin and ſinners have done to it, and thereby affronted Heaven; what inſuperable difficulty can be ſuppoſed, that will render it neceſſarily impoſſible? Does not the importance of the ſubject plead ſtrongly in its favour, as the eternal ſalvation of hundreds of millions of Immortals are concerned in it?

If there be Joy in Heaven over *one* ſinner that repenteth, what tranſports of joy and tides of pleaſure muſt overflow thoſe heavenly happy ſpirits upon ſuch an occaſion!

Let us for a moment ſuppoſe, that Providence had ſent us into the moſt barbarous parts of the world

world—to receive the first notice of immortality by finding ourselves in *Hades* immortal—being both here and hereafter for ever debarred from hearing the gospel, or enjoying Gospel-privileges—What idea could we entertain of the amiable attributes of God—of the all sufficient merits of Christ—or the rectitude of a governing Providence—when we had found ourselves in life abandoned to invincible ignorance, and at our death doomed to endless sufferings? The supposition above affords us a hope for a Hottentot; and that in future, the scales of providential favours may be turned towards them in opportunities superior to what we now enjoy; seeing that all the Dispensations of Heaven advance from darker to brighter, from less to more glorious. And can humanity object to this?

If the scriptures are not so explicit on this head as some others, we need not wonder at it. Our Saviour informed his disciples, that he had many things to say to them, which, while he lived, they were not able to bear: But when, by many infallible Proofs, he had shewed himself alive after his passion, we may reasonably suppose, that in the space of those forty days in which he frequently conversed with his disciples, "Speaking of the Things that pertain to the kingdom of God," and though no particulars are related, notwithstanding it is very probable that the extent of it—its subjects—how to be governed—what the nature of its government, politically considered, would be—the principal Persons to be employed under him in that divine government—its privileges—its duration, &c. &c. would be the subjects of conversation in that considerable time for information therein. *See Acts* i. 1, 8.

So far as I can perceive, Promises may extend into Eternity, but Prophecies must terminate in Time.

Time. Prophecies are a Revelation of the ſecret purpoſes of God, who, as the Sovereign of the Univerſe, ſees and calls the end from the beginning. His divine Preſcience ſaw all the events and iſſues of Time before its commencement; therefore not only all the evils of the Fall, but how to provide the moſt ſalutary and ample remedies. That Omniſcience which at one glance compriſes every latent Cauſe, and every poſſible Conſequence reſulting from it, however diſtant in time or place. The abſolute Perfection of his knowledge admits of no limitation from what are called caſual or fortuitous events. The ſpontaneous actions of free Agents, with all their minuteſt circumſtances, are previouſly known to Him. To ſuppoſe otherwiſe, as ſome do, is to ſuppoſe that the creatures he has made have ſet bounds to theſe very Perfections they were intended to illuſtrate, and thus to defeat his original deſign by the very means made uſe of to promote it.

To have created human nature immutable, without option, and impeccable, would have been to make engines of Providence, but not voluntary ſubjects of moral government: Their actions would have been neceſſary, and therefore the agents not accountable. Upon ſuch a ſuppoſition, neither virtue nor vice could have had any exiſtence, nor conſequently Rewards and Puniſhments. This would have precluded the neceſſity both of Promiſes and Prophecies. What kind of Theatre would the world have been in ſuch a caſe? What would infinite love and goodneſs have had to diſplay their inimitable Glories in, except a world of Puppets, influenced by ſecret and inviſible ſprings? What contracted intellects! How incapable of happineſs, and advancement in it!

As

As the caſe now ſtands, how widely different! How much more eligible! The various and ſucceſſive periods of Time, producing ſuch a ſeries of events, only to be comprehended by an infinite Mind; yet the parts, and actors through the aſtoniſhing Piece, in their principal characters, propheſied of ſome of them many thouſands of years before their introduction upon the ſtage! Many of theſe Prophecies, yea the principal of them, wait a future accompliſhment; ſome of which will not be fulfilled till a long ſeries of Ages have run their deſtined rounds.

As infinite Wiſdom concerted, omnipotent Power and Grace will effect and finiſh the God-like deſign. Satanical wiſdom will then appear folly— Helliſh and tyrannical Uſurpations, ſubſiſting here only for a time, muſt very rapidly give way to the equitable, mild, and gracious Government of the Son of God. Then a world of Miſeries will vaniſh from the face of the Earth. The happy days that ſucceed will demonſtrate, that the whole concerted ſcheme of Creation, Redemption, and Providence, are worthy of him by whom are all Things, and for whom are all Things.

DIALOGUE XI.

Philotheos. MY dear Didafcalos, I have frequently bemoaned the narrow contracted fyftems of Divinity commonly received among us. But it is certainly our bounden duty, fo foon as we perceive our error, to abandon it; and at any rate to buy the Truth, coft what it will, and to fell it not, whatever price may be obtained for it.

Didas. True. But few, I fear, are humble and candid enough to do this. To conquer the prejudices of education—relinquifh plaufible favourite fentiments—fentiments fanctioned by time—efpecially when great and good men, and bodies of men, have formed them into Articles of Faith, &c. Many, rather than be at the pains thoroughly to inveftigate the fubject, will tread in the track of their predeceffors, purfuing the line of their fyftem however eccentric, without any fear of it's leading them from the line of Truth.

"That to have mercy upon all—that Chrift died for all—gave himfelf a ranfome for all—muft only mean a very few at the moft, though fome of *all Sorts*." Do not fuch gloffes as thefe, "Mould the Scriptures into a nofe of wax," fuited to every fentiment, by which any thing or nothing may be proved at pleafure, as Cardinal Cajetan told John Calvin.

Phil. Moft certainly they do. Neverthelefs, the fenfe of fcripture muft be uniform and confiftent with itfelf, being all dictated by one fpirit. The literal fenfe ought to be followed, unlefs fome abfurdity, oppofition to fome plain paffage, the evident fcope of the writer, or the like caufe forbid it, as I think every one will, at leaft ought to allow.

Didas.

Didas. They were written in languages God gave unto mankind, and certainly contain a true, full, and necessary Revelation of his will. But if, when He plainly says one thing, we, in conformity to our system, suppose that He means another, how may his will be known by his written words?

Thus the Son of God informs us of his errand into the world, and who can suppose that he would give us wrong information? "God sent not his Son into the world to condemn the world," altho' He is the appointed Judge of it. But how shall we reconcile this negative design with the positive effects, if it be true that but few will be benefited in the issue? To annihilate them, is to condemn them, whether Infants, as Dr. Watts seemed to suppose; or Adults, as hundreds have done, in order to avoid the more dreadful consequence of dooming them to a hell, which a resurrection, the consequence of his coming, capacitates them for. He adds, "But that the world through him might be saved." And hence his Title is, "The Saviour of the World," *Joh.* iv. 42. But it seems that this Title stands for almost a nullity, if the World will not be saved through him. I ask, how is it possible for his Title to be valid as the Saviour of the world; or, how could the world ever possibly be saved *through him*, or one tenth part of it, upon any other hypothesis than the above, without running into the greatest absurdities?

"The Son of Man came to seek and to save that which was lost." But were the lost sheep of the house of Israel lost alone? Were not the sheep of every house or family under heaven lost? If he came to *seek* them, what place is there in the vast sheep-walk of the earth, in which millions may lie and perish and he not find them? But if he finds them either *on* the earth or *in* the earth, is he unable or unwilling to save them, although

he

he seeks them on purpose? In either case, what sort of Shepherd or Bishop of Souls must he be? Surely not a Hireling that careth not for the sheep. His office is to *seek* and to *save* that which is lost, but all mankind have gone astray and are lost, Ergo. After all, shall the far greatest part be for ever lost? How then does he execute his office?

Christ humbled himself—made himself of no reputation—became obedient unto the death of the Cross in the Form of a Slave—wherefore God hath highly exalted him, and given him a Name which is above every Name: That at the name of Jesus every knee, in heaven, in earth, and under the earth, should bow—that every tongue, in heaven, in earth, and under the earth, should confess, that Jesus Christ IS LORD, to the Glory of God the Father, *Phil.* ii. 7, 11.

1. Where has this Lord any other Dominions than in heaven, in earth, and under the earth?

2. Throughout this vast Domain, Christ is Crowned Lord of All!

3. But Christ the Lord is also *Jesus*, a Restorer, a Deliverer, a Saviour. A Name which is *above* every Name. A Name, to which every knee must bow, in token of Submission and Obedience; while every tongue, as well as every bended knee, shall confess, openly and verbally acknowledge, that Jesus Christ is LORD of every thing, both Place and Person—Heathens, Jews, Christians, &c. I ask,

1. If now we make the enquiry, How many Persons, upon their bended knees, will be hardy enough to say, "we will not have THIS MAN to Rule over us?" Reason will answer, dare any, except devils, tell Him so to his Face? Will there be any then who would not rather kiss him?

2. If *every tongue* must confess him to be Lord, I appeal again to reason—Is it not to be *their* Lord,

Lord, *their* Governor? If any should say no,

3. Is not this a flat denial of the Text? If every tongue must confess, how many will be silent? Or will there be any feigned hypocritical confessions then and there? Or if there should be supposed to exist either feigned Submissions or Confessions, would such be "to the Glory of God the Father?" What Glory can redound to the Father of all, or to the Lord and Governor of all, from such feigned pretensions to obedience, &c.? As such could not pass without Detection, it is evident they argue no small degree of submission unto that exalted LORD of All!

Can reason suppose, that in "Ages to come," coercive measures alone will produce such Confessions and Submissions? If so, why should they not as well be used here also, as hereafter? But would coercion, without Grace, produce Voluntary Submissions in rational creatures? If not, will Grace be conferred without the proper Means of Grace? Is not the foundation of the Dominion of Emmanuel here laid in his voluntary obedience and sufferings? How can *these* foundation truths ever be known in Heaven, in Earth, and under the Earth, without being publicly preached there? Is there not reason to believe, that then and there, as well as now and here, Faith will come by Hearing, and that Faith will work by love, so as to produce the Submissions and Confessions mentioned in the Text? As this will take place in Ages to come, or in Christ's proper Seasons, so is it not that Testimony then to be produced, "That he gave himself a Ransome for All, &c." that will effect this grand design of God the Father, redounding so much to his own Honour and Glory, thro' that of his Son? And now let reason and scripture say whether these were not the ultimate Ends of Creation, Redemption, and Providence.

To compaſs theſe ends, as a part of the vaſt Deſign, St. Paul informs us of an Apoſtolical Adage, "This is a faithful ſaying, and worthy of all acceptation, that Chriſt Jeſus came into the World to ſave Sinners," 1 *Tim.* i. 15. In what age or part of the world will you find any ſinners excluded from this grand Deſign, obſtinate Unbelievers excepted? All mankind are ſinners. And did our Saviour ſo far miſs of the end of his coming into the world as only to ſave a comparative few? If this is a faithful ſaying, why is it credited by ſo few? It ſeems that either St. Paul, or thoſe who diſcredit it, muſt have been miſtaken, as he ſpeaks of ſinners indefinitely. If it be "Worthy of all acceptation," ſurely that worth only wants to be known, in order to gain it a General Acceptance! But can either the important Fact, its Faithfulneſs, or eminent Worth be known to ſinners, unleſs by teaching? But muſt not theſe leſſons either be taught in a future ſtate, or not at all, to by far the greateſt number of ſinners? And do not their Salvation depend upon hearing them, and believing? Elſe, how can they be condemned for not believing?

Again, St. John informs us, that "For this Purpoſe the Son of God was manifeſted," viz. in the Fleſh, "that he might deſtroy the Works of the Devil," 1 *Joh.* iii. 8. But to deceive and deſtroy mankind is the end of all the Devil's Works. Let Reaſon, guided by Scripture—Prophecies and Promiſes, in the iſſue, when the Son of God has executed his Purpoſe, produce a ſchedule of the Devil's works that will be undeſtroyed; or patiently wait to ſee the Deſtruction that He will make. What! will this Purpoſe miſcarry in four parts out of five? If it does, to what cauſe will you attribute it? Whether is the Son of God or the Devil poſſeſt of the greater abilities, the one to

erect

erect works, or the other to destroy them? and when destroyed, build up better out of the ruins? Will not Sin, Death, and Hades, be destroyed? Will not the Devil himself be taken, chained, imprisoned, and finally executed, in the burning Lake? After all, take the whole of Mankind, shall hell have ten, or even two for one? Reason forbids it—Humanity recoils at the thought—and who can press Revelation into their service, to prove the affirmative, with consistency?

Phil. But does not our Saviour decide the affirmative, when he informs us, that few are chosen—few enter in at the strait gate?

Didas. His Authority would be decisive, if it could be proved that he speaks absolutely *of all Mankind in every Age.* But who will undertake the task? He who would be hardy enough, almost every page in the Bible would confront and confute him: The first Promise, (*Gen.* iii. 15.) leads the Van, and is followed by an invincible Army of Arguments drawn out of the main body of scripture prophecies, promises, types, assertions, invitations, &c. which all the arts of Criticism and Wit, in league together, can never vanquish or drive from the field of conquest.—Great is Truth, and will prevail! With respect to his own People, in the time of his public Ministry, these were notorious Facts; which, in a great degree, have existed hitherto, even where christianity has been publicly professed. But in his own Times, the Tables will be turned—the Beast and false Prophet destroyed—the Devil bound—and the Lord alone exalted. Happy change! Christianity, in all its life and purity, will then gain the ascendant, while iniquity will be sought for and not found. The ends of the earth shall see his great Salvation!

Phil. Say, my dear Didas, does that sentence, (*Gen.* iii. 15.) past upon the Old Serpent, regard the

the Devil Perſonally, or his conqueſt of Mankind; and his uſurped Government over them principally?

Didas. Both, beyond all diſpute. His Headſhip over mankind, principally; to cut off which, and recover mankind unto an union with Himſelf, was and is the grand deſign of the Son of God. But how greatly muſt this deſign fail in its execution, upon the Plan of our common ſyſtems of divinity? If, from the Creation to the ultimate end of time, only *a few were choſen, &c.* would not our Saviour's undertaking be rendered futile and vain, in ſo far as hell would be abundantly more peopled with mankind than heaven; and the Devil's Headſhip or Government ſo far from being overthrown, that, in fact, it would be eſtabliſhed for ever? And, upon this ſuppoſition, how would the Devil triumph over Chriſt—Sin over Grace—the Second Death over Eternal Life—And, in one word, how would Hell triumph over Heaven! Doctrines that infer ſuch conſequences, can by no means be reconciled with the authority and deſign of the Woman's Seed. If the hypotheſis, here contended for, be admitted, every difficulty vaniſhes in a moment; and if any can advance one ſuperior to it, I ſhould greatly rejoice and thank them.

Did not St. Peter underſtand the will of his Maſter? He informs us, that "He is not willing that any ſhould Periſh, but that all ſhould come to Repentance," 2 *Pet.* iii. 9. If this be true, then it follows, that all thoſe who do periſh, periſh contrary to the will of Chriſt. His will, on the contrary, is, "That all ſhould come to Repentance." Will not Chriſt, whoſe authoritative Office it is to give Repentance, afford grace, means, time, and opportunity, that all may come to Repentance, ſo agreeable to his will, ſo neceſſary to a proper diſcharge of his Office, and to human happineſs?

But,

But, in fact, is this grace, these means of grace, together with proper opportunities of improving them, afforded in this life to any but a very small proportion of mankind? If not, then certainly they will in the Ages to come. But how can this be, unless they Rise again to enjoy them, or else enjoy them in *Hades?*

If such be his Will, and such the salutary ends of our Saviour's coming into the world; and after all, this Will, and these Ends be defeated; there must a sufficient cause lodge somewhere. This cause cannot originate in the Will of God—the want of an All-sufficiency in Christ's Person—Offices—Merits—Grace and Good-will—the Operations of the Holy Spirit—or, lastly, in any incapacity in human Nature, or absolute diabolical Cunning and uncontrollable Power of the Devil over Mankind in general.

Phil. But as man is a free agent, does not the true cause originate in the Option, Ignorance, and Obstinacy of the human Mind and Will—in the influence of his Passions—and their almost insuperable attachments to objects of time and sense?

Didas. No doubt these, and such as these, are the proper causes assignable for such a supposed dreadful event. But in this case, have we no reason to believe, that infinite goodness will excite, infinite wisdom contrive, and infinite grace, power, and providence, provide and execute such means and measures as may be sufficient to reduce the most obstinate Rebels in future, without exerting such a force as shall effectually destroy their free agency? He who made the human mind, is he void of, or can he find no key to suit its most intricate wards, and open every lock in the House of David, without ruining or destroying it? When He employs his cords of Love, and human Bands, sweetly and secretly to draw; where is that sinner,

except

except in Hell, that will not, cannot feel the divine attraction, even as the needle does the magnetic loadstone? Will not this in fact be the case in future?

"Thy People shall be Willing in the *Day of thy Power*;" that is, when our Lord Jesus Christ, "*in His own Times*, shall shew, who is the blessed and only Potentate, the King of kings, and Lord of lords," 1 *Tim*. vi. 14, 15, 16. The Heathen will then be his willing People, his Inheritance. The womb of the morning will then bring forth the bright and morning Star, (*Rev.* xxii. 16.) and this will usher in *Hemeran Aionos*, (2 *Pet.* iii. 18.) a glorious *Aionian Day*, such as the world has yet never seen. Christ's willing People will cover the face of the earth, and vie in number with the drops of pearly dew, *Psa*. cx. 3. Glorious morning this! and glorious will be the day, or following Season of Grace, to all the world of Mankind!

Hitherto we only have had the first fruits, the harvest will then commence, and "A nation be born in a day." "The Ends of the Earth shall see the Salvation of God; and all shall know Him from the least unto the greatest." The Jewish High Priest prophesied, that Jesus should die for that Nation, and not for that nation only, but that also, He should gather together in One, the children of God that were scattered abroad. Is not God the Father of the spirits of all flesh? Ought we not then to take this last clause, *Pro singulis hominibus omnium generum*, for every individual of human kind? What is this gathering together *in one*, but the same with St. Paul's reheading of all Things in Christ in the fulness of Times, as is above observed? At which time, Christ will be confessed the Head over All to His Body the Church, which is His FULNESS.

This

This is the good pleasure of God—this is his original Purpose, to Restore all Things in Christ, the Second Adam, after the First had fallen, and all things into confusion with him. With a view to this, God, in all ages, has gradually gathered a few out of the general Mass of Mankind, more or less, according to the Dispensations they were under. And herein a vast variety of circumstances must naturally occur, far above the foresight or comprehension of mortals: Such as to Elect certain Persons and Nations, for Ages together, and to confer upon them extra and peculiar privileges; while others, in comparison, seemed to be abandoned by their Maker in no small degree. But notwithstanding these present unfavourable appearances, they all of them are, in reality, no other than so many parts of a great and glorious Plan, drawn in the Mind of that omnipotent and omniscient Workman, who worketh All Things according to the Counsel of his own Will, which Will is holy, just, and good. The principal parts of this Plan are hid from the wicked, who, at the present, shall not understand, but the wise will understand (*Dan.* xii. 10.) so much of it, as at the present may conduce to their comfort and edification in Faith, Hope, and Love: The rest are vailed in futurity, and shaded in Prophecies, Promises, and Types. These, in Christ's proper Seasons, will all be fully exhibited by a pointed and circumstantial accomplishment, to the Praise of the Glory of His GRACE, who will, I doubt not, accept the far greatest part of Mankind in the Beloved, at the grand close and winding up of all things, by Grace through Faith.

Phil. Pray, my dear Didas. does not the Prophet Ezekiel touch upon this Subject at this very season, in the xlviith Chapter of his Prophesy?

Didas. This is certain, that the last thirteen Chapters

Chapters of his Prophesy have never to this day had their proper accomplishment. The important events therein contained are reserved for Christ's own Times or Seasons. The passage you refer to, belongs to the first of these Times, before the Ages of Ages, but includes them also. The subject of this Chapter and the following, is partly the same with that in *Rev.* xx, xxi, xxii, in some great measure. I shall select a few passages to my present purpose, respecting all those ages, in what follows.

I. The City of Ezekiel is exactly four-square. It has three Gates on every side, equi-distant one from another. These Gates are for the twelve Tribes of the Children of Israel, three on every side, one peculiar to each Tribe. This City will be founded on the present earth, at the beginning of the Millennium; and, according to its name, JEHOVAH SHAMMA, or JEHOVAH IS THERE, will be the Metropolis of the Kingdom when it is Restored to Israel—the Royal Residence of Christ in his Kingdom, when he will Reign with his Ancients gloriously; and which he will leave his Saints and Elders in Possession of, together with the Camp around it, when he returns to Heaven at the End of the Millennium, or *Sabbatismos*, properly so called.

But here my dear Phil. may observe, that as Moses left the seventh day unlimited, never saying that the "Evening and the Morning were the seventh day," as he had said of all the former six days; so in like manner this Sabbatismos is not, strictly speaking, limited within the bounds of the Millennium, but extends throughout all the Time of Satan's little Season, until the descent of Christ to Create all Things new. This is the very City that Satan intended to storm with his Gog—Magog Army. It is not the very identical City with the New

New Jerusalem, for that will be situated on the New earth, (posterior to this in Time and superior to this in glorious Privileges) nevertheless modeled much in the same manner, of a quadrangular form, yet cubical, and immensely more rich in its materials.

II. Ezekiel's City, &c. belongs equally to the Times of the Restitution of all Things, but to the more early of those Times than St. John's City. Hence in some things they exactly agree, though in others they differ. And wherein they differ, the latter always exceeds the former. Restoration advances from lesser to greater degrees of Glory. St. John exhibits Restitution in its last Times, and advances it to the summit of Perfection in Time— the next step will be into the Glories of Eternity, properly so called; the happiness, glory, and duration of which, beggar all description, but will most assuredly succeed the Son's surrendering up the Kingdom to the Father, when the "Constituted Ages" end with the *Sæcula Sæculorum*, and God will be *all in all!*

Phil. Alas! what is Time, when drawn out to its utmost length in the Ages of Ages, compared with Eternity? Not so much as a moment compared with a million of Ages! Never-ending Eternity! solemn, incomprehensible subject! Let us not be surprised, if the whole of Time be taken up, however long its line may prove, in properly preparing subjects for such an endless duration, and almost an infinite degree of happiness and honour!

But pray, my dear Didas, what is Ezekiel's Holy Water which issued out from under the threshold of the House, and increased in depth in proportion to its distance from the fountain? Is this the same with St. John's "Pure River of water of Life, clear as crystal, proceeding out of the Throne of God and the Lamb?"

 Didas.

Didas. It is the very fame when in its laft meafurement, unfordable, "a River to fwim in." I take Ezekiel's River myftically to intend the out-pouring of the fpirit from the time that he was firft given, after that Jefus was Glorified, (*Joh.* vii. 37. 40.) that is, from the day of Pentecoft, throughout all the "Ages to come," (*Eph.* ii. 7.) in which God will fhew the "Exceeding riches of his grace in his kindnefs toward all through Chrift Jefus," but more efpecially towards Gentile Nations, towards whom the Apoftle confidered God's kindnefs towards the Ephefians as a pattern.

Thefe Ages to come are *Tou Pleromatos ton Chairon*, the fulnefs of Times, (*Ibid* i. 10.) which, without difpute, extend to the end of all Time.

III. This Holy Water, emblem of the Holy Spirit, proceeding from the Father and the Son, or from the Throne of God and the Lamb, iffued from the right Side of the Sanctuary, and from that place the man began to meafure, *Ezek.* xlvii. 3, 4, 5. For the firft thoufand Cubits, the Waters were only ancle-deep. This may properly enough reprefent the prefent Gentile-Difpenfation, from Pentecoft to the commencement of the Millennium, by our Saviour's next advent. In this whole age, the Holy Spirit's extra operations lafted but a fmall time from his firft out-pouring; and ever fince, has flowed very fhallow, as all Church Hiftory evidences. The fecond fpace of a thoufand cubits, the increafing river was knee-deep: For at the next advent of Chrift, and the beginning of the Millennium, the Spirit of Grace and Supplication will be much more poured out upon the Jews, and the divine effufion will flow much farther, and the work of grace fink far deeper than it has done hitherto among the Gentiles. Thefe healing ftreams will heal their apoftafy and backflidings, yea every mental diforder; infomuch that "All Ifrael will then

then be saved." Yes, my friends, "Every thing shall *live* whither the River cometh." It will reach this present Desert Nation, and then "What shall the Receiving of them be but Life from the Dead?" *Rom.* xi. 15.

IV. The third space, being a thousand Cubits farther distant from the sacred Spring, "The Waters were to the Loins," being at the least double the former depth. In every Dispensation of Time, the farther distant from Pentecost, the more abundantly will the Holy Spirit flow from the holy Fount. In the little Season, from the loosing of Satan to the devouring of Gog and Magog, being the third Age from the days of the Apostles, these healing streams will restore Life and Health to the Gentile Nations; at which time, many of the glorious Promises respecting those Nations in particular will then be fulfilled, Satan in the mean time practising every possible art to delude them. But, however he may impose upon multitudes in the latter part of his limited Time, yet he will never be able to erect a Kingdom, like that of the Beast, to promote and support his interests in that age as he hitherto has done. On the contrary, "The kingdom and dominion, and the greatness of the kingdom *under the whole heaven*, shall be given to the People of the Saints of the Most High at the beginning of the Millennium; and at this Time, the Saints will Possess the Kingdom, and the twenty-four Elders will reign upon the Earth.

V. Upon the devouring of Gog and Magog, and casting of Satan into the burning Lake, the Ages of Ages commences, in which the Prophet beheld, that "The waters were risen, waters of swimming, a River that could not be passed over." This is the same with St. John's "Pure River of water of Life, clear as crystal, proceeding out of the Throne of God and the Lamb"—an unanswer-

able

able demonstration, that the Lamb was upon the Throne *with*, and had not as yet delivered the Kingdom up to the Father, and of course exists in Time.

Phil. But how far does St. John's River or Rivers run?

Didas. Ezekiel gives a pointed answer. "They go down into the Desert, and go into the Sea (of Sodom,) which being brought forth into the Sea, the waters shall be healed. And it shall come to pass, that every thing that liveth, (or that did formerly live) whithersoever the Rivers shall come, shall Live," (*ver.* 8, 9.) or be Restored unto Life. By these two Rivers, for so is the Hebrew, when they reach the Waters, or People, in the Desert, i. e. in the Time of Satan's little Season; and in the Dead Sea, or in the last of the Ages of Ages, "The Waters (or People) shall be *healed*; and there shall be a very great multitude of Fish, because these waters shall come thither; for they shall be healed," that is, the Waters, and the Fish in them. But if healed, it must be by receiving the spirit of a sound mind, by which these dead fish in the deadly waters of the Dead Sea shall be quickened and saved. Thus our Saviour intimated, saying, "It shall be more tolerable for Sodom, &c.

Can any Prophetical emblem, with greater propriety and plainness, set forth the immense multitudes of poor lost sinners, in number "As the Fish of the great sea, (the Mediterranean) exceeding many," (*ver.* 10.) all of which, by the life-giving streams of these Rivers, shall be Restored to Life, and finally saved?

Phil. But will there be any appointed Ordinances to catch these Fish?

Didas. Most certainly there will. The Prophet expresly informs us of Fishers who were to spread forth their Nets, in which they would catch fish according

according to their kinds, of all ſorts and ſizes, ſuch as are in the great Sea, *ver.* 10. Theſe Fiſhers, like our Saviour's Apoſtles, are "Fiſhers of Men:" Their nets are like the Apoſtles, and they *spread* them, (*ver.* 10) and catch Fiſh by preaching the Goſpel of the riches—the unſpeakable riches of Chriſt. And in theſe Ages, theſe Riches will be fully diſplayed, and will entirely unfold the "Myſtery of God," as you have heard above.

St. John informs us who theſe Fiſhers will be: "The Spirit and the Bride ſay, Come. And let him that *heareth*, (the Invitation of the Spirit and the Bride) ſay, Come. And let him that is athirſt, (are there any ſuch in Heaven?) Come! And whoſoever will, let him take the Water of Life Freely," *Rev.* xxii. 17. See more of this below.

Phil. My dear Didas. if this be not Preaching the Goſpel, I beg to be informed what is. But will theſe countleſs multitudes, as numerous as the Fiſhes of the great ſea, *all* be healed and live?

Didas. Yes. The Angel ſays expreſsly, that every thing ſhall Live whither the River cometh. The Sea is the world; the Fiſh are the People of Sodom, and other Heathen, &c. God and the Lamb are the Fountain; the Rivers that flow from this exhauſtleſs fountain is the Holy Spirit of Grace; theſe Rivers heal all the Fiſh in the Deſert and the Dead Sea; they alone can heal the world of Mankind, and the natural world; they alone can Reſtore or Recover both to that holy and happy ſtate, originally and ultimately intended by the great Creator for Mankind.

Theſe different ſpecies of Fiſh, and their multitude, point plainly enough at the different people, places, and foregoing ages, who never enjoyed the benefit of Revelation, the Goſpel, or Goſpel Ordinances, in this life. Perhaps the ſpecies of fiſh are not more numerous, or their ſpecified diffe-

 rences

rences greater, than thoſe that have ſubſiſted among mankind from Adam to the Time when this viſion will be fully accompliſhed.

Phil. Our Saviour told his Diſciples, that he would make them Fiſhers of Men. Do you think that he made any alluſion to Ezekiel's Fiſhermen?

Didas. It is highly probable, that the real Proprietor of theſe Fiſh, Fiſhermen, and Nets, intended his Conduct and Language to be the true Key to the viſion. God uſually works by inſtruments, and conveys Goſpel Grace by Goſpel Channels or Ordinances, eſpecially Preaching, becauſe "Faith comes by hearing, and hearing by the Word of God" Preached.

Phil. St. John had a viſion of Many Waters: Theſe the Angel interpreted to be "Peoples, and Multitudes, and Nations, and Tongues," *Rev.* xvii. 1, 15. Do you ſuppoſe that St. John's evangelical Interpreter alluded to Ezekiel's Waters?

Didas. Beyond doubt theſe Waters of the Apoſtle allude to one ſort of the Prophet's Waters. For the Prophet has two very different kinds of Water, which by no means muſt be confounded.

1. *A Sea of Waters* which wanted Healing, *ver.* 8. To theſe Waters St. John's Interpreter alluded; both mean Peoples, and Multitudes, and Nations, and Tongues. But thoſe of the Prophet vie with Fiſhes for number, in which they almoſt infinitely exceed St. John's, and take in a much larger ſpace.

2. The other Waters iſſued out of the Sanctuary, *ver.* 12. and flowed from the ſouth ſide of the Altar, *ver.* 1. Theſe laſt are the Waters meaſured by the Angel, which running into the Waters of the Sea, healed them.

Phil. Do you then ſuppoſe, that theſe Waters of the Sanctuary, running through the Deſert, and falling

falling into the Dead Sea, will finally heal, and save all mankind in the issue?

Didas. By no means. In this Wilderness, an irreversible Sentence is passed upon "*The Miry Places thereof and the Marshes thereof,*" which sentence is two-fold, 1st. "They shall not be *Healed*." 2nd. "They shall be given to Salt," *ver.* 11. The sanative waters of the Sanctuary never reach them.

Phil. And why so, think you?

Didas. Because the Persons intended by these Places had heard the Gospel—enjoyed the benefits of Revelation—but had always "Resisted the Holy Ghost," both in his internal influences, and external evidences, to prove, "That there is no other Name given under Heaven among Men, whereby we can be Saved, but the Name of JESUS." And as to this Name, they had obstinately Refused to bow in this Dispensation of the Holy Spirit, and blasphemed him here in all his kind endeavours to convince them: They must now bend and break under the weight of the Wrath of the Lamb; these sanative Rivers will pass them by, as Places not capable of Cultivation; incurable; not forgiven in this Age; not to be forgiven in the Age to come, (*Matt.* xii. 32.) but like land given to Salt, will be made sacrifices to vindictive vengeance, and salted with the Fire of Gehenna, *Mark* ix. 49.

Phil. These will be dreadful and durable sufferings indeed!

Didas. Dreadful above all conception! And of the end of them, it appears to me, that Revelation is silent.

Phil. Have we not reason to fear, that the proud and obstinate Pharisee is of this number; who, as tenaciously as Mire and Clay, adheres to his own Righteousness for Justification, and will not *submit* to the Righteousness of God; but goes about

about in an unmeaning round of legal performances, till he sinks and perishes in the quagmire of his own inventions, destitute of evangelical Righteousness, that approved wedding Garment? Do not final Apostates, who deny the Lord that bought them, for whom there remains no more sacrifice for sin, bid fair for those *Marshes*, in the mystical Prophecy; who, like ground absolutely incapable of cultivation, being no more visited by these life-giving streams, are given to the salting fire of Gehenna?

Didas. Little doubt can be entertained, but that such as these are principally intended: At the end of the ages of ages, when the Time of human *probation ends*, and Time itself is about to expire, the last Sentence of the Judge finally fixes the Fate of Mankind—"He that is unjust, let him be unjust *still*: And he which is filthy, let him be filthy *still*," *Rev.* xxii. 11. And who they are, the 15th verse informs you.

Phil. You suppose, then, that St. John's crystalline River of Water of Life is the same with Ezekiel's which issued out of the Sanctuary, in its last measurement, "A River of Swimming?"

Didas. I do. This very plainly appears by the following comparison.

1. They both have one Fountain. The Prophet's river issued from out of the Sanctuary which had God's Throne in it; the Apostle's, out from the Throne of God and the Lamb.

2. The quality of the Prophet's River gave name to St. John's. It gave Life to every thing whithersoever it went: Hence, from its effects, the Apostle terms his a River of Water of Life.

3. Both the sides of these Rivers are ornamented with the same Trees, and therefore the Rivers are the same. The Prophet informs us, that "On the bank of the river were very many trees on this

 side

side and on that side." The Apostle says, "On either side of the river was there the Tree of Life"—The singular for the plural, Tree for Trees.

4. These Trees are all the same; 1st. for situation, on both sides of the River. 2nd. For the Time of fruit-bearing: The Trees of the Prophet bear new fruit *according to his Month*; St. John's, *every Month*. 3rd. The leaf of the Prophet's Tree is for *Medicine*; but the leaves of the Apostle's Tree were for *the Healing of the Nations*; by which word he explains the Prophet's both Desert, Dead Sea, and his multitudes of Fishes. 4th. The Fruit of the Prophet's Trees was for Meat; and thus said he "Who walketh in the midst of the seven golden Candlesticks," "To him that overcometh will I give to eat (the Prophet's Meat) of the Tree of Life, which is in the PARADISE of God," *Rev.* ii. 7. *Comp. Rev.* xxii. 14. Where, note well, that as St. John, by the word *Nations*, explains the Prophet's Desert, &c. before it was healed, so the word Paradise here proves, that the whole, both of the Prophet's and the Apostle's description, relate to the *Times* of the Restitution of all Things, and consequently not to ETERNITY, properly so called, but to Paradise Restored.

These most glorious events will mark the Times of which God hath spoken by the unanimous voice of all his Prophets, since the prophetic Age began. These are their universal Themes—Grand objects, of which they never lost sight. The important end of Creation, Providence, and Redemption. For these purposes, the "Constituted Ages were framed," or adjusted in due course, (*Comp. Heb.* i. 2. with xi. 3.) according to His own good Pleasure or Purpose; which was, according to the Œconomy or Dispensation of the Fulness of Times, such as were contained in those Constituted Ages, that He might Reunite or REHEAD *all-Things in Christ*; (*Eph.* i. 9, 10.) who is the Centre of all; by whom and for whom all things were made that have an existence, Deity alone excepted.

Phil. Pray, my dear Didas, do you suppose that any of the Jews will have an offer of Salvation in future Ages, when raised again, as well as some of the Gentiles will?

Didas. Most certainly I do. Is any thing impossible with God? What line of human wisdom or understanding can sound the depths of the divine counsels? Such a depth in fact is in them, respecting the subject before us, as astonished an inspired Apostle, when the *Mystery* was first laid open to his view. By this the Apostle discovered,

1st. That a partial temporary blindness had happened unto Israel, until the Fulness of the Gentiles, in this present Dispensation, be brought in.

2d. That whenever that period arrives, then "All Israel shall be saved."

To prove this last proposition, he adduces the following arguments: 1st. A Deliverer shall come out of Sion, and shall turn away ungodliness from Jacob. This Deliverer is the Messiah, who, at his next coming and his kingdom, will fulfil every stipulated covenanted blessing. 2d. This covenant is, that he will take away their sins. 3rd. God hath not finally rejected his People whom he foreknew or approved; no: They are beloved for their Fathers sakes. 4th. The gifts and calling of God are without Repentance. 5th. If the first-fruit be holy, so is the whole lump, or collected harvest. 6th. If the Root be holy, (Abraham) so are the Branches, notwithstanding their temporary excision from their own Olive Tree. 7th. For God is able, i. e. willing, to graff *them* in again, viz. those very identical branches that He had broken off. 8th. For God hath shut up all in Disobedience:

ence: Why? That he might have *Mercy upon all!* 9th. It was confonant to the divine counsel—part of a grand Plan, to permit, for a Time, a leffer evil, in order to fecure a greater and more lafting good. For firft, by the Fall of the Jews, Salvation came to the Gentiles,—Riches and Reconciliation to the World! 10th. What fhall the receiving of them be? Life from the Dead!

On this important period and miraculous work, the Prophet Hofea fixed his eye. "After two days will He *revive us*: In the *third day* He will RAISE US UP, and we fhall LIVE *in his Sight*," *Hos*. vi, 2. Here obferve,

This paffage refers to *Judah*. "I will be as a young Lion to the Houfe of Judah. *I will tear*, viz. in pieces; *I will take away*, viz. into Captivity, *and none fhall Refcue*." The Lion of the Tribe of Judah executed this dreadful threatening by the Roman Armies at the Deftruction of Jerufalem, A. M. 4074. After this deftruction of People, City, and Temple, "I will go return to my Place," viz. in Heaven, until the Times of the Reftitution of all Things. Then faid Peter, God fhall fend Jefus to blefs them, &c. Upon this, they will fee and confefs their fins, and "Seek my Face," or Favour. Then they unanimoufly cry to one another, "Come, and let us Return unto Jehovah, for he hath Torn, and he will Heal *us*!" namely, the very identical People that were torn fo long before. If, with St. Peter, you, my dear Phil., underftand thefe of the Lord's Days of a thoufand years each, then you know it falls out, that *in the third Day* God will *Raife them up* to live in his fight, in the *Sabbatifmos*.

DIALOGUE XII.

Philotheos. PRAY, my dear Didaſcalos, what Book is that which the Angel informed Daniel of, and in which he told him ſome of his People were written? *Dan.* xii. 1.

Didas. Doubtleſs there are many Regiſters kept in the Court of Heaven. This before us appears to be a ſpecial one, written upon ſome very extraordinary occaſion, like that in *Malachi* iii. 16. Evident it is, that it concerns Daniel's People, as diſtinguiſhed from others in the verſe following. The Promiſe to Daniel was, "Thy People ſhall be delivered, *every one found written in the Book.*" Now what deliverance can this be which is *peculiar* to Daniel's People, except it be from ſome trouble and bondage which is alſo *peculiar* to that ſame People?

Phil. And is there any bondage or confinement peculiar to that People, and upon any ſpecial occaſion?

Didas. Moſt certainly, and ſuch as never befel any other People, nor yet themſelves at any other Time.

Phil. Pray, my dear friend, what can it be?

Didas. It is an Act of God which the Holy Ghoſt himſelf terms *Severity*; and ſuch ſeverity as is oppoſed to the eſſential goodneſs of God. Severity towards the Jews—ſuperabundant goodneſs towards the Gentiles! At one ſevere ſtroke, infinite Wiſdom lopped off almoſt a whole nation, as ſo many branches from a good Olive Tree: Then He concluded, or rather, *Shut them all up together*, like ſo many State Priſoners, in Unbelief! There they remain, have, and will remain, near two thouſand years together! *Rom.* xi. 22, 32.

Phil.

Phil. Aftoniſhing! No doubt, among the Archieves of Heaven, all theſe Priſoners are enrolled. But after ſo long a confinement, what will their Deliverance be, which the Angel promiſed Daniel?

Didas. Such as he intended when he ſhut them all up. This was, "That He might have Mercy upon ALL." O the depth of the Riches both of the wiſdom and knowledge of God! Let us humbly adore what we cannot comprehend, not having been of the number of his Counſellors!

Phil. You ſuppoſe, then, that thoſe Branches lopped off by *ſeverity*, and ſo long treated as *enemies*, while the currents of divine favour ran through ſome Gentile Nations, were and are ſtill beloved for their Father's ſake?

Didas. Moſt aſſuredly. If I ſuppoſed otherwiſe, I ſhould differ widely from St Paul, and contradict the moſt ſolemn Proclamation the world ever heard.

Phil. What Proclamation, my dear friend?

Didas. It was iſſued by Jehovah, Sovereign of the Univerſe and God of Iſrael. It was made when he kept his Court on Mount Sinai, in Arabia, and bears date, according to the Hebrew Chronology, A. M. 2513. It is found, being Preſerved in the Code of his Laws, and Regiſtered in *Exod.* xx. 5, 6, and is as follows:

"I AM JEHOVAH THY GOD, a jealous God, viſiting the Iniquity, or guilt, of the Fathers upon the Children unto the Third and Fourth Generation of them that HATE ME; and ſhewing MERCY unto *Thouſands* (in ſucceſſion) of them that LOVE ME, and keep my Commandments." Now theſe Thouſands of Generations extend down to the loweſt limits of Time; and yet Time muſt laſt ſo long, or this moſt ſolemn Proclamation cannot be true. But who will aver this,

 that

that pretends to believe the Bible? This long ſeries of Time is termed, by St. Paul, "All the Generations of the Age of Ages," perhaps in alluſion to this Proclamation, as it is certain that he had his eye upon it when he aſſerted, that they were beloved for their Fathers ſakes, and thence inferred *Mercy* for them all, agreeable to this gracious Proclamation.

Phil. Indeed it is ſufficiently evident to me, that theſe Children of the Prophets, and Heirs of the Covenant which God made with their Fathers, will have their ſins blotted out when the Times of Revivification ſhall come from the Face or perſonal Preſence of the Lord, *Acts* iii. 19, 25. They ſtand in the ſame relation to their Fathers as the branches do to the root, or the harveſt to the firſt fruits. Hence it appears, that in Chriſt's own Times, the whole will be made holy and acceptable, when Jeſus comes to bleſs them by turning them every one from their iniquities.

Didas. Yea, and though they have not *now believed*, but lie under a ſpirit of ſlumber, will not God pour upon them a ſpirit of Grace and Supplication *when* they look upon him whom they had pierced? And while they mourn for Him with "A-ſorrow of a godly ſort," the ſight will conſtrain them to cry with their *Quondum* brother in unbelief, My Lord, and my God!

Phil. But do you ſuppoſe that the whole nation will be delivered, including all who lived in the days of our Saviour and his Apoſtles?

Didas. By no means. In thoſe days, multitudes of Scribes, Phariſees, and Hypocrites, could hardly eſcape the Condemnation of Gehenna! Will the Judge of all the Earth make no difference between thoſe who hindered, and thoſe who were hindered by them, from entering into the kingdom?

Phil.

Phil. Without doubt he will. But permit me to aſk, whether Ezekiel's Viſion of dry bones had not a farther proſpect than the returning Tribes from the Babyloniſh Captivity? Whether the ultimate views of the Prophet might not extend to the preſent ſubject?

Didas. The language of the Prophet in my ears breathes a very different ſound than that of the returning Tribes from Babylon. *See Ezek.* xxxvii. In the ten firſt verſes, you have the Viſion related. But what language can deſcribe a literal Reſurrection more clearly? The Expoſition of the Viſion God himſelf gives us in the four following verſes. Let us attend unto it one moment. 1ſt. "Theſe bones are the whole Houſe of Iſrael." But a very ſmall part of that Houſe ever returned to this day. 2nd. Attend to their deſponding language; "Behold, our bones are dried, and our *hope is loſt.*" How could this comport with their ſtate in Babylon, when Jeremiah had aſſured them of a Return in ſeventy years? "We are cut off for our parts." So ſaid St. Paul, as you have juſt heard. 3rd. Now attend to a chain of precious pertinent Promiſes which are made, not to the two only, but to the twelve Tribes, or the whole houſe of Iſrael. Firſt, "Thus ſaith Jehovah-God, Behold, O my People, I will open your Graves, and cauſe you to come up out of your Graves." Will not this have a literal, if it has at all a metaphorical fulfilment? Second, "I will bring you into the land of Iſrael," juſt as Iſrael did the bones of Joſeph out of Egypt, "And ye ſhall know that I am Jehovah," a faithful Performer of all my Promiſes, as your Fathers found me, *Exod.* vi. 3. Third, "Shall put my ſpirit in you, *and ye ſhall Live.*" Can words more expreſsly declare both their Reſurrection and Converſion? Fourth, "And I will place you in your own Land," viz. the

the whole House of Israel, *ver.* 11. But this has never yet been done, but most assuredly will take place in every tittle in Christ's own Times.

These are positive Promises, neither limited nor suspended upon any stipulated terms or conditions whatever. And such are the Promises in general made to this People respecting their future Restoration. An observation the more worthy of our regard, because if attended to duly it might tend to soften and sweeten the asperities of those disputes about the conditionality of divine Promises, by distinguishing which do and which do not belong to this People upon this occasion. I query whether, upon an intelligent and impartial enquiry into this subject, it would not be found, that the principal passages in holy writ, which many pious Writers have prest, contrary to their real meaning, into the Service of Calvinism, would not be found to refer entirely to this people upon past and future occasions.

Phil. But, my dear Didas, did not the Angel Gabriel inform Daniel of this Resurrection in the last Chapter of his Prophecy?

Didas. Yes, my friend, beyond a doubt. To demonstrate which, you have only to take the first year of our Saviour's Life, and lay this down as the ground of your Demonstration. Then call to your assistance St. John's Number of the Beast and of Man, *Rev.* xiii. 18. This Key of mystical calculation will unlock the secret Wards of Daniel's Prophetical Numbers, and to your astonishment lay open the Cabinet of his calculations in that chapter. His two numbers are both *dated* from the establishment of Antichristianism in both East and West in the seventh Century. Then was the daily Sacrifice taken away from the Christian Church in both parts of the Empire, and the abomination that maketh desolate set up.

Of

Of these two numbers of Daniel, the *expiration* of the former fixes the year of the commencement of that tremendous Time of Trouble, when Michael the Great Prince shall stand up for the Jews. This Time of unexampled Trouble will continue forty-four years, at the end of which Daniel's People will be delivered, as you heard above, and the first Resurrection take place. *See Dan.* xii. *the three first and three last verses.*

	A. M.
The first year of our Saviour's Life,	4000
St. John's mystical Key, — —	666
Daniel's first number when the troubles begin,	1290
TOTAL,	5956

The first year of our Saviour's Life,	4000
St. John's mystical Key, — —	666
Daniel's last number when the troubles end,	1335
	6001

"But go thou thy way till the End be," the End of these Wonders, *ver.* 1, 2, 3, 6. the end of this present evil Age; "for thou shalt Rest" in the Grave, "and *stand* in thy Lot at the End of the Days" last mentioned.

Phil. As the *Sabbatismos* now commences, and Daniel rises to keep it—the Beast and false Prophet destroyed—the Dragon bound and imprisoned—*Theocracy* restored by Christ reigning among his Ancients gloriously, viz. The blessed and holy, the just, the dead in Christ, all now with Daniel standing in their Lot with Abraham, Isaac, and Jacob, in the Kingdom of God. Now, I suppose, Ezekiel's Holy Water will rise from the Ancles, run up the Legs to the Knees, and a spirit of

Grace and Supplication be poured upon Daniel's delivered People, now again graffed into their own good Olive Tree, and received "Alive from the dead." Will not the Stone in Nebuchadnezzar's Dream accumulate in bulk in proportion to Ezekiel's swelling stream?

Didas. No doubt it will. By the Destruction of the Beast and the false Prophet, the splendid Figure in that Monarch's Dream was entirely annihilated: The smallest vestiges of worldly honour and pompous pride are not to be traced around the Globe!

The Stone cut out of the Mountain without Hands discovers its divine extraction, and the Hand that cut it out is now visible to all the Earth. The Kingdoms of this World have changed their Sovereigns—are no longer under the Government of "The Basest of Men," *Dan.* iv. 17. The Wicked will no longer "Walk on every side, when the Vilest men are exalted," *Psa.* xii. 8. For the "Kingdom and Dominion, and the greatness of the Kingdom *under the whole Heaven*, shall be given to the People of the Saints of the Most High, whose Kingdom is an everlasting Kingdom, and all Dominions (Governed by the 24 Elders) shall serve and obey Him," *Dan.* vii. 27. "Thy Kingdom Come!" Amen.

The first size of the Stone represents Christ's spiritual kingdom of Grace. This kingdom is *within*—a kingdom of righteousness, peace, and joy in the Holy Ghost, erected in the heart of every real christian; consequently it is hid from the Vulture's Eye. The Martyrs' blood, the Confessors' courage, and the Persecuted Christians' patience, are the usual Ensigns of this spiritual Royalty. Holiness within, and Persecution without, have, in every age, from Abel to this day, marked the Subjects of this kingdom.

Phil.

Phil. How should it be otherwise, when to this day, for the most part, the Dragon and his Vassals, "The Beast and false Prophet," have maintained an Aristocratical Sway, both in Church and State, the greatest part of the world over!

Didas. Very true. In every age hitherto, righteous Abel has suffered under the bloody hands of those who "Have gone in the way of Cain." This will not always be the case. When all the glittering metals, and other materials that composed the monstrous Colossian Image, are "Broken to pieces together," reduced to Powder, and carried away with the wind, the *Regnum Lapidis*, or kingdom of the Stone, will be erected with this royal Motto, "The Lord is King, let the Earth rejoice!" For his Kingdom will never be destroyed, it shall stand for ever, *Dan.* ii. 44.

By the conversion of the Jews, and the saving of all Israel in the Time of the Millennium, the accumulating stone will acquire a visible and very great accession to its size. In the Time of Satan's little season, this growing stone will become a great Mountain, from the effects of Ezekiel's life-giving streams, which being now in the third measured distance from the sacred Fount, will run loin deep, and, in their passage down the Desert, heal abundance of Fish according to their kinds. But we are very much mistaken if we imagine this *Regnum Montis*, or kingdom of a mountain, is the largest size of this stone, as much as we should be if we were to dream that Ezekiel's Rivers when loin deep were at the deepest. This Mountain is yet very far from covering the whole Earth. This is demonstrable. Satan's Authority is not yet subdued; for he is now practising his Arts to Deceive the Nations. His Head is indeed bruised, but not utterly broken. In the four quarters of the earth, if under the Civil or Political Government of the divine

divine Theocracy, moſt evidently they are not under the ſpiritual; if they were, how could Satan muſter ſuch an Army from among them as he judged ſufficient to ſtorm the Holy City, and deſtroy the Camp of the Saints? To whatever ſize the Mountain ſwells in theſe two periods, Gog and Magog muſt be devoured--Satan caſt into the burning lake—and the laſt Times of the Reſtitution of all Things take place in "All the Generations of the Age of Ages," (*Eph.* iii. *ult.*) before the Mountain-ſtone can ſpread and cover the whole Earth.

That this will be in the Time of the new Heavens and new Earth, or the laſt Periods of the Reſtitution of all Things, and not in Eternity, but within the Time of the Conſtituted Ages and within the bounds of our Saviour's Mediatorſhip, with me admits of no doubt.

Phil. What conceptions many Divines and Expoſitors entertain of ſupernal and endleſs happineſs, I am little acquainted with. But I confeſs my ſurpriſe, that it ſeems to be taken for granted, that St. John has given us a ſatisfactory and ſufficient deſcription of it in *Revelations, Chapters* xxi *and* xxii.

Didas. True. But this muſt be inadvertence. Supernal and endleſs happineſs is by no means deſcribed in "The Revelation of Jeſus Chriſt, which God gave unto Him." No; that happineſs is above all verbal or hieroglyphical deſcription! Beſides, it is what that Revelation never promiſes in its Title, and is even contrary unto it. What this Revelation promiſes, is "To ſhew unto his Servants," not ſupernal and eternal Glory, but "*Things which muſt* SHORTLY COME TO PASS," *Rev.* i, 1. Now here I ſhould be very glad to know, Firſt, by what rule of criticiſm or ſound reaſoning ſupernal Glory can poſſibly be

crowded

crowded in among these *Things*. Secondly, If the Things here Revealed are "Shortly to come to pass," I should be also glad to know, 1st. How long their Eternity will be. 2nd. What those Things are that are here Revealed that are incompatible with Time. 3rd. How the Things that are to come to pass, or how they are to come to pass *Shortly*, that are of endless duration in the supernal Heavens, surpass my very limited comprehension, I confess.

Phil. Why the Book should be supposed to discover more than God revealed to his Son—his Son to the Angel—the Angel to St. John—or St. John to the Churches, I know not; especially as none of the hands that it either then did pass thorough, or ever since, durst either add to or diminish the contents of it, without the utmost peril. To me it appears in a very different light, and a few of your thoughts upon this very interesting passage will greatly oblige me.

Dodus. You have heard above, that, according to St. Peter, the Antediluvian heavens and earth *Perished* at the Flood. And as they were by him termed Old, it is fairly implied, That when the present Earth emerged out of the Waters, it was most certainly New. Yet that which perished at the Deluge, curst by its Maker for Adam's crime, was very far from its original state when all things were *very good*. The present is therefore its third state. Yet in all the three, its *substance* has always been the same. This appears from its first produce compared with the present. But the qualities, no doubt, have been very different in all these different states.

The change that Grace makes in turning sinners into saints, is it not termed *a new Creation?* Yet, are they not the very same individual numerical persons in both states? What reason is there to

suppose,

suppose, that St. John's New Heaven and New Earth are any other than a Restoration to their primeval State? Why may not the substance be the same, however improved? What is there in the Mosaical account of the Creation, in the least to countenance a supposition, that the Heavens and Earth he speaks of were ever intended to be of endless duration, in case sin had never entered? The Fathers, in the *Nicene* Council, A. D. 325, inform us, that "This World or Earth was made the smaller, as God foresaw that Man would sin; wherefore, say they, we look for new Heavens and a new Earth, according to the Sacred Scriptures, wherein shall be gloriously manifested the Kingdom of the great God and our Saviour Jesus Christ; and then, as Daniel prophesies, the Saints of the Most High shall possess the Kingdom: And the Earth shall be a pure and holy Habitation, the Land of the Living and not of the Dead, &c."

These Fathers, we see, supposed, and well they might, that they were only intended to be of temporary duration. And why should we suppose that St. John's New Heavens and Earth should be any other? The duration of Time in the primitive, the present, and the new Heaven and Earth, and the Sæcula Sæculorum, or Ages of Ages, are all measured by day and night. But Day and Night are measured by the Sun's diurnal motion. Must the Sun for ever measure day and night? Are Time and Eternity of the same mode of existence? Can Eternity, in any sense, be measured by days and nights, by months and years? Is it not natural and rational to conclude, that none of them were ever intended by their Maker to continue for Perpetuity?

Phil. After Adam by Sin had forfeited his inheritance, and the Son of God was appointed the Heir of all Things, the Apostle informs us that the Ages were then constituted; what ages, pray?

Didas. Certainly not the Ages of Angels, for we know nothing of them, as above ſaid; but the different ages of this created world, in its different mutations; the different diſpenſations of Grace and Providence, to take place in theſe different mutations, until the *Ton Trochon*, or *Wheel* of Nature ſtands ſtill, *Jam*. iii. 6. This includes the whole Time of our Saviour's Mediation for Mankind, and the time that the ſun and moon will endure; for ſo long and no longer the Machine will go.

Since the Fall there have elapſed, 1ſt. the Antediluvian Age. 2nd. The Patriarchal Age, from the Flood to Moſes. 3rd. The Levitical or Jewiſh Age, from the Baptiſm of Moſes in the Cloud and in the Red Sea to the Baptiſm of Jeſus in Jordan. 4th. The Gentile or preſent Age, extending to the next advent of Chriſt to ſet up his Kingdom. 5th. The Millennium. 6th. The little Seaſon of Satan, from his liberation to his deſtruction in the lake of fire. Theſe two laſt are future, and ſo is 7th. The Ages of Ages, or the longeſt of all Ages; nevertheleſs will have an end, and time with them, when heaven and earth will paſs away; the purpoſes of their Creation and Preſervation being perfectly completed, and the Plans of Redemption and Providence finiſhed.

Then will the whole Poſterity of Adam, except thoſe that Periſh through final obſtinacy and unbelief in the miry and marſhy Places of Ezekiel's Deſert where his Healing Life-giving Waters never came, theſe excepted, all the reſt will, from the fulneſs of the Body, Reheaded by the ſecond Adam—an indiſſoluble Union formed between Member and Member—Body and Head—and Deity the Head of All, be ALL in ALL to endleſs duration!!

So far as I can ſee, this will be the ſummit of Perfection of human Nature. The ſcale or climax of of gradual advancement is this—Man is the Head of the Woman—Christ is the Head of Man—God is the Head of Christ. The Woman is Man's Fulness—The whole Church is Christ's Fulness—And Christ is God's Fulness. Thus will Deity fill *all in all*, and that to endless duration!! Behold the dignity of Man! *See* 1 *Cor*. xi. 3.

The Marriage of the Lamb and his Bride will be celebrated upon the new earth in the Paradise of God, though Consummated in Heaven, just as the Marriage of the first Adam with his Bride was Celebrated in the newly-created Earth, in the Paradise of Adam. The Paradise of God is the Paradise of Adam Restored, and completes the Times and the Restitution of all Things. If any Person doubts this Fact, let him carefully and candidly weigh the following Remarks upon the Type and Antitype, &c. of this very interesting subject.

1. Adam's Paradise was made at the Old Creation; the Paradise of God (*Rev*. ii. 7.) at the New. "He that sat upon the Throne said, Behold! I make all Things new," Paradise among the rest, for the second Adam.

2. The Paradise of Adam was a sacred enclosure, very different from the Gound out of which he was made, and into which he was banished after his rebellion; the Paradise of God is enclosed with a Wall, quite distinct from the earth around it, and from which the Kings bring their glory and honour into it. *Ch*. xxi. 24, 26.

3. ADAM, upon his Marriage in Paradise, received a *new* Name, viz. ISH, confirmed by his Maker, as a Title of honour, *Gen*. ii. 23, 24, 25. The second Adam will have the same, "Him that overcometh, I will write upon him My New Name," *Rev*. iii. 12.

4. Upon the Marriage of Adam, he said, when the common Parent brought the virgin couple together,

together, "This is now Bone of my Bones, and Flesh of my Flesh;" in like manner the Bride, the Lamb's Wife, will be "Members of his body, of his flesh, and of his bones;" and in both cases, "They two are one Flesh," *Gal.* v. 30, 31. Astonishing mysterious Union!

5. The first name that the woman had at her *creation* was *Bekebah*, being expressive of her sex, *Gen.* i. 27. Upon her marriage and extraction from her husband's side in Paradise, she received a new Name, ISHAH; this was honorary—expressive both of natural and social Identity with her husband who gave it her: In like manner, Christ will give, in Paradise Restored, to his Bride, "A white Stone, and in the Stone a New Name," with this farther inscription written upon it, "The Name of my God, and the Name of the City of my God, the New Jerusalem," *Comp. Rev.* ii. 17. *with* iii. 12. An evidence to each of being a citizen of that City which *cometh down out of heaven* to the new earth.

6. Adam's Paradise had the Tree of Life in the *midst of the Garden*, *Gen.* ii. 9. In like manner in the Paradise of God, "In the *midst of the street of it*, and on either side of the River, there was the Tree of Life," *Rev.* xxii. 2.

7. Adam's Paradise was enriched with the finest Gold and precious Stones, "And the gold of that Land is good: There is Bdellium and the Onyx-Stone," *Gen.* ii. 12. These were the Materials for building with, which Adam's rebellion prevented. Not so the second Adam's Capital; "The building of the wall of it was of *Jasper*; and the City was pure Gold," *Rev.* xxi. 18. Thus the second Adam finished what the first failed in, who formed it into "A City, whose Builder and Maker is God."

8. Adam's Paradise was well watered, for "A River went out of Eden to water the Garden,"

which having performed, was divided into four great rivers, *Chap.* ii. 10, 14. The Angel ſhewed John its antitype, being "A clear River of Water of Life, clear as Cryſtal, proceeding out of the Throne of God and the Lamb," *Chap.* xxii. 1. Being now "Set down with his Father on His Throne," *Chap.* iii. 21. So that he had not yet delivered up the Kingdom to his Father; for the End was not yet come.——*N. B.* This River is the ſame with Ezekiel's in its greateſt depth, and is intended for all who are athirſt, *ver.* 17. But ſurely there will be none ſuch in Heaven; even the Saints in Paradiſe will thirſt no more.

This is the Kingdom *Prepared*, in its Type; "*Apo kataboles koſmou*," (*Matth.* xxv. 34.) *from* the foundation of the world, or immediately after Adam was formed out of the duſt, (*See Gen.* ii. 7, 8) and intended for him, probably, all the Time of his probation upon Earth, and in which his Maker placed him inveſted with dominion over the Creatures. This was the type of the Millenniel Kingdom which Chriſt intended, being Paradiſe *Reſtored*, or the Paradiſe of God, (*Rev.* ii. 7.) of which the Sheep, or the Righteous, being the proper Heirs would henceforth inherit until their Removal into a more glorious Manſion in their heavenly Father's Houſe, more glorious than Adam would have been removed into if he had never ſinned. Here you may obſerve, that St. John uſes the very ſame greek phraſe in *Rev.* xiii. 8. and in the xvii. 8. In both which places mention is made of the Book of Life of the Lamb; (*See alſo Chap.* xxi. 27.) In the former place, the Lamb is ſaid to be *ſlain* "From the foundation of Koſmos." This could only be in Type, *after* the fall of Adam, when he was ſlain figuratively in thoſe animals, which probably were ſheep or lambs ſacrificed, with the ſkins of which Adam and Eve were clothed immediately

diately before their expulsion from Paradise, *Gen.* iii. 21. It has been above observed, that the moment the first Adam fell, the second Adam took upon him the administration of the World with respect to its future Restoration. The Ensign of this Office is the Hieroglyphic of a Lamb—A Lamb of God, who alone could bear away the Sin of Kosmos or the World. Ever since the first Sacrifice for Sin was offered, this Lamb was slain in Figure; and so long as he will act the Part of a Mediator, he will bear that ensign of his office. "*From* the Foundation of the World," then, must mean from the Time of those typical Sacrifices being offered in Paradise; at which Time, or *immediately* before, Kosmos was founded, when the Ground was cursed. In *Heb.* ix. 26, the same expression is rendered "*Since* the foundation of the world." What Blood of a Prophet was ever shed *before* the blood of Abel? Yet this is said to be "*From the Foundation of the World,*" *Luk.* xi. 50. What Secrets are contained in any of the Parables in *Matth.* xiii. except that of the Tares being sown in the Field (the World) among the good Seed, which sowing is dated "From the *Foundation* of the World," *ver.* 35, while Adam *slept* and the Devil deceived Eve? Therefore, except those that the Redeemer may, at the *End* of the Millennium, take into other and higher Mansions along with Himself, this Aionion Kingdom the Righteous shall possess, (*Ibid ver.* 46.) extending, in point of duration, to "All the Generations *Tou Aionos ton Aionon*, of the Age of Ages. *Comp. Eph.* iii. 21, *with Rev.* xxii. 5. *in the Greek*, All this Time the Throne of God and the Lamb shall be erected in the Holy City, where his Servants shall serve Him, until, at the end of this Period, the Son himself will deliver up this Mediatorial Kingdom unto the Father, every Enemy my of Chriſt and Mankind being deſtroyed, and Time itſelf be no more.

9. In Adam's Paradiſe, Time was meaſured by Days, Months, &c. In like manner, the age of ages, like all preceding ages, will be meaſured by day and night, and moons—"The Tree of Life yielded her fruit every month," *Ibid* xxii. 2. The age of ages is included in St. Peter's Times of Refreſhing, or rather *Reanimation*, and the Times of the Reſtitution of all Things, (*Acts* iii. 21.) being Chriſt's own Times, 1 *Tim*. ii. 6. In theſe Times all Things will be *Reſtored* without a Poſſibility of a ſecond Relapſe. This will be plain by an induction of many particulars which will take place in thoſe Times.

1. Adam was a diſobedient Servant of God; yea, he rebelled againſt him in his Paradiſe: But in Paradiſe Reſtored, God's "Servants ſhall ſerve Him."

2. Adam by Sin forfeited his right to the Tree of Life: Here the forfeited Right is reſtored to them that do his Commandments, for "They ſhall have Right to the Tree of Life."

3. Adam was baniſhed from his Paradiſe, and prohibited re-entering into it: Paradiſe Reſtored removes the prohibition, for "The Gates of it ſhall not be ſhut" at all againſt thoſe who feed upon the ſacred fruit, for they "May enter in through the Gates into the City."

4. Adam, as a ſinner, was driven *without*, and kept *without* his Paradiſe, being defiled and unholy, and ſo no longer qualified to dwell in it: In like manner, nothing *that defileth* can in any *wiſe enter into* Paradiſe Reſtored; ſuch are without, as you ſee in *Chap*. xxii. 15.

5. The ground was curſed for the ſin of Adam: But here, "There ſhall be no more Curſe, or curſed thing."

6. Sorrow,

6. Sorrow, Pain, &c. were introduced into Man and Beaſt in the firſt Paradiſe; but they had no exiſtence before the Fall: Paradiſe Reſtored removes them entirely from all its happy Inhabitants; there ſhall be "Neither ſorrow, nor crying, neither ſhall there be any more pain, for God ſhall wipe all tears from every eye."

7. Death paſſed into Mankind, and into the World, in the firſt Paradiſe: But in the Paradiſe of God, "There ſhall be no more Death." This does not prove that this Paradiſe is in Heaven, only that its Inhabitants (for of them it is ſpoken) "Shall die no more;" death ſhall have no dominion in the age of ages, but in Gehenna, where the ſecond death exiſts.

8. Adam by Creation was God's Son and Heir; by rebellion he forfeited both privileges: To the Conqueror the Inheritance is reſtored; "I will be his God, and he ſhall be my Son, he ſhall inherit all Things."

9. Adam, before he ſinned, was highly favoured and bleſt with the company of his Maker in his Paradiſe. This was the greateſt Bleſſing and Privilege of his nature and ſituation. He forfeited this exalted privilege by Rebellion. In the Paradiſe of God, this happineſs, honour, and unſpeakable bleſſing, is reſtored; "They ſee his Face, and He will dwell with them."

10. A flaming Cherubim guarded the firſt Paradiſe, brandiſhing the ſword of Juſtice to hinder the Rebel's return: The Gates of the Paradiſe of God are guarded by Angels, and they who do his commandments "Enter in through the Gates into the City," but without are Dogs, Sorcerers, &c. who are not admitted.

11. It is by many ſuppoſed, and in itſelf very probable, that the divine Preſence exhibited an outward ſplendid glory in Adam's Paradiſe, ſuch as

afterward appeared in the Wilderneſs, Tabernacle, &c. Is not this the ſame of which we read in the Paradiſe of God? "The Glory of God did lighten it, and the Lamb is the Light thereof;" that is, the glorious *Shechinah!*

12. When God created the World, he created the glorious materials found in the Paradiſe of Adam; afterwards he planted it with all its choice and incomparable Fruit-trees, Plants, Herbs, Flowers, &c. And of the new Creation, He that ſat upon the Throne ſaid, "Behold! I make all things new!" This will be done with unſpeakable advantage and improvement.

Phil. Glorious things are ſpoken of this City of our God! From the few obſervations above, it appears to me, I confeſs, that you may fairly commit it to the judgment and deciſion of common ſenſe and unbiaſſed reaſon, whether theſe be not the "Times of the Reſtitution of all Things," if ever there will be ſuch Times, or if ever all things will be Reſtored.

Upon the cloſeſt examination of Scriptures I am able to make, I frankly confeſs, That every forfeiture made by the Diſobedience of the firſt Adam is here reſtored, with immenſe advantage, by the ſecond Adam in the Paradiſe of God. What evil, moral, ſpiritual, or natural, did the firſt Tranſgreſſion introduce into the old Creation, that you can trace the leaſt veſtiges of in the new? yea, that are not expreſsly removed and remedied?

It is true, that the Glory here deſcribed is ſo exceeding great, and the deſcription of it ſet off in ſuch pompous language, that few, ſince the primitive times of Chriſtianity, have viewed it in any other light than as deſcriptive of never-ending happineſs in heaven.

Didas. True. But I have long been at a loſs to find a ſolid and ſufficient reaſon for it. That it cannot

cannot be what they ſuppoſe it to be, beſides what has been above advanced, the reaſons contained in the following queries have long convinced me to the contrary.

1. Is the glory here deſcribed abſolutely incompatible with a ſtate upon the renewed earth, or Paradiſe Reſtored? If it be, wherein does it conſiſt?

2. Is the Glory and Happineſs in the New Jeruſalem ſuperior to that which our Saviour promiſed to his Diſciples in many of his diſcourſes, reſpecting the kingdom which we daily pray to come, which when come, the "Will of God will be done ON EARTH as it is in Heaven?"

3. Did not our Saviour promiſe greater things to his followers than any that we find them enjoy in Paradiſe Reſtored? For inſtance, "Then ſhall the Righteous ſhine forth like the Sun in the Kingdom of their Father." We read of the Glory of God and the Lamb ſhining thus in the New Jeruſalem; but where of any other, either ſaint or angel? Beſides, the New Jeruſalem is the Kingdom of our God and his Chriſt; and not of the Father *only*. This will not take place until the End, when the Son delivers up the Kingdom to the Father. In this very paſſage our Saviour clearly diſtinguiſhes between his Kingdom and his Father's, *See Matth.* xiii. 41, 43. The Kingdom of Chriſt will commence at the end of this age, *ver.* 40.

4. Is not a Lamb the Hieroglyphic of Chriſt *only* as He is Mediator? Does He not bear that enſign in the New Jeruſalem? But what reaſon is there to ſuppoſe, that he will bear the enſigns of his office, when the office itſelf is utterly at an end; for ſo it will be when he delivers up the Kingdom to his Father?

5. But

5. But it is plain that this He does not do in the New Jerusalem-State, *Chap.* xxi. 10, 14, 22. "For the Lord God Almighty and the *Lamb* are the Temple of it; yea, "The *Lamb* is the Light thereof," (*ver.* 23.) just as He is the Light of the World; which, if this does not belong to his prophetical office, I ask what does it belong to?

6. Is heaven walled about with a "Wall great and high, having twelve Gates," and an angel as a Centinal at each Gate, and one of the Names of the twelve Tribes inscribed on each Gate? A city four square, with three Gates on each Side? Is there any danger that heaven should either be stormed, or some enemy or spy steal in unawares, that it should be so strongly walled and strictly watched? A wall of one hundred and forty-four Cubits high, and of twelve thousand Furlongs in circuit, who can believe that this should circumscribe that *Topon* or Place (*Joh.* xiv. 2, 3.) which our Saviour is gone to prepare for his followers?

7. How can this City be in heaven, when we are expressly told, that it "Came down from God out of Heaven?" Is not this an uncommon way of describing any thing that is situated in heaven?

8. If New Jerusalem be situated in heaven, and not on the Restored earth; what earth is that, and what Kings are they, who bring their Glory and Honour into it? Are there earthly kingdoms in heaven?

9. Around this Holy City there are two very different kinds of Nations. There are nations that *are saved*, and who will walk in the light of it, (*Chap.* xxi. 24.) or of the divine Shechinah residing within it; and it is the Kings of these Nations that bring their glory and honour into it. But "The Leaves of the Tree of Life are for the Healing of the Nations," xxii. 2. Are these nations in Heaven? Surely not. Are there no nations,

nations, then, want Healing? What, then, are the sanative virtues of these leaves for? Do they grow in vain? Surely no. Are not these Nations the very same with Ezekiel's Fish that wanted quickening and healing? The word Healing is taken from the Prophet, and like an Index points unto him. See therefore what has been said upon *Ezek.* xlvii.

10. If ever the Kingdom of God so come as that His Will shall be done on *earth* as it is done in heaven, and if such time never will come, why do we pray for it? But if it will, where do we find any thing like it, except in the New-Jerusalem State?

11. Is not a Sun of Righteousness the Title of Christ as he is a Mediator? Is not his being the light of the world a branch of this office? When ever had this Prophecy a literal accomplishment, except in this holy city, where his personal glory is such as to preclude the necessity of the solar light? Is not the Lamb the Light of it? A light so eminently glorious, that the Nations of them that are saved walk in this light?

12. Is such a state compatible with a heavenly state, or in what sense can it be said that he has delivered up the kingdom, while he is thus reigning among his ancients gloriously? Or how can God be *all in all*, when the *Lamb* is such a light to such a City, and to so many Nations? Does not the word Lamb of necessity include his human nature? While this reigns, how is Deity all in all? Again,

13. Is not Thirst an evidence of *want?* What want can there be in heaven? But it seems that there are vast multitudes upon this new earth labouring under this want. And for what other purpose does that pure River of water of life flow with a crystalline transparency, but to supply that want?

want? Does not this River proceed from the Throne (one Throne) of God and the Lamb, where of course they both reign (*Chap.* iii. 21.) together upon it? Is this River any other than a very large Efflux, like Ezekiel's when deepest, of the Holy Spirit proceeding from the Father and the Son? Surely not.

14. Does not this River now flow far and wide among those poor Gentile Nations, who in this World never either tasted its life-giving virtues, or washed in its regenerating purifying streams? Raised from the dead, they find of both a pressing want. And here a rich provision is made for them in the healing leaves of the Tree of Life, and the crystal river! Thus we read,

15. "And the Spirit and the Bride (the Inhabitants of the City, *Chap.* xxi. 9, 10.) say, Come! And let him that heareth (the call of the Bride, &c.) say, Come! And let him that IS ATHIRST, Come! And whosoever will, let him take the Water of Life FREELY."

Permit me here to ask the unbiassed candid enquirer after truth, can any deny this fact, that in the ages of ages (*ver.* 5.) there will exist Persons who will be Athirst, and consequently in Want? But what can any person want, or be athirst for, in supernal glory? Does not the water of life mean the spirit that proceedeth from the Father and the Son? Is not that the water which these Persons thirst after? And are not these the Nations that need healing? Where else in the whole Bible do we find such an Invitation as this? Where else will you find such a multitude at once crying Come? Where a more general Invitation—Whosoever will, or is willing—A more special frank Invitation, Him that is athirst, take the Water of Life *Freely*?

Phil.

Phil. That all these things will exist in the Times of the Restitution of all Things, or in Christ's own Times, who can possibly doubt? The series of the Prophecy—the existence of the Bride in her then glorious bridal State—the Paradise Restored with the Tree of Life and the River of Water of Life—the unequaled Invitation given to the Nations, &c. &c. all demonstrate that now that Testimony is adduced, That Christ gave Himself a Ransome for all; and that there is no other Name given under Heaven whereby Men CAN be saved, but the Name of JESUS.

Surely, from what has been said upon this Subject, we may safely assert, That now is the grand Jubilee—now are the Times of Refreshing, or Reanimation from (Prosopou) the Face of the Lord—And they shall see his Face, and his Name shall be on their Foreheads. These Ages will finish the Mystery of God—the Mystery of Christ—the Mystery of Providence respecting Mankind—and fully exhibit the unsearchable Riches of Christ's Mercy, Merits, Grace, and Goodness, to Worlds visible and invisible!

Didas. The Times of Refreshing or Reanimation are three:

1st. The Time of Christ's next advent. Then the Sabbatismos commences with the binding of Satan; and now is the Resurrection of the Just.

2nd. The second Resurrection takes place, and Satan is let loose among this newly-raised world of People; but the Holy City and the Camp of the Saints continue, as in the Time of the Millennium. But hitherto the kingdom of Christ is very incomplete. The stone is accumulating, like a rolling snow-ball, into a vast Mountain, but Gog and Magog are a Demonstration, that it has not yet filled the Earth. No, Satan's influence is still very great in all the four quarters of it, his Head being

being not yet fully bruifed—his Works not yet wholly deftroyed.

3rd. When Gog and Magog are devoured, Satan's little feafon expired, and himfelf caft into the burning lake, all things will be created anew; and, as you have heard above, the Paradife of God, &c. Reftored, and the ages of ages will complete the Times of Reftitution. This laft, as it will be by far the longeft, fo alfo much more the happieft of all the preceding: For, as I take it, the two former of thefe Periods will reftore all Things to their primeval State, but with very great improvement. And as Adam, newly created, fpent the firft day of his life, being the firft Sabbath of the world, in the worfhip of his Maker, who probably was perfonally prefent with him; but, not unlikely, the very next polar day or year, Satan deceived Eve: So, in like manner, the Millennium being over, Chrift perfonally returned to heaven, having raifed fome of the heathen Nations and will others in fucceffion, the Devil will be let loofe among them, once more to try his hellifh arts, who in time will fucceed with great numbers.

Phil. St. John informs us, that, upon the binding of Satan, "He fhould deceive the Nations *no more*, until the thoufand years fhould be fulfilled." Now what particular Nations do you fuppofe the Apoftle intends?

Didas. Thofe nations that he formerly had *fuffered* to walk in their own ways, at the Times of whofe Ignorance he *winked*; becaufe in the whole Courfe of his Providence, or the Difpenfation of the Fulnefs of Times, or in "Ages to come," he intended "To call them all every where to Repent." The words *no more*, plainly imply, that he means the fame nations that he had formerly deceived. Indeed, in this prefent evil

ftate,

ſtate, he deceives the whole world, (*Chap*. xii. 9.) but they have not in this life a fair trial, therefore God winks at their ways. But when raiſed again, they will be called upon every where to Repent, in Satan's little Seaſon, and in the Ages of Ages. Then will be their proper Time of Probation. And thus will God approve himſelf no Reſpecter of Perſons—not willing that any ſhould periſh—being Love itſelf—Goodneſs eſſential—whoſe tender mercies are over all his works.

Thus, both in Satan's little Seaſon will the everlaſting Goſpel be preached unto the Nations, and in the Ages of Ages ſuch an Invitation will be given, as the like is not to be found in all the "Scripture of Truth" beſide, that I remember. I look upon it, that of all Adam's Race, few, in Compariſon of all the nations who want healing in thoſe ages, will miſs of the life-giving River, and the healing virtues of the Leaves of the Tree of Life. Who will then refuſe to do His Commandments? All who do them will be made free of the City—drink the living Water at the Fountain-Head—Eat of the immortalizing Fruit until Mortality is ſwallowed up of Life—and God IS ALL IN ALL! Amen. Hallelujah! My ſimple aim has been,

"That to the height of this great Argument
"I might aſſert eternal Providence,
"And juſtify the Ways of God to Man."

MILTON.

FINIS.

ERRATA.

Preface,	Page iv, Line 14,	after *into*	read *it*.
	xiii, Line 38,	for *has*	read *have*.
Dialogues,	22, Line 22,	for *were*	read *was*.
	34, Line 20,	after *Blind*	read *World*.
	38, Line 35,	before *Word*	read *his*.
	44, Line 33,	after *but*	read *to*.
	50, Line 25,	after *upon*	read *it*.
	57, Line 4,	for *dody*	read *body*.
	57, Line 26,	for *Prehead*	read *Rehead*.
	61, Line 33,	after *limits*	read *of*.
	69, Line 20,	for *its*	read *their*.
	75, Line 37,	for *Ban*	read *Bane*.
	97, Line 30,	for *mortal*	read *moral*.
	139, Line 30,	for *the*	read *his*.
	154, Line 21,	for *now*	read *know*.
	156, Line 35,	after *that*	read *neither*.
	180, Line 18,	for *know*	read *known*.
	190, Line 35,	for *Counſel*	read *Council*.
	218, Line 15,	for *many*	read *Mary*.
	219, Line 4,	for *Anaſtaris*	read *Araſtaſis*.
	275, Line 27,	after *Adam*	read *be ſaved*.
	275, Line 31,	for *from*	read *form*.

☞ In Conſequence of the Author dying ſhortly after the Work was put to preſs, together with ſome other concurrent Circumſtances, ſeveral Errors, literal and grammatical, have unavoidably occurred, excluſive of thoſe above-mentioned, which the candid Reader is humbly requeſted to excuſe.

CPSIA information can be obtained
at www.ICGtesting.com
Printed in the USA
BVHW081614260819
556817BV00021B/3191/P

9 781407 603681